Indonesian

D1057029

lonely planet

phrasebooks
and
Laszlo Wagner

Indonesian phrasebook
5th edition – March 2006

Published by
Lonely Planet Publications Pty Ltd ABN 36 005 607 983
90 Maribyrnong St, Footscray, Victoria 3011, Australia

Lonely Planet Offices
Australia Locked Bag 1, Footscray, Victoria 3011
USA 150 Linden St, Oakland CA 94607
UK 2nd fl, 186 City Road, London, EC1V 2NT

Cover illustration
Sawah, sawah! Feeds my hunger and soothes my soul by Yukiyoshi
Kamimura

ISBN 1 74059 297 2

text © Lonely Planet Publications Pty Ltd 2006
cover illustration © Lonely Planet Publications Pty Ltd 2006

10 9 8 7 6 5 4 3

Printed by Hang Tai Printing Company Limited
Printed in China

acknowledgments

Editor Jodie Martire would like to acknowledge the following people for their contributions to this phrasebook:

Laszlo Wagner for his translating precision and his excellent suggestions for valuable cultural material. Laszlo left a boring life of teaching English to spend a decade in much of Asia, captivated especially now by the diversity and hospitality of Indonesia. He spends most of his time in the eastern islands of Maluku and Papua, where he would never have had such a good time without speaking Indonesian. He also developed a deep appreciation of the fascinating wealth of native languages spoken in the region.

   Laszlo would like to thank all those involved in the creation of this book, especially Ukirsari Manggalani Brodjokaloso for her invaluable help and sense of humour when looking for the proper slang for improper situations. He'd also like to thank Mark, Kemal and Sarah for assistance with some *bahasa daerah*, and his good friend Said Samad, who not only taught him more Indonesian than anyone else but also patiently introduced him to his wonderfully difficult native Galelarese.

   He also insists on saying thanks to his editors for their encouragement, flexibility and openness to including topics previously not planned in this phrasebook.

Kusnandar from Lonely Planet for language and cultural advice, and Yukiyoshi Kamimura for the illustrations.

Lonely Planet Language Products

Publishing Manager: Chris Rennie
Commissioning Editor: Ben Handicott
Editor: Jodie Martire
Assisting Editor: Branislava Vladisavljevic
Layout Designer: Jacqui Saunders
Managing Editor: Annelies Mertens

Managing Layout Designer: Sally Darmody
Layout Manager: Adriana Mammarella
Series Designer: Yukiyoshi Kamimura
Cartographer: Wayne Murphy
Project Manager: Annelies Mertens
Production Manager: Jo Vraca

make the most of this phrasebook ...

Anyone can speak another language! It's all about confidence. Don't worry if you can't remember your school language lessons or if you've never learnt a language before. Even if you learn the very basics (on the inside covers of this book), your travel experience will be the better for it. You have nothing to lose and everything to gain when the locals hear you making an effort.

finding things in this book

For easy navigation, this book is in sections. The Tools chapters are the ones you'll thumb through time and again. The Practical section covers basic travel situations like catching transport and finding a bed. The Social section gives you conversational phrases, pick-up lines, the ability to express opinions – so you can get to know people. Food has a section all of its own: gourmets and vegetarians are covered and local dishes feature. Safe Travel equips you with health and police phrases, just in case. Remember the colours of each section and you'll find everything easily; or use the comprehensive Index. Otherwise, check the two-way traveller's Dictionary for the word you need.

being understood

Throughout this book you'll see coloured phrases on each page. They're phonetic guides to help you pronounce the language. You don't even need to look at the language itself, but you'll get used to the way we've represented particular sounds. The pronunciation chapter in Tools will explain more, but you can feel confident that if you read the coloured phrase slowly, you'll be understood.

communication tips

Body language, ways of doing things, sense of humour – all have a role to play in every culture. 'Local talk' boxes show you common ways of saying things, or everyday language to drop into conversation. 'Listen for …' boxes supply the phrases you may hear. They start with the language (so local people can point out what they want to say to you) and then lead in to the pronunciation guide and the English translation.

social 113

indonesian

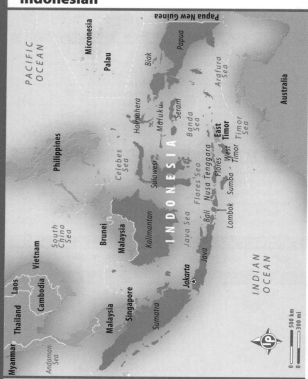

■ official language

For more details, see the **introduction**.

Indonesian, or *Bahasa Indonesia* as it's known to the locals, is the official language of the Republic of Indonesia. It's used in administration, education, business and the media, although less than 10 per cent of the population claim it as their mother tongue. For the majority of speakers it's actually the second language, but as such it represents a uniting force for the hundreds of ethnic groups scattered across the world's largest archipelago.

Indonesian, and its closest relative Malay, both developed from Old Malay, an Austronesian language spoken in the kingdom of Srivijaya on the island of Sumatra. The earliest written records of this Buddhist kingdom date from the 7th century AD. Over time Malay became the principal language of trade in the archipelago, a lingua franca for traders from China, India and Arab nations. The Arab traders also brought Islam to the archipelago, and Malay was the language which disseminated it throughout the islands. Alongside Bazaar Malay, the language spoken by common Indonesians, a variety called Classical Malay held sway as the court language in the Muslim sultanate of Malacca and was prized as the language of literature.

The Dutch and British colonisers, the most successful of the European traders who arrived in the 16th century, consolidated the influence of Malay by using it to

at a glance ...

language name: Indonesian

name in language:
Bahasa Indonesia
ba·ha·sa in·do·ne·si·a

language family:
Austronesian

approximate number of speakers: 220 million (of which 20 million are native speakers)

close relatives:
Malay & related dialects

key country:
Republic of Indonesia

donations to English:
(run) amok, cockatoo, orang-utan

introduction

communicate with indigenous populations. These contacts, together with the distinctions that emerged during the evolution of the language, ultimately resulted in the development of two separate modern forms – Indonesian (influenced by Dutch) and Malay (which borrowed more from English).

At the start of the 20th century, a modified version of Persio-Arabic script (in use since the 14th century) was replaced by the Latin alphabet under European influence. The term *Bahasa Indonesia* (Indonesian language) was first introduced in 1928 by the nationalist movement which aimed for the language's official recognition. Finally, with the Declaration of Independence in 1942, Indonesian was proclaimed the country's official language.

In addition to the vocabulary Indonesian adopted from its foreign interactions – such as *istana* (Sanskrit for 'palace'), *hakim* (Arabic for 'judge'), *meja* (Portuguese for 'table'), *mie* (Chinese for 'noodle'), *kantor* (Dutch for 'office') and *otomatis* (English for 'automatic') – it continues to be influenced by Indonesia's hundreds of languages known as *bahasa daerah* (local languages). For more information, see **local languages** on page 45.

Indonesian is usually described as an easy language to learn, thanks to its phonetic spelling, simple pronunciation and the fact that verbs don't change for tense and nouns don't change for singular or plural. It's also often said that it takes a lifetime to master, as you'll probably understand when you get into its plethora of affixes and infinite exceptions to rules.

As a starter, though, this book gives you the practical phrases you need to get by, as well as the fun social phrases that lead to a better understanding of Indonesia and its people. The contacts you make through speaking Indonesian will make your travel experience unique. Local knowledge, new relationships and a sense of satisfaction are on the tip of your tongue, so don't just stand there, say something!

abbreviations used in this book

a	adjective	inf	informal	pl	plural
adv	adverb	lit	literal	pol	polite
excl	exclusive		translation	sg	singular
f	feminine	m	masculine	v	verb
incl	inclusive	n	noun		

TOOLS > pronunciation

You shouldn't have any problems pronouncing Indonesian – not only do the sounds have equivalents in English, but they're also written in the Latin alphabet.

vowel sounds

Indonesian vowels are generally pronounced as crisp sounds.

| symbol | english equivalent | indonesian | | transliteration |
		letter	example	
a	park	*a*	*lagu*	la·goo
ai	aisle	*ai*	*ramai*	ra·mai
e	bed	*e*	*helm*	helm
ee	need	*ie*	*mie*	mee
ey	they	*ei*	*Brunei*	broo·ney
i	pit	*i*	*mirip*	mi·rip
o	for	*o*	*pohon*	po·hon
oo	book	*u*	*surat*	soo·rat
ow	how	*au*	*harimau*	ha·ri·mow

consonant sounds

Most consonants in Indonesian have equivalents in English, but there are a few things to keep in mind. The r and h sounds are pronounced more distinctly than in English.

The ng combination, which is found in English at the end or in the middle of words like 'ringing', also appears at the beginning of words in Indonesian. You can learn how to make the

11

sound by saying 'sing along' slowly, then dropping the 'si-' at the beginning. With a little practice, it should come easily. If you see ng·g the second g is also pronounced like in the word 'English' – eg *punggung* poong·goong (back).

symbol	english equivalent	indonesian letter	indonesian example	transliteration
b	better	b	rambut	ram·boot
ch	chat	c	catur	cha·toor
d	dog	d	darah	da·rah
f	friend	f	fajar	fa·jar
g	good	g	gambar	gam·bar
h	hat	h	hidung	hi·doong
j	joke	j	jelek	je·lek
k	kick	k	kamus	ka·moos
kh	loch (guttural sound)	kh	khayal	kha·yal
l	loud	l	langit	lang·it
m	man	m	meja	me·ja
n	no	n	nomor	no·mor
ng	sing	ng	bintang	bin·tang
ny	canyon	ny	nyamuk	nya·mook
p	pig	p	pagi	pa·gi
r	right (rolled)	r	roti	ro·ti
s	slow	s	sedih	se·dih
sh	ship	sy	syukur	shoo·koor
t	tale	t	kota	ko·ta
w	win	w	warna	war·na
y	yes	y	sayang	sa·yang

regional variations

Indonesian and Malay developed from one language, Old Malay, which is why they're often considered regional variations instead of separate languages. They share a common sound system and grammatical structures, the main differences being found in the vocabulary.

Of course, there are many regional variations within Indonesia itself. This is partly due to geographical factors (Indonesian is spoken across an archipelago of some 18,000 islands), but this is also the result of contact with many local languages. Speakers of over 700 local languages use Indonesian as a lingua franca, alongside their own mother tongues.

For more on local languages, see **local languages** on page 45.

For more on local languages, see **local languages** on page 45.

idiom-speak

To find out how Indonesian speakers really feel about life, you should get familiar with some of their idioms …

Like bees to the honey pot.
Ada gula ada semut.   a·da goo·la a·da se·moot
(lit: where there's sugar, there are ants)

No one's perfect.
Tiada gading yang   ti·a·da ga·ding yang
tak retak.   tak re·tak
(lit: there's no ivory that isn't cracked)

You can't turn the clock back.
Nasi sudah menjadi   na·si soo·dah men·ja·di
bubur.   boo·boor
(lit: the rice has already become porridge)

A bad apple spoils the barrel.
Karena nila setitik rusak   ka·re·na ni·la se·ti·tak roo·sak
susu sebelanga.   soo·soo se·be·lang·a
(lit: a drop of indigo ruins the pot of milk)

pronunciation

word stress

Indonesian is a monotonal language, with a slight rise in the tone of your voice towards the end of a sentence. Stress in individual words isn't as strong as in English – in general, all syllables are given the same emphasis, so we haven't marked stressed syllables in our pronunciation guide.

reading & writing

Indonesian uses the Latin script. The spelling is mostly phonetic – each letter always represents the same sound – so the correspondence between letters and their pronunciation is regular. The only letters which change their sounds slightly are *e* (when unstressed, it sounds like the 'a' in 'about' rather than the 'a' in 'park') and *o* (at the end of a syllable, it changes from the 'o' in 'for' to the 'o' in 'hot').

The alphabet was standardised in 1972, when a few spelling changes were introduced by the Ministry of Education (although some old, Dutch-influenced spellings are still found in people's names and placenames). The letters *f*, *q* (pronounced as k), *v*, *x* and *z* (pronounced the same as in English) are very rare in Indonesian and only found in loan words.

alphabet						
A a a	*B b* be	*C c* che	*D d* de	*E e* e	*F f* ef	*G g* ge
H h ha	*I i* i	*J j* je	*K k* ka	*L l* el	*M m* em	*N n* en
O o o	*P p* pe	*Q q* ki	*R r* er	*S s* es	*T t* te	
U u oo	*V v* ve	*W w* we	*X x* eks	*Y y* ye	*Z z* zed	

contents

The list below shows grammatical structures you can use to say what you want. Look under each function – in alphabetical order – for information on how to build your own phrases. For example, to tell a taxi driver where your hotel is, look for **giving instructions**, and you'll be directed to information on **demonstratives, imperatives**, etc. A glossary of grammatical terms is included at the end of this chapter.

adjectives & adverbs

Adjectives never change their form and appear after the noun they refer to. When there's more than one adjective, the word *yang* (who/which) is used between the adjectives.

a good car
  mobil bagus   mo·bil ba·goos
  (lit: car good)

a good, fast car
  mobil bagus yang cepat   mo·bil ba·goos yang che·pat
  (lit: mobil good which fast)

Adjectives can also function as adverbs. They can go anywhere in the sentence.

That car travels quickly.
  Mobil itu jalan cepat.   mo·bil i·too ja·lan che·pat
  (lit: car that travel quick)

articles

Indonesian doesn't have articles as English does. You can use the word *satu* (one) for 'a' or 'an', and for 'the' you have a couple of options. You can add the suffix *-nya* (his/her/its) to the noun, or use demonstratives ('this' or 'that') to refer to something specific or familiar (like the word 'the' does in English).

a shop
  satu toko   sa·too to·ko
  (lit: one shop)

Where's the shop?
Di mana tokonya?   di ma·na to·ko·nya
(lit: where shop-its)

Di mana toko ini/itu?   di ma·na to·ko i·ni/i·too
(lit: where shop this/that)

See also **demonstratives**.

be

The verb 'be' isn't necessary in simple Indonesian statements.

I'm Australian.
Saya orang Australia.   sa·ya o·rang ow·stra·li·a
(lit: I person Australia)

For a negative statement, use *tidak* (no) before the word you're negating.

I'm not Australian.
Saya bukan orang Australia.   sa·ya boo·kan o·rang ow·stra·li·a
(lit: I not person Australia)

See also **negatives** and **there is/are**.

classifiers

Classifiers (sometimes called 'counters') are words used when counting that identify what kind of thing it is you're tallying up. An English equivalent would be 'two *bottles* of beer' – to order beer, you say the container it comes in, and 'bottles' are the container or 'classifier' you use. Though there are quite a few classifiers in Indonesian, the most used ones are *orang* (person) for people, *ekor* (tail) for animals, *buah* (fruit) for things and *butir* (grain) for small, round objects. The classifier is placed between the number and the noun.

two students
   dua orang mahasiswa   doo·a o·rang ma·ha·sis·wa
   (lit: two person student)

three monkeys
   tiga ekor monyet   ti·ga e·kor mo·nyet
   (lit: three tail monkey)

two books
   dua buah buku   doo·a boo·ah boo·koo
   (lit: two fruit book)

six eggs
   enam butir telur   e·nam boo·tir te·loor
   (lit: six grain egg)

When you have only one item, *satu* (one) changes to *se-* and is added to the beginning of the classifier.

one student
   seorang mahasiswa   se·o·rang ma·ha·sis·wa
   (lit: one-person student)

one book
   sebuah buku   se·boo·ah boo·koo
   (lit: one-fruit book)

For information on plurals, see **nouns**.
For general information on counting, see the **numbers & amounts** chapter, page 31.

demonstratives

giving instructions • indicating location • pointing things out

To point something out, place the word *ini* (this/these) or *itu* (that/those) after the noun.

this seat
   tempat duduk ini   tem·pat doo·dook i·ni
   (lit: seat this)

those bags
   tas-tas itu   tas tas i·too
   (lit: bag-bag those)

As Indonesian doesn't have articles, demonstratives can also be used where you would say 'the' in English (see **articles**).

the passport
   paspor ini   pas·por i·ni
   (lit: passport this)

have

making a statement • negating • possessing

To talk about ownership, use the words *punya* (have) or *tidak punya* (not have). The word *punya* doesn't change its form – it's the same for 'I', 'you', etc.

I have a car.
   Saya punya mobil.   sa·ya poo·nya mo·bil
   (lit: I have car)

I don't have a car.
   Saya tidak punya mobil.   sa·ya ti·dak poo·nya mo·bil
   (lit: I not have car)

The word *ada* (exist) can also translate the word 'have' when talking about something that exists or is available (see also **there is/are**).

Do you have a single room?
   Ada kamar untuk satu   a·da ka·mar oon·took sa·too
   orang?   o·rang
   (lit: exist room for one person)

For more on expressing possession, see **possessive pronouns**.

imperatives

Simply use the dictionary (root) form of the verb for imperatives. To make the request more polite, you need to use the active form of the verb instead (like *menolong* in the last example). Other key words are *tolong* ('please' to request something), *silakan* ('please' to give permission to do something) or *bisakah* (lit: can?). *Tolong* and *silakan* go before the verb, and *bisakah* goes before the pronoun (as in the last example).

Stop here.
   Berhenti di sini.   ber·hen·ti di si·ni
   (lit: stop here)

Please stop.
   Tolong berhenti.   to·long ber·hen·ti
   (lit: help stop)

Please sit down.
   Silakan duduk.   si·la·kan doo·dook
   (lit: please sit)

Help me.
   Tolong saya.   to·long sa·ya
   (lit: help me)

Can you help me?
   Bisakah Anda   bi·sa·kah an·da
   menolong saya?   me·no·long sa·ya
   (lit: can you-sg-pol help me)

For information on the different forms of verbs, see **verbs**, and for negative forms of commands, see **negatives**.

negatives

To negate a verb or an adjective, use the word *tidak* (no) before the word negated. In commands, *jangan* (don't) should be used instead.

I don't speak Indonesian.
  Saya tidak bicara   sa·ya ti·dak bi·cha·ra
  Bahasa Indonesia.   ba·ha·sa in·do·ne·si·a
  (lit: I no speak language Indonesia)

Don't drink that water.
  Jangan minum air itu.   jang·an mi·noom a·ir i·too
  (lit: don't drink water that)

The word *bukan* (not) is used to negate nouns and numerals. Place it before the item you're talking about.

This isn't my bag.
  Ini bukan tas saya.   i·ni boo·kan tas sa·ya
  (lit: this not bag my)

See also **be** and **have**.

nouns

naming people/things

Indonesian nouns have just one form for both singular and plural. Whether or not there's one or more than one is usually indicated by context, or words such as *semua* (all), *banyak* (many) etc. Nouns can also be repeated to indicate plural, but with numbers repetition is not necessary.

a ticket
  satu tiket   sa·too ti·ket
  (lit: one ticket)

child's tickets
  tiket-tiket anak   ti·ket ti·ket a·nak
  (lit: ticket-ticket child)

three tickets
  tiga tiket   ti·ga ti·ket
  (lit: three ticket)

See also **classifiers** for more information on expressing quantity.

personal pronouns

Indonesians often use personal names, kinship terms or titles instead of the pronouns 'I' or 'you' when they're referring to others or themselves. It may take you a while to get used to someone named Rudy saying *Rudy mengantuk* (Rudy is sleepy) when what he means is *Saya mengantuk* (I'm sleepy).

However, Indonesian does have personal pronouns which you can use to address someone or refer to them (given in the table below). Note that there are four words for 'you'. In polite conversation, use *Anda* for one person and *Anda sekalian* for more than one. With friends and peers your age, you can use the informal *kamu* for individuals and *kalian* for groups.

There are also two words for 'we' in Indonesian – one is used to include the person you're speaking to (we incl), and the other excludes them (we excl).

Each pronoun in Indonesian plays the role of four in English – the word *saya* means 'I', 'me', 'my' and 'mine'. This is the same for all pronouns in the table below. See also **possessive pronouns**.

I/me/my/mine		*saya*	sa·ya
you/your/yours	sg inf	*kamu*	ka·moo
	sg pol	*Anda*	an·da
he/him/his/ she/her/hers/it/its		*dia*	di·a
we/us/our/ours	incl	*kita*	ki·ta
	excl	*kami*	ka·mi
you/your/yours	pl inf	*kalian*	ka·li·an
	pl pol	*Anda sekalian*	an·da se·ka·li·an
they/them/their/theirs		*mereka*	me·re·ka

Note that 'it' and 'its' have no direct translation. You can use *dia* as shown in the previous table, *-nya* as shown in the table below, or the words *ini* (this) or *itu* (that). See also **demonstratives**.

For more on politeness and how to address people (including other terms you can use) see the box on page 108, and **meeting people**, page 115.

possessive pronouns

naming people/things • possessing

Possessive pronouns are the same as personal pronouns (see the table on the previous page). They're placed after the thing that's possessed.

their hotel	*hotel mereka* (lit: hotel their)	ho·tel me·re·ka
my bag	*tas saya* (lit: bag my)	tas sa·ya

For 'my', 'your sg inf', 'his' and 'her', you can also show possession by adding the suffixes listed in the table below to the thing that's owned. After *-nya* (his/her/its) you may also hear people adding *dia* (he/she/it) for more emphasis.

my	*-ku*	-koo
your sg inf	*-mu*	-moo
his/her/its	*-nya*	-nya

my bag	*tasku* (lit: bag-my)	tas·koo
his medicine	*obatnya (dia)* (lit: medicine-his (he))	o·bat·nya (di·a)

See **have** for more on possession.

prepositions

Prepositions show the relationships between words in a sentence, just like in English. Some useful ones are listed below:

about	*tentang*	ten·tang	inside	*di dalam*	di da·lam
at (place)	*di*	di	on (place)	*di*	di
at (time)	*pada jam*	pa·da jam	on (time)	*pada*	pa·da
for (purpose)	*untuk*	oon·took	outside	*di luar*	di loo·ar
for (time)	*selama*	se·la·ma	since	*sejak*	se·jak
from	*dari*	da·ri	to (place)	*ke*	ke
in (place)	*di*	di	until	*sampai*	sam·pai
in (time)	*dalam*	da·lam	with	*dengan*	deng·an

questions

Statements can be turned into yes/no questions simply by raising your tone at the end of the sentence. Alternatively, use the question word *apakah* (lit: is-it-that) at the start of the sentence. When asking about people or things (ie with nouns), you can also place the word *bukan* (not) at the end of the sentence. The different ways you can do this are shown on the next page.

This is your child
   Ini anak Anda.   i·ni a·nak an·da
   (lit: this child yours-sg-pol)

Is this your child?

Ini anak Anda?　　　　i·ni a·nak an·da
(lit: this child yours-**sg-pol**)

Apakah ini anak Anda?　　a·pa·kah i·ni a·nak an·da
(lit: is-it-that this child yours-**sg-pol**)

Ini anak Anda, bukan?　　i·ni a·nak an·da boo·kan
(lit: this child yours-**sg-pol** not)

These question words can be used either at the start or the end of a sentence.

What?	*Apa?*	a·pa
Who?	*Siapa?*	si·a·pa
When?	*Kapan?*	ka·pan
Why?	*Mengapa?*	meng·a·pa
Where? (direction)	*Ke mana?*	ke ma·na
Where? (location)	*Di mana?*	di ma·na
How?	*Bagaimana?*	ba·gai·ma·na
How much/many?	*Berapa?*	be·ra·pa

there is/are

making statements • negating • pointing things out

To say that something does or doesn't exist, just use the words *ada* (there is/are) or *tidak ada* (there isn't/aren't).

There's a mistake in the bill.

Ada salah di kuitansi.　　a·da sa·lah di koo·i·tan·si
(lit: there-is mistake in bill)

There's no hot water.

Tidak ada air panas.　　ti·dak a·da a·ir pa·nas
(lit: not there-is water hot)

TOOLS

verbs

Many verbs are formed by adding different suffixes and prefixes to root words, depending on the verb and the context. Others don't require any affixes. Indonesian speakers often use root words instead of active verbs (verbs with affixes), so both are given in the **dictionary** where applicable. You'll usually be understood if you just use the root word.

Verbs don't change their form to show person or number, or even tense. Whether an action is past or present is indicated by the context. You can use words that describe time or place – *hari ini* (today), *kemarin* (yesterday) or *besok* (tomorrow) at the start or end of a sentence, or adverbs such as *sedang* (currently), *sudah* (already) or *belum* (not yet) before the verb. For the future you can also add the word *akan* (will) before the verb.

I've already eaten.
    Saya sudah makan.   sa·ya soo·dah ma·kan
    (lit: I already eat)

I'm arriving tomorrow.
    Saya datang besok.   sa·ya da·tang be·sok
    (lit: I arrive tomorrow)

I will help you.
    Saya akan bantu kamu.   sa·ya a·kan ban·too ka·moo
    (lit: I will help you-sg-inf)

word order

The word order in Indonesian is the same as in English sentences: subject–verb–object.

I have a friend here.
    Saya punya teman di sini.   sa·ya poo·nya te·man di si·ni
    (lit: I have friend at here)

See also **negatives** and **questions**.

glossary

adjective	a word that describes something – 'they stepped onto the **endless** beach …'
adverb	a word that explains how an action is done – 'and walked **slowly** towards the setting sun'
active verb	a verb form which has affixes attached – 'ed' is an affix in 'the sky glow**ed** pink and gold'
affix	syllable(s) added to the beginning (prefix) or end of a word (suffix) to modify its meaning
article	the words 'a/an' or 'the'
demonstrative	word that means 'this/these' or 'that/those'
noun	a thing, person or idea – 'romance'
personal pronoun	word that means 'you', 'she', 'we', 'they', etc
possessive pronoun	word that means 'mine', 'yours', 'ours', etc
prefix	syllable(s) added to the beginning of a word to modify its meaning – 'they **re**traced their steps to their favourite place'
preposition	word that precedes a noun to show its relation to other words in a sentence – 'from', 'after', etc
root word	the part of a verb that doesn't change – prefixes or suffixes are added to create new words, like 'stroll' in '**stroll**ed' and '**stroll**ing'
suffix	syllable(s) added to the beginning of a word, to modify its meaning, like 'ably' in 'they sat themselves comfort**ably** on the sand'
verb	the word in a sentence that describes the action – 'and **watched** the final rays of light disappear'

TOOLS

28

language difficulties

Do you speak (English)?
Anda bisa Bahasa (Inggris)?   an·da bi·sa ba·ha·sa (ing·gris)

Does anyone speak (English)?
Ada orang yang bisa   a·da o·rang yang bi·sa
Bahasa (Inggris)?   ba·ha·sa (ing·gris)

Do you understand?
Anda mengerti?   an·da meng·er·ti

Yes, I understand.
Ya, mengerti.   ya meng·er·ti

No, I don't understand.
Tidak mengerti.   ti·dak meng·er·ti

I (don't) understand.
Saya (tidak) mengerti.   sa·ya (ti·dak) meng·er·ti

I speak (English).
Saya bisa Bahasa (Inggris).   sa·ya bi·sa ba·ha·sa (ing·gris)

I don't speak (Indonesian).
Saya tidak bisa Bahasa   sa·ya ti·dak bi·sa ba·ha·sa
(Indonesia).   (in·do·ne·si·a)

I speak a little.
Saya bisa sedikit.   sa·ya bi·sa se·di·kit

Pardon?
Maaf?   ma·af

no, not yet ...

To questions about status or experience – like 'Are you married?' or 'Have you ever been to Iceland?' – the common answer is either *sudah* soo·dah (already) or *belum* be·loom (not yet). Saying *ya* ya (yes) or *tidak* ti·dak (no) isn't incorrect, but it suggests you won't ever marry or get to Iceland. Regardless of your intentions, *sudah* and *belum* are seen as more optimistic and positive responses.

I would like to practise (Indonesian).
    Saya ingin praktekkan   sa·ya ing·in prak·te·kan
    Bahasa (Indonesia).   ba·ha·sa (in·do·ne·si·a)

Let's speak (Indonesian).
    Mari kita berbahasa   ma·ri ki·ta ber·ba·ha·sa
    (Indonesia).   (in·do·ne·si·a)

Please speak slowly.
    Tolong, bicara pelan-pelan.   to·long bi·cha·ra pe·lan pe·lan

What does (pahit) mean?
    Apa artinya (pahit)?   a·pa ar·ti·nya (pa·hit)

How do you …?	*Bagaimana*	ba·gai·ma·na
	Anda …?	an·da …
pronounce this	*sebutkan ini*	se·boot·kan i·ni
write (boleh)	*tulis (boleh)*	too·lis (bo·leh)

Could you please …?	*Tolong, bisa …?*	to·long bi·sa …
repeat that	*ulangi*	oo·lang·i
speak more slowly	*bicara lebih pelan*	bi·cha·ra le·bih pe·lan

---

say your please & thank you

There are two words for 'please' in Indonesian – say *tolong* to·long (lit: help) when making a request or asking someone to do something for you, but if you're offering something or giving permission to somebody, use the word *silakan* si·la·kan (lit: be-my-guest).

Please open the window.
    Tolong buka jendela.   to·long boo·ka jen·de·la

Please sit down.
    Silakan duduk.   si·la·kan doo·dook

The meaning of *terima kasih* te·ri·ma ka·sih (thank you) is straightforward – it shows appreciation. Be careful, however, when you're offered food or drink. If you accept with *terima kasih*, you'll probably go hungry, as that means 'no, thanks'. To accept, say *ya* ya (yes) or *boleh* bo·leh (may).

cardinal numbers

Indonesian numbers are very logical. For numbers between 11 and 19, add -belas -be·las (lit: -teen) to the numbers one to nine – 13 is *tigabelas* (lit: three-teen). For the 'tens', you do the same trick with the word -puluh -poo·looh (lit: ten) – 30 is *tigapuluh* (lit: three-ten). The only thing to watch out for is that *satu* (one) usually becomes *se-* when attached to the beginning of a word – 11 is *sebelas* (lit: one-teen).

0	*nol*	nol
1	*satu*	sa·too
2	*dua*	doo·a
3	*tiga*	ti·ga
4	*empat*	em·pat
5	*lima*	li·ma
6	*enam*	e·nam
7	*tujuh*	too·jooh
8	*delapan*	de·la·pan
9	*sembilan*	sem·bi·lan
10	*sepuluh*	se·poo·looh
11	*sebelas*	se·be·las
12	*duabelas*	doo·a·be·las
13	*tigabelas*	ti·ga·be·las
14	*empatbelas*	em·pat·be·las
15	*limabelas*	li·ma·be·las
16	*enambelas*	e·nam·be·las
17	*tujuhbelas*	too·jooh·be·las
18	*delapanbelas*	de·la·pan·be·las
19	*sembilanbelas*	sem·bi·lan·be·las

20	*duapuluh*	doo·a·poo·looh
21	*duapuluh satu*	doo·a·poo·looh sa·too
22	*duapuluh dua*	do·a·poo·looh doo·a
30	*tigapuluh*	ti·ga·poo·looh
40	*empatpuluh*	em·pat·poo·looh
50	*limapuluh*	li·ma·poo·looh
60	*enampuluh*	e·nam·poo·looh
70	*tujuhpuluh*	too·jooh·poo·looh
80	*delapanpuluh*	de·la·pan·poo·looh
90	*sembilanpuluh*	sem·bi·lan·poo·looh
100	*seratus*	se·ra·toos
200	*dua ratus*	doo·a ra·toos
1000	*seribu*	se·ri·boo
1,000,000	*satu juta*	sa·too joo·ta

for-sight

Is it 'for' three days or 'for' your friend? Indonesian has two translations of the word 'for', so if it's a period of time, use the word *selama* se·la·ma, but if it introduces a purpose or doing something on behalf of someone, use *untuk* oon·took.

I'm here for three days.

Saya di sini selama tiga hari. sa·ya di si·ni se·la·ma ti·ga ha·ri

(lit: I at here for three day)

This drink is for you.

Minuman ini untuk Anda. mi·noo·man i·ni oon·took an·da

(lit: drink this for you)

ordinal numbers

For numbers above 'first', simply add *ke-* ke (to) to the beginning of the cardinal number – as shown below, 'second' is *kedua* (to-two). The only exception to this rule is 1,000,000th, which becomes *kesejuta* ke·se·joo·ta.

TOOLS

32

1st	*pertama*	per·ta·ma
2nd	*kedua*	ke·doo·a
3rd	*ketiga*	ke·ti·ga
4th	*keempat*	ke·em·pat
5th	*kelima*	ke·li·ma

fractions & decimals

a quarter	*seperempat*	se·pe·rem·pat
a third	*sepertiga*	se·per·ti·ga
a half	*setengah*	se·teng·ah
three-quarters	*tiga perempat*	ti·ga pe·rem·pat
all	*semua*	se·moo·a
none	*kosong*	ko·song

Indonesian decimals are straightforward, with the only major difference being that a *koma* (comma) is used instead of a full stop. Read the first number, say *koma*, then read the next numbers as a group – the first example literally means 'three comma fourteen'.

3.14	*tiga koma empatbelas (3,14)*	ti·ga ko·ma em·pat·be·las
4.2	*empat koma dua (4,2)*	em·pat ko·ma doo·a
5.1	*lima koma satu (5,1)*	li·ma ko·ma sa·too

classifiers

penolong bilangan

Indonesian uses the classifiers overleaf when counting people, animals and objects. For more information, see the **phrasebuilder**, page 18.

numbers & amounts

classifiers		
people	*orang*	o·rang
	(lit: person)	
3 travellers	*tiga orang turis*	ti·ga o·rang too·ris
	(lit: three person tourist)	
animals	*ekor*	e·kor
	(lit: tail)	
three rats	*tiga ekor tikus*	ti·ga e·kor ti·koos
	(lit: three tail rat)	
large objects	*buah*	boo·ah
	(lit: fruit)	
3 houses	*tiga buah rumah*	ti·ga boo·ah roo·mah
	(lit: three fruit house)	
small, round objects	*butir*	boo·tir
	(lit: grain)	
3 eggs	*tiga butir telur*	ti·ga boo·tir te·loor
	(lit: three grain egg)	

useful amounts

jumlah yang berguna

How much/many?	*Berapa?*	be·ra·pa
Please give me ...	*Tolong kasih saya ...*	to·long ka·sih sa·ya ...
(100) grams	*(100) gram*	(se·ra·toos) gram
half a kilo	*setengah kilo*	se·teng·ah ki·lo
a kilo	*satu kilo*	sa·too ki·lo
a bottle	*satu botol*	sa·too bo·tol
a packet	*satu paket*	sa·too pa·ket
a slice	*sepotong*	se·po·tong
a tin	*satu kaleng*	sa·too ka·leng
a few/some	*beberapa*	be·be·ra·pa
less	*kurang*	koo·rang
(just) a little	*sedikit (saja)*	se·di·kit (sa·ja)
a lot/many/much	*banyak*	ba·nyak
more	*lebih banyak*	le·bih ba·nyak

telling the time

Telling the time in Indonesian is quite straightforward. To say 'o'clock', say *jam* (lit: clock) before the hour – *jam enam* is 'six o'clock'. For minutes past the hour, say the hour plus *lewat* (past), then the number of minutes plus *menit* (minute). For minutes to the hour, use *kurang* (minus) instead of *lewat*. For a quarter to or past the hour, use *lewat* or *kurang* as described, but say *seperempat* (one-quarter) instead of 15 minutes. For half-past the hour, think of it as 'half to' and say *setengah* before the following hour – 6.30 is *setengah tujuh* (lit: half seven).

What time is it?
   Jam berapa?   jam be·ra·pa

It's (ten) o'clock.
   Jam (sepuluh).   jam (se·poo·looh)

Five past (ten).
   Jam (sepuluh) lewat   jam (se·poo·looh) le·wat
   lima menit.   li·ma me·nit

Quarter past (ten).
   Jam (sepuluh) lewat   jam (se·poo·looh) le·wat
   seperempat.   se·pe·rem·pat

Half past (ten).
   Setengah (sebelas).   se·teng·ah (se·be·las)

Twenty to (eleven).
   Jam (sebelas) kurang   jam (se·be·las) koo·rang
   duapuluh menit.   doo·a·poo·looh me·nit

Quarter to (eleven).
   Jam (sebelas) kurang   jam (se·be·las) koo·rang
   seperempat.   se·pe·rem·pat

At what time …?
Jam berapa …? jam be·ra·pa …

At (ten).
Pada jam (sepuluh). pa·da jam (se·poo·looh)

At (7.57)pm.
Pada jam (delapan kurang pa·da jam (de·la·pan koo·rang
tiga menit) malam. ti·ga me·nit) ma·lam
(lit: at clock (eight minus three minute) night)

the calendar

kalendar

days

You might hear Indonesians talking about *Senin* (lit: Monday) or *hari Senin* (lit: day Monday) – they both mean the same thing. This works for all days of the week except *hari Minggu* (lit: day Sunday). In this case, make sure you add *hari*, as *minggu* on its own means 'week'.

Monday	*hari Senin*	ha·ri se·nin
Tuesday	*hari Selasa*	ha·ri se·la·sa
Wednesday	*hari Rabu*	ha·ri ra·boo
Thursday	*hari Kamis*	ha·ri ka·mis
Friday	*hari Jumat*	ha·ri joo·mat
Saturday	*hari Sabtu*	ha·ri sab·too
Sunday	*hari Minggu*	ha·ri ming·goo

months

January	*Januari*	ja·noo·a·ri
February	*Februari*	feb·roo·a·ri
March	*Maret*	ma·ret
April	*April*	ap·ril
May	*Mei*	mey
June	*Juni*	joo·ni
July	*Juli*	joo·li
August	*Agustus*	a·goo·stoos
September	*September*	sep·tem·ber
October	*Oktober*	ok·to·ber
November	*November*	no·vem·ber
December	*Desember*	de·sem·ber

dates

What date is it today?
   Tanggal apa hari ini?   tang·gal a·pa ha·ri i·ni

It's (18 October).
   Tanggal (18 Oktober).   tang·gal (de·la·pan·be·las ok·to·ber)

seasons

For countries which have 'spring', 'summer', etc, Indonesians use the following terms:

spring	*musim semi*	moo·sim se·mi
summer	*musim panas*	moo·sim pa·nas
autumn/fall	*musim gugur*	moo·sim goo·goor
winter	*musim dingin*	moo·sim ding·in

For their own seasons, Indonesians have two basic terms – *musim hujan* moo·sim hoo·jan (the 'rainy season' falling between October and April) and *musim kemarau* moo·sim ke·ma·row (the 'dry season' between May and September).

Here are other seasons you may hear locals talking about:

harvest season	*musim panen*	moo·sim pa·nen
windy season	*musim angin*	moo·sim ang·in
western wind season	*musim angin barat*	moo·sim ang·in ba·rat

present

masa ini

now	*sekarang*	se·ka·rang
today	*hari ini*	ha·ri i·ni
tonight	*malam ini*	ma·lam i·ni
this ...	*... ini*	... i·ni
morning	*pagi*	pa·gi
afternoon	*sore*	so·re
week	*minggu*	ming·goo
month	*bulan*	boo·lan
year	*tahun*	ta·hoon

past

masa lalu

since (May)	*sejak (bulan Mei)*	se·jak (boo·lan mey)
(three days) ago	*(tiga hari) yang lalu*	(ti·ga ha·ri) yang la·loo
day before yesterday	*kemarin dulu*	ke·ma·rin doo·loo
yesterday	*kemarin*	ke·ma·rin
yesterday morning	*kemarin pagi*	ke·ma·rin pa·gi
yesterday afternoon	*kemarin sore*	ke·ma·rin so·re
last night	*tadi malam*	ta·di ma·lam

last ...	... *yang lalu*	... yang la·loo
week	*minggu*	ming·goo
month	*bulan*	boo·lan
year	*tahun*	ta·hoon

future

tomorrow	*besok*	be·sok
day after tomorrow	*lusa*	loo·sa
in (six days)	*(enam hari) lagi*	(e·nam ha·ri) la·gi
until (June)	*sampai (bulan Juni)*	sam·pai (boo·lan joo·ni)

tomorrow ...	*besok ...*	be·sok ...
morning	*pagi*	pa·gi
afternoon	*sore*	so·re
evening	*malam*	ma·lam

next ...	... *depan*	... de·pan
week	*minggu*	ming·goo
month	*bulan*	boo·lan
year	*tahun*	ta·hoon

during the day

afternoon	*sore*	so·re
dawn	*subuh*	soo·booh
day	*hari*	ha·ri
evening	*malam*	ma·lam
midday	*siang*	si·ang
midnight	*tengah malam*	teng·ah ma·lam
morning	*pagi*	pa·gi
night	*malam*	ma·lam
sunrise	*matahari terbit*	ma·ta·ha·ri ter·bit
sunset	*matahari terbenam*	ma·ta·ha·ri ter·be·nam

There are many religious dates observed and celebrated by Indonesia's various communities. For most celebrations, you can wish people a happy day by saying *Selamat* se·la·mat (a standard greeting word), plus *Hari* ha·ri (day of celebration) and then the name of the festival – 'Merry Christmas' would be *Selamat Hari Natal* se·la·mat ha·ri na·tal.

Here are some greetings you'll hear locals using at other festivities:

Hari Proklamasi   ha·ri prok·la·ma·si
Kemerdekaan   ke·mer·de·ka·an
Indonesia's Independence Day on 17 August each year. Indonesians will wish each other *Selamat Hari Proklamasi! Merdeka!* se·la·mat ha·ri prok·la·ma·si mer·de·ka (Happy Proclamation Day! Independence!).

Lebaran   le·ba·ran
The first day of the 10th lunar month marks the end of *Ramadan* and the celebration of *Lebaran* (also known as *Idul Fitri* i·dool fi·tri). It's a time when people ask forgiveness from each other for wrongdoings, using the words *Mohon maaf lahir batin* mo·hon ma·af la·hir ba·tin (Forgive my sins). Any Muslim can be greeted at this time with *Selamat Hari Raya Idul Fitri* se·la·mat ha·ri ra·ya i·dool fi·tri (Happy Lebaran), and close friends and relatives can add *Maaf lahir batin*.

Ramadan   ra·ma·dan
The ninth month of the Muslim calendar is the month of *Ramadan*, also known as *bulan puasa* boo·lan poo·a·sa (the fasting month). During *Ramadan*, many Muslims abstain from drinking, eating, smoking, sex and other pleasures during daylight hours. On the eve or first day of Ramadan, Muslims will greet each other with *Selamat menunaikan ibadah puasa Ramadan* se·la·mat me·noo·nai·kan i·ba·dah poo·a·sa ra·ma·dan (lit: Successful prayers for the fast of Ramadan). Once the fasting is in progress, the greeting becomes *Selamat Puasa* se·la·mat poo·a·sa (Happy Fasting).

How much is it?
  Berapa harganya?   be·ra·pa har·ga·nya

Can you write down the price?
  Bisa Anda tulis harganya?   bi·sa an·da too·lis har·ga·nya

Do you accept …?	*Anda menerima …?*	an·da me·ne·ri·ma …
credit cards	*kartu kredit*	kar·too kre·dit
debit cards	*debit card*	de·bit kard
travellers cheques	*cek perjalanan*	chek per·ja·la·nan

I'd like …, please.	*Tolong, saya mau …*	to·long sa·ya mow …
a refund	*minta kembali*	min·ta kem·ba·li
	uang saya	oo·ang sa·ya
my change	*uang kembalian*	oo·ang kem·ba·li·an
to return this	*kembalikan ini*	kem·ba·li·kan i·ni

magic medicine

If your money worries just won't go away, you can't find your true love or you've lost your car keys, it might be time to make a date with a *dukun* doo·koon (faith healer and mystic). The *dukun* tradition is alive and well in Indonesia, with methods of treatment varying greatly between or even within regions. Generally speaking, there are two types of healers – *dukun putih* doo·koon poo·tih (white shamans), who use tools like *doa* do·a (prayers), and *dukun hitam* doo·koon hi·tam (black shamans), who may use *roh* roh (spirits) or spells involving a symbolic *kris* kris (dagger). Indonesians may consult a *dukun* for many reasons, even to place a curse on an enemy.

I'd like to ...	*Saya mau ...*	sa·ya mow ...
cash a cheque	*tukar satu cek*	too·kar sa·too chek
change a travellers cheque	*tukar cek perjalanan*	too·kar chek per·ja·la·nan
change money	*tukar uang*	too·kar oo·ang
get a cash advance	*minta cash advance*	min·ta kesh ad·vans
withdraw money	*menarik uang*	me·na·rik oo·ang

quick chat ups

Here are some abbreviations your Indonesian friends might use to *ngobrol di internet* ngo·brol di in·ter·net (chat) with you or in *SMS* es·em·es (SMS messages). The trick to most of these short forms is to delete the vowels in each word.

bhs	*bahasa*	ba·ha·sa	language
dgn	*dengan*	deng·an	with
dlm	*dalam*	da·lam	in/inside
dst	*dan seterusnya*	dan se·te·roos·nya	and so on
byk	*banyak*	ba·nyak	many/much
jml	*jumlah*	joom·lah	quantity
kmrn	*kemarin*	ke·ma·rin	yesterday
sdg	*sedang*	se·dang	now
slmt tngl	*selamat tinggal*	se·la·mat ting·gal	goodbye
sm	*sama*	sa·ma	same/with
tdk	*tidak*	ti·dak	no
tp	*tetapi*	te·ta·pi	but
tsb	*tersebut*	ter·se·boot	above-mentioned
utk	*untuk*	oon·took	for
yg	*yang*	yang	which/that

Where's a/an ...?	*Di mana ...?*	di ma·na ...
automated teller machine	*ATM*	a·te·em
foreign exchange office	*kantor penukaran* *mata uang asing*	kan·tor pe·noo·ka·ran ma·ta oo·ang a·sing

What's the ...?	*Berapa ...?*	be·ra·pa ...
charge	*biayanya*	bi·a·ya·nya
exchange rate	*kursnya*	koors·nya

How much is it per ...?	*Berapa per ...?*	be·ra·pa per ...
day	*sehari*	se·ha·ri
game	*satu game*	sa·too gem
hour	*satu jam*	sa·too jam
(five) minutes	*(lima) menit*	(li·ma) me·nit
page	*satu lembar*	sa·too lem·bar
person	*seorang*	se·o·rang
visit	*satu kunjungan*	sa·too koon·joong·an
week	*satu minggu*	sa·too ming·goo

It's ...	*Ini ...*	i·ni ...
free	*gratis*	gra·tis
(12,000) rupiah	*(duabelas ribu) rupiah*	(doo·a·be·las ri·boo) roo·pi·ah

For more money-related phrases, see **banking**, page 101.

local languages of indonesia

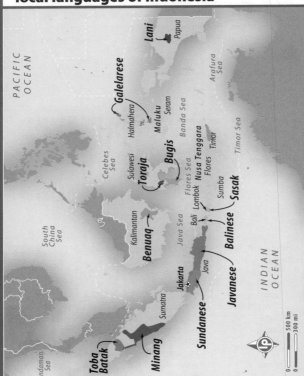

To use this chapter, simply locate your destination on the map and find out the local language spoken there. Look up the appropriate page number in the box on page 45, and start speaking. For more details about local languages, also see the introduction opposite.

Speaking Indonesian, you can easily travel throughout the archipelago – but don't forget that *Bahasa Indonesia* is a second language for 90% of Indonesians. Instead, their mother tongue will be one of Indonesia's more than 700 *bahasa daerah* (local languages), a diversity which ranks Indonesia second only to Papua New Guinea in linguistic diversity. When people go to a multicultural town or deal with the government, they'll use *Bahasa Indonesia*, but back at home and in traditional ceremonies they'll speak *bahasa daerah* – it's an important marker of cultural identity. Many of these languages are spoken by small populations, while others are used by huge numbers of people. Javanese, for example, ranks among the world's top 12 languages.

As a visitor to Indonesia, you'll never be expected to speak any local languages, but there's no doubt that Indonesians will appreciate your extra effort. For this phrasebook we've selected the languages you're most likely to come across in your travels. Look up the area you're going to on the map opposite, and find the local language below. Many of these languages don't use phrases for civilities like 'hello', 'goodbye' or 'thank you'. Instead, people may ask how you are or where you're going. Happy language travelling!

Balinese	46	Minang	52
Benuaq	47	Sasak	53
Bugis	48	Sundanese	54
Galelarese	49	Toba Batak	55
Javanese	50	Toraja	56
Lani	51		

balinese

number of speakers: 4 million
key area: Bali
notes: Balinese has levels of language like *Javanese* (see page 50) – we've included the middle level understood by all Balinese speakers.

one	*besik*	be·sik	six	*nenem*	ne·nem
two	*due*	doo·e	seven	*pitu*	pi·too
three	*telu*	te·loo	eight	*kutus*	koo·toos
four	*papat*	pa·pat	nine	*sie*	si·e
five	*lime*	li·me	ten	*dase*	da·se

How are you?
Kenken kabare? — ken·ken ka·ba·re

Thank you.
Matur suksma. — ma·toor sook·sma

Do you speak Balinese?
Bisa ngomong Bali sing? — bi·sa ngo·mong ba·li sing

I speak a little Balinese.
Tiang bisa akidik. — ti·ang bi·sa a·ki·dik

I don't understand.
Tiang sing ngerti. — ti·ang sing nger·ti

What do you call this in Balinese?
Ne ape adane di Bali? — ne a·pe a·da·ne di ba·li

Which is the way to (Ubud)?
Kije jalan lakar kel (Ubud)? — ki·je ja·lan la·kar kel (oo·bood)

How much is this?
Ji kude niki? — ji koo·de ni·ki

What's your name?
Sire wastene? — si·re wa·ste·ne

My name is …
Adan tiange … — a·dan ti·ang·e …

benuaq

number of speakers: 100,000
key area: Lower Mahakam basin, East Kalimantan

one	*erai*	e·rai	**six**	*jawat*	ja·wat
two	*duaq*	doo·ak	**seven**	*turu*	too·roo
three	*toluu*	to·loo·oo	**eight**	*walo*	wa·lo
four	*opaat*	o·pa·at	**nine**	*sie*	si·e
five	*limaq*	li·mak	**ten**	*sepuluh*	se·poo·looh

Do you speak Benuaq?
Iko dulik ngecarang   iko doo·lik nge·cha·rang
bahasa Benuaq?   ba·ha·sa be·noo·ak

I speak a little Benuaq.
A'ap dulia ngecarang   a·ap doo·li·a nge·cha·rang
bahasa Benuaq kedik.   ba·ha·sa be·noo·ak ke·dik

I don't understand.
A'ap awea ngerti.   a·ap a·we·a nger·ti

What do you call this in Benuaq?
Nai ohoa sua bahasa   nai o·ho·a soo·a ba·ha·sa
Benuaq o'on?   be·noo·ak o·on

Which is the way to (Isuy)?
Kalau kakat ke (Isuy),   ka·low ka·kat ke (i·sooy)
lalo lame?   la·lo la·me

How much is this?
Ohoq berapa raga no?   o·hok be·ra·pa ra·ga no

What's your name?
Encek nai iko?   en·chek nai i·ko

My name is …
Nai a'ap …   nai a·ap …

bugis

number of speakers: 3.5 million
key area: South Sulawesi

one	*ceddi*	che·di	**six**	*ennang*	e·nang
two	*dua*	doo·a	**seven**	*pitu*	pi·too
three	*tellu*	te·loo	**eight**	*arwa*	ar·wa
four	*eppa*	e·pa	**nine**	*asera*	a·se·ra
five	*lima*	li·ma	**ten**	*seppulo*	se·poo·lo

Do you speak Bugis?
Iko maccako mabahasa
Ogi?
i·ko ma·cha·ko ma·ba·ha·sa
o·gi

I speak a little Bugis.
Iya maccaka mabahasa
Ogi cedde.
i·ya ma·cha·ka ma·ba·ha·sa
o·gi che·de

I don't understand.
De pa uwisseng.
de pa oo·wi·seng

What do you call this in Bugis?
Asenna iye bahasa Ogi aga?
a·se·na i·ye ba·ha·sa o·gi a·ga

Which is the way to (Sengkang)?
Koloki joka (Sengkang)
labe tegaki?
ko·lo·ki jo·ka (seng·kang)
la·be te·ga·ki

How much is this?
Siaga ellina yae?
si·a·ga e·li·na ya·e

What's your name?
Iga assemu?
i·ga a·se·moo

My name is …
Asseku …
a·se·koo …

galelarese

number of speakers: 80,000
key area: parts of North Maluku

one	*moi*	moy	**six**	*butanga*	boo·tang·a
two	*sinoto*	si·no·to	**seven**	*tumding*	toom·ding
three	*saange*	sa·ang·e	**eight**	*tupaange*	too·pa·ang·e
four	*iha*	i·ha	**nine**	*sio*	si·o
five	*motoha*	mo·to·ha	**ten**	*mogiowo*	mo·gi·o·wo

Where are you going?
Kiaka notagi?   ki·a·ka no·ta·gi

Thank you.
Sukkur dala-dala.   soo·koor da·la da·la

Do you speak Galelarese?
Ngona idadi nogogalela?   ngo·na i·da·di no·go·ga·le·la

I speak a little Galelarese.
Ngohi tanako o Galela   ngo·hi ta·na·ko o ga·le·la
ma demo ma cunu.   ma de·mo ma choo·noo

I don't understand.
Ngohi tanakowa.   ngo·hi ta·na·ko·wa

What do you call this in Galelarese?
Manena ma ronga   ma·ne·na ma rong·a
isigogalela o kia?   i·si·go·ga·le·la o ki·a

Which is the way to (Soasio)?
Nako o (Soasioka)   na·ko o (so·a·si·o·ka)
kiano pamote?   ki·a·no pa·mo·te

How much is this?
Manena o kiamoi ma ija?   ma·ne·na o ki·a·moy ma i·ja

What's your name?
Ani ronga naguuna? **m**   a·ni rong·a na·goo·oo·na
Ani ronga nagumuna? **f**   a·ni rong·a na·goo·moo·na

My name is …
Ai ronga o …   ai rong·a o …

javanese

number of speakers: 80 million

key area: Central & East Java

notes: Javanese has *krama* (high), *madya* (middle) and *ngoko* (low) levels of language – the differences are related to the social status of the speakers. For the numbers 1 to 10 we've included 'high' and low' levels where appropriate, but all other phrases are 'middle level'. *Balinese* (page 46) and *Sundanese* (page 54) also use this structure.

one	*setunggal/ siji*	se·toong·gal/ si·ji	**six**	*nem*	nem
two	*kalih/loro*	ka·lih/lo·ro	**seven**	*pitu*	pi·too
three	*tigo/telu*	ti·go/te·loo	**eight**	*wolu*	wo·loo
four	*sekawan/ papat*	se·ka·wan/ pa·pat	**nine**	*songo*	song·o
five	*gangsal/ limo*	gang·sal/ li·mo	**ten**	*sedoso/ sepulu*	se·do·so/ se·poo·loo

How are you?
Piye kabare? — pi·ye ka·ba·re

Thank you.
Matur nuwun. — ma·toor noo·woon

Do you speak Javanese?
Sapeyan saged basa Jawi? — sa·pe·yan sa·ged ba·sa ja·wi

I speak a little Javanese.
Kula namung saged basa Jawi sakedhik. — koo·la na·moong sa·ged ba·sa ja·wi sa·ke·dik

I don't understand.
Kula mboten mangertos. — koo·la mbo·ten mang·er·tos

What do you call this in Javanese?
Napa namine ing basa Jawi? — na·pa na·mi·ne ing ba·sa ja·wi

How much is this?
Pinten regine? — pin·ten re·gi·ne

What's your name?
Nami panjenengan sinten? — na·mi pan·je·neng·an sin·ten

My name is …
Nami kula … — nami koo·la …

lani

number of speakers: 200,000
key area: north & west of the Baliem Valley, Papua

one	*ambiret*	am·bi·ret
two	*bire*	bi·re
three	*kenagandak*	ke·na·gan·dak
four	*beredak-beredak*	be·re·dak be·re·dak
five	*penok liginik*	pe·nok li·gi·nik

Hello!
 Waa!   wa·a

Can you speak Lani?
 Kat Lani wene yurak ndak?   kat la·ni we·ne yoo·rak ndak

I can speak a little Lani.
 An Lani wene mbuluk nenu.   an la·ni we·ne mboo·look ne·noo

I don't understand.
 An negolek.   an ne·go·lek

What do you call this in Lani?
 Yi nano Lani wene paga?   yi na·no la·ni we·ne pa·ga

Which is the way to (Tiom)?
 (Tiom) norak kenok tu   (ti·om) no·rak ke·nok too
 ngepago norak?   nge·pa·go no·rak

How much is this?
 Yi onggo made?   yo ong·go ma·de

What's your name?
 Kat kandege ta?   kat kan·de·ge ta

My name is …
 An nedage yio …   an ne·da·ge yi·o …

Thank you.
 Waa nore.   wa·a no·re

I am going/Goodbye.
 An nagi waa.   an na·gi wa·a

minang

number of speakers: 6.5 million
key area: West Sumatra

one	*cio*	chi·o	**six**	*anam*	a·nam
two	*duo*	doo·o	**seven**	*tujuah*	too·joo·ah
three	*tigo*	ti·go	**eight**	*lapan*	la·pan
four	*ampe*	am·pe	**nine**	*sambilan*	sam·bi·lan
five	*limo*	li·mo	**ten**	*sapuluah*	sa·poo·loo·ah

How are you?
    Ba'a kabanyo?   ba·a ka·ba·nyo

Thank you.
    Terimo kasih.   te·ri·mo ka·sih

Do you speak Minang?
    Bisa baso Minang?   bi·sa ba·so mi·nang

I speak a little Minang.
    Bisa sakete baso Minang.   bi·sa sa·ke·te ba·so mi·nang

I don't understand.
    Ambo indak tau.   am·bo in·dak ta·oo

What do you call this in Minang?
    Kalo iko baso   ka·lo i·ko ba·so
    Minangnyo apo?   mi·nang·nyo a·po

Which is the way to (Maninjau)?
    Kalo jalan ke (Maninjau)   ka·lo ja·lan ke (ma·nin·jow)
    ke mano?   ke ma·no

How much is this?
    Iko hargonyo bara?   i·ko har·go·nyo ba·ra

What's your name?
    Namonyo siapo?   na·mo·nyo si·a·po

My name is …
    Namo ambo …   na·mo am·bo …

sasak

number of speakers: 2 million
key area: Lombok

one	*sekek*	se·kek	**six**	*enam*	e·nam
two	*due*	doo·e	**seven**	*pituk*	pi·took
three	*telo*	te·lo	**eight**	*baluk*	ba·look
four	*empat*	em·pat	**nine**	*siwak*	si·wak
five	*lime*	li·me	**ten**	*sepulu*	se·poo·loo

Thank you.
Tampak asih.　　　　　　　　　tam·pak a·sih

Do you speak Sasak?
Side taom bahase Sasek?　　　si·de ta·om ba·ha·se sa·sek

I speak a little Sasak.
Aku taongkah bahase　　　　　a·koo ta·ong·kah ba·ha·se
Sasek sekedik.　　　　　　　　sa·sek se·ke·dik

I don't understand.
Endek ngerti.　　　　　　　　en·dek nger·ti

What do you call this in Sasak?
Ape aran sak iyak elek　　　　a·pe a·ran sak i·yak e·lek
bahase Sasek?　　　　　　　　ba·ha·se sa·sek

Which is the way to (Kuta)?
Lamun lek (Kute), embe　　　　la·moon lek (koo·te) em·be
eak langantah?　　　　　　　　e·ak lang·an·tah

How much is this?
Pire ajin sak iyak?　　　　　　pi·re a·jin sak i·yak

What's your name?
Saik aranm side?　　　　　　　sa·ik a·ranm si·de

My name is …
Arankah aku …　　　　　　　　a·ran·kah a·koo …

sundanese

number of speakers: 30 million
key area: West Java & Banten
notes: Sundanese has levels of language like *Javanese* (see page 50) – we've included the middle level understood by all speakers.

one	*hiji*	hi·ji	six	*genep*	ge·nep
two	*dua*	doo·a	seven	*tujuh*	too·jooh
three	*tilu*	ti·loo	eight	*dalapan*	da·la·pan
four	*opat*	o·pat	nine	*salapan*	sa·la·pan
five	*lima*	li·ma	ten	*sapuluh*	sa·poo·looh

How are you?
  Kumaha damang?　　　　koo·ma·ha da·mang

Thank you.
  Hatur nuhun.　　　　ha·toor noo·hoon

Do you speak Sundanese?
  Tiasa nyarios Sunda?　　　　ti·a·sa nya·ri·os soon·da

I speak a little Sundanese.
  Abdi tiasa nyarios Sunda　　　　ab·di ti·a·sa nya·ri·os soon·da
  sakedik-sakedik.　　　　sa·ke·dik sa·ke·dik

I don't understand.
  Abdi teu terang.　　　　ab·di te te·rang

What do you call this in Sundanese?
  Dina basa Sunda ieu　　　　di·na ba·sa soon·da i·e
  naon namina?　　　　na·on na·mi·na

Which is the way to (Ciater)?
  Upami bade ka (Ciater)　　　　oo·pa·mi ba·de ka (chi·a·ter)
  ngalangkung kamana?　　　　nga·lang·koong ka·ma·na

How much is this?
  Sabaraha pangaosna?　　　　sa·ba·ra·ha pang·a·os·na

What's your name?
  Namina saha?　　　　na·mi·na sa·ha

My name is …
  Nami abdi …　　　　na·mi ab·di …

toba batak

number of speakers: 2 million
key area: North Sumatra

one	*sada*	sa·da	**six**	*onom*	o·nom
two	*dua*	doo·a	**seven**	*pitu*	pi·too
three	*tolu*	to·loo	**eight**	*walu*	wa·loo
four	*opat*	o·pat	**nine**	*sia*	si·a
five	*lima*	li·ma	**ten**	*sappulu*	sa·poo·loo

Hello!
Horas! — ho·ras

Thank you.
Mauliate. — mow·li·a·te

Do you speak Batak?
Ai marbahasa Batak do ho? — ai mar·ba·ha·sa ba·tak do ho

I speak a little Batak.
*Boi do ahu marbahasa
Batak saotik.* — boy do a·hoo mar·ba·ha·sa
ba·tak sa·o·tik

I don't understand.
Dang huantusi. — dang hoo·an·too·si

What do you call this in Batak?
*Behama mandokkon on
molo hata Batakna?* — be·ha·ma man·do·kon on
mo·lo ha·ta ba·tak·na

Which is the way to (Parapat)?
Ai dia do dalan to (Parapat)? — ai di·a do da·lan to (pa·ra·pat)

How much is this?
Sadia argana on? — sa·di·a ar·ga·na on

What's your name?
Ai ise do goarmu? — ai i·se do go·ar·moo

My name is …
Ia goarhu … — i·a go·ar·hoo …

toraja

number of speakers: 500,000
key area: Tanatoraja district, South Sulawesi

one	*misa*	mi·sa	**six**	*annan*	a·nan
two	*dadua*	da·doo·a	**seven**	*pitu*	pi·too
three	*tallu*	ta·loo	**eight**	*karua*	ka·roo·a
four	*apa*	a·pa	**nine**	*kasera*	ka·se·ra
five	*lima*	li·ma	**ten**	*sangpulo*	sang·poo·lo

Hello!
Salama! — sa·la·ma

Thank you.
Kurre sumanga. — koo·re soo·mang·a

Do you speak Toraja? ·
Bisa ko mabasa Toraya? — bi·sa ko ma·ba·sa to·ra·ya

I speak a little Toraja.
Bisa na mabasa Toraya sidi. — bi·sa na ma·ba·sa to·ra·ya si·di

I don't understand.
Tae ku tandai. — ta·e koo tan·dai

What do you call this in Toraja?
Apa sanganna te lan — a·pa sang·a·na te lan
basa Toraya? — ba·sa to·ra·ya

Which is the way to (Makale)?
Kale male lako (Makale), — ka·le ma·le la·ko (ma·ka·le)
umba di olai? — oom·ba di o·lai

How much is this?
Pira alinna te? — pi·ra a·li·na te

What's your name?
Minda sangamu? — min·da sang·a·moo

My name is …
Sanganku … — sang·an·koo

getting around

Which ... goes to (Cirebon)?	... yang mana menuju ke (Cirebon)?	... yang ma·na me·noo·joo ke (chi·re·bon)
boat	Kapal	ka·pal
train	Kereta api	ke·re·ta a·pi
Is this the ... to (Ketapang)?	Ini ... yang ke (Ketapang)?	i·ni ... yang ke (ke·ta·pang)
bus	bis	bis
car	mobil	mo·bil
minibus	bemo	be·mo
When's the ... (bus)?	Jam berapa (bis) ...?	jam be·ra·pa (bis) ...
first	pertama	per·ta·ma
last	terakhir	te·ra·khir
next	yang berikutnya	yang be·ri·koot·nya
Where can I get a ...?	Di mana saya bisa dapat ...?	di ma·na sa·ya bi·sa da·pat ...
bicycle-rickshaw	becak	be·chak
motorcycle-rickshaw	bajaj	ba·jaj
motorcycle-taxi	ojek	o·jek
horse-cart	dokar	do·kar

What time does it leave?
Jam berapa berangkat? jam be·ra·pa be·rang·kat

What time does it get to (Denpasar)?
Jam berapa sampai di (Denpasar)? jam be·ra·pa sam·pai di (den·pa·sar)

time & distance

Knowing how far away a place is doesn't help you know how long it takes to get there – travelling 20km on a rough road can take as long as 100km on a *jalan tol* ja·lan tol (toll road). Here are some phrases to help you get on top of 'how long' a journey is.

How long does the trip take?
Berapa lama perjalanannya?
be·ra·pa la·ma per·ja·la·nan·nya

How far is the journey?
Berapa jauh perjalanannya?
be·ra·pa ja·ooh per·ja·la·nan·nya

It's (50) kilometres away.
Jaraknya (50) kilometer.
ja·rak·nya (li·ma·poo·looh) ki·lo·me·ter

The trip takes two hours.
Lamanya dua jam.
la·ma·nya doo·a jam

How long will it be delayed?
Berapa lama keterlambatannya?
be·ra·pa la·ma ke·ter·lam·ba·tan·nya

Is this seat free?
Tempat duduk ini masih kosong?
tem·pat doo·dook i·ni ma·sih ko·song

That's my seat.
Itu tempat duduk saya.
i·too tem·pat doo·dook sa·ya

Please tell me when we get to (Wonosobo).
Tolong, beritahu waktu kita sampai di (Wonosobo).
to·long be·ri·ta·hoo wak·too ki·ta sam·pai di (wo·no·so·bo)

Please stop here.
Tolong, berhenti di sini.
to·long ber·hen·ti di si·ni

How long do we stop here?
Berapa lama berhenti di sini?
be·ra·pa la·ma ber·hen·ti di si·ni

tickets

Where's the ticket window?
Di mana loket tiket?   di ma·na lo·ket ti·ket

Where do I buy a ticket?
Di mana saya bisa beli tiket?   di ma·na sa·ya bi·sa be·li ti·ket

Do I need to book (well in advance)?
Harus pesan (jauh)   ha·roos pe·san (ja·ooh)
lebih dulu?   le·bih doo·loo

A ... ticket	*Satu tiket ...*	sa·too ti·ket ...
(to Medan).	*(ke Medan).*	(ke me·dan)
1st-class	*kelas satu*	ke·las sa·too
2nd-class	*kelas dua*	ke·las doo·a
child's	*anak*	a·nak
one-way	*sekali jalan*	se·ka·li ja·lan
return	*pulang-pergi*	poo·lang per·gi

I'd like a/an	*Saya mau tempat*	sa·ya mow tem·pat
... seat.	*duduk ...*	doo·dook ...
aisle	*dekat gang*	de·kat gang
nonsmoking	*di ruang yang*	di roo·ang yang
	bebas asap rokok	be·bas a·sap ro·kok
smoking	*di ruang yang*	di roo·ang yang
	boleh merokok	bo·leh me·ro·kok
window	*dekat jendela*	de·kat jen·de·la

cheap students

As a general rule, there aren't any transport discounts for students, but you could always try asking for *satu tiket mahasiswa* sa·too ti·ket ma·ha·sis·wa (one student ticket) and see if you're in luck ...

Is there (a) …?	*Ada …?*	a·da …
air conditioning	*AC*	a·se
blanket	*selimut*	se·li·moot
sick bag	*kantong muntah*	kan·tong moon·tah
toilet	*kamar kecil*	ka·mar ke·chil

How much is it?		
Ongkosnya berapa?		ong·kos·nya be·ra·pa

Is it a direct route?		
Ini rute langsung?		i·ni roo·te lang·soong

Can I get a stand-by ticket?		
Bisa dapat tiket stand-by?		bi·sa da·pat ti·ket stand bai

Can I get a sleeping berth?		
Bisa dapat tempat tidur?		bi·sa da·pat tem·pat ti·door

What time should I check in?		
Jam berapa harus lapor untuk check-in?		jam be·ra·pa ha·roos la·por oon·took chek in

I'd like to … my ticket, please.	*Tolong, saya mau … tiket saya.*	to·long sa·ya mow … ti·ket sa·ya
cancel	*batalkan*	ba·tal·kan
change	*ganti*	gan·ti
collect	*ambil*	am·bil
confirm	*konfirmasi*	kon·fir·ma·si

listen for …

agen perjalanan	a·gen per·ja·la·nan	**travel agent**
bagasi bawaan di kabin	ba·ga·si ba·wa·an di ka·bin	**carry-on luggage**
dibatalkan	di·ba·tal·kan	**cancelled**
ini	i·ni	**this one**
itu	i·too	**that one**
jadwal	jad·wal	**timetable**
kelebihan bagasi	ke·le·bi·han ba·ga·si	**excess baggage**
loket tiket	lo·ket ti·ket	**ticket window**
penuh	pe·nooh	**full**
peron	pe·ron	**platform**
terlambat	ter·lam·bat	**delayed**

luggage

Where can I find a/the …?	*Di mana …?*	di ma·na …
baggage claim	*klaim bagasi*	klaim ba·ga·si
left-luggage office	*ruang penyimpanan barang*	roo·ang pe·nyim·pa·nan ba·rang
luggage locker	*loker penitipan barang*	lo·ker pe·ni·ti·pan ba·rang
trolley	*kereta bagasi*	ke·re·ta ba·ga·si

My luggage has been …	*Bagasi saya …*	ba·ga·si sa·ya …
damaged	*rusak*	roo·sak
lost	*hilang*	hi·lang
stolen	*dicuri*	di·choo·ri

That's (not) mine.
Itu (bukan) milik saya.   i·too (boo·kan) mi·lik sa·ya

Can I have some coins?
Boleh saya dapat uang logam?   bo·leh sa·ya da·pat oo·ang lo·gam

plane

Where does flight (ME777) arrive/depart?
Di mana tempat keberangkatan/kedatangan penerbangan (ME777)?   di ma·na tem·pat ke·be·rang·ka·tan/ke·da·tang·an pe·ner·bang·an (em e too·jooh too·jooh too·jooh)

Where's (the) …?	*Di mana …?*	di ma·na …
airport shuttle	*bis bandara*	bis ban·da·ra
arrivals hall	*kedatangan*	ke·da·tang·an
departures hall	*keberangkatan*	ke·be·rang·ka·tan
duty-free	*bebas bea*	be·bas be·a
gate (number two)	*pintu (nomor dua)*	pin·too (no·mor doo·a)

bus, coach & minibus

bis dan bemo

How often do buses come?
Berapa sering ada bis di sini?   be·ra·pa se·ring a·da bis di si·ni

Where do I catch a minibus?
Di mana saya bisa naik bemo?   di ma·na sa·ya bi·sa na·ik be·mo

Does the bus stop at (Gianyar)?
Bisnya berhenti di (Gianyar)?   bis·nya ber·hen·ti di (gi·a·nyar)

How much to (Ubud)?
Ongkos ke (Ubud) berapa?   ong·kos ke (oo·bood) be·ra·pa

I might just walk.
Mungkin saya jalan kaki saja.   moong·kin sa·ya ja·lan ka·ki sa·ja

How many people can ride on this?
Berapa orang bisa naik ini?   be·ra·pa o·rang bi·sa na·ik i·ni

Are you waiting for more people?
Anda masih menunggu orang lagi?   an·da ma·sih me·noong·goo o·rang la·gi

Can you take us around the city, please?
Bisa antar kami keliling kota?   bi·sa an·tar ka·mi ke·li·ling ko·ta

I'd like to get off at (Kuta).
   Saya mau turun di (Kuta).   sa·ya mow too·roon di (koo·ta)

What's the next stop?
   Apa nama halte berikutnya?   a·pa na·ma hal·te be·ri·koot·nya

Next stop, please.
   Tolong, berhenti di halte   to·long ber·hen·ti di hal·te
   yang berikut.   yang be·ri·koot

You're on my foot.
   Anda injak kaki saya.   an·da in·jak ka·ki sa·ya

city n&a	*kota*	ko·ta
intercity a	*antarkota*	an·tar·ko·ta
local a	*lokal*	lo·kal

For bus numbers, see **numbers & amounts**, page 31.

---

wanna lift?

If you're looking for someone to take you for a ride, ask for an *opelet* o·pe·let, *angkot* ang·kot or *bemo* be·mo – they're all local words for 'minibus'.

---

train

What station is this?
   Ini stasiun apa?   i·ni sta·si·oon a·pa

What's the next station?
   Stasiun apa yang berikut?   sta·si·oon a·pa yang be·ri·koot

Does it stop at (Tegal)?
   Di (Tegal) berhenti?   di (te·gal) ber·hen·ti

Do I need to change?
   Saya harus ganti kereta?   sa·ya ha·roos gan·ti ke·re·ta

Is it direct/express?
   Ini langsung/ekspres?   i·ni lang·soong/eks·pres

Which carriage is …?	*Kereta yang mana …?*	ke·re·ta yang ma·na …
for (Semarang)	*ke (Semarang)*	ke (se·ma·rang)
1st class	*kelas satu*	ke·las sa·too
for dining	*restorka*	re·stor·ka

boat

kapal

What's the sea like today?
Bagaimana kondisi laut hari ini?
ba·gai·ma·na kon·di·si la·oot ha·ri i·ni

Are there life jackets?
Ada baju pelampung?
a·da ba·joo pe·lam·poong

What island/beach is this?
Ini pulau/pantai apa?
i·ni poo·low/pan·tai a·pa

---

writing home

Indonesian city addresses look similar to the one on the left below. It means that the addressee lives in:

Jl. Banda 23	23 Banda Street (*Jl.* is short for *Jalan*, or 'street')
RT 08 RW 10	Neighbourhood (*Rukun Tetangga*) number 8, in Bandung, also known as Administrative Unit (*Rukun Warga*) number 10
Ciumbuleuit	Ciumbuleuit
Bandung 40142	Bandung, postcode 40142
Jabar	the province of West Java (*Jabar*, short for *Jawa Barat*)

Other abbreviated province names include *Jatim* (*Jawa Timur*) and *NTT* (*Nusa Tenggara Timur*). Addresses may also include *kampung* (village), *desa* (village area), *kecamatan* or *kec.* (subdistrict) and *kabupaten* or *kab.* (regency).

As you'd expect from an archipelago of more than 18,000 islands, there's a wide variety of waterborne transport. Here are some boats you could find yourself floating in …

kapal kayu	ka·pal ka·yoo	wooden ship
kapal Pelni	ka·pal pel·ni	large, government-run passenger ship
ketinting	ke·tin·ting	canoe with outboard propeller
longboat	long·bot	wooden boat with an engine
perahu layar	pe·ra·hoo la·yar	sailing boat
sampan	sam·pan	canoe
spid	spid	fibreglass speedboat with several engines

I feel seasick.

   Saya mabuk.   sa·ya ma·book

Can I dine at the captain's table?

   Boleh saya makan di   bo·leh sa·ya ma·kan di
   meja kapten?   me·ja kap·ten

boat (general)	*kapal*	ka·pal
boat (local)	*perahu*	pe·ra·hoo
cabin	*kamar*	ka·mar
captain n	*kapten*	kap·ten
(car) deck	*dek (mobil)*	dek (mo·bil)
ferry n	*kapal feri*	ka·pal fe·ri
lifeboat	*sekoci penolong*	se·ko·chi pe·no·long
life jacket	*baju pelampung*	ba·joo pe·lam·poong
yacht	*kapal pesiar*	ka·pal pe·si·ar

taxi

taksi

I'd like a taxi …	*Saya mau taksi …*	sa·ya mow tak·si …
at (9am)	*pada (jam sembilan pagi)*	pa·da (jam sem·bi·lan pa·gi)
now	*sekarang*	se·ka·rang
now tomorrow	*besok*	be·sok

Where's the taxi rank?
Di mana pangkalan taksi?   di ma·na pang·ka·lan tak·si

Is this taxi available?
Taksi ini kosong?   tak·si i·ni ko·song

Please put the meter on.
Tolong, pakai argo!   to·long pa·kai ar·go

How much is it to (block M)?
Berapa ongkosnya kalau sampai (Blok M)?   be·ra·pa ong·kos·nya ka·low sam·pai (blok em)

Please take me to (this address).
Tolong antar saya ke (alamat ini).   to·long an·tar sa·ya ke (a·la·mat i·ni)

How much is it?
Berapa?   be·ra·pa

Please …	*Tolong …*	to·long …
slow down	*lebih pelan*	le·bih pe·lan
stop here	*berhenti di sini*	ber·hen·ti di si·ni
wait here	*tunggu di sini*	toong·goo di si·ni

For other useful phrases, see **directions**, page 73.

car & motorbike

car & motorbike hire

I'd like to hire a/an ... (car).	Saya mau sewa (mobil) ...	sa·ya mow se·wa (mo·bil) ...
4WD	berpenggerak empat roda	ber·peng·ge·rak em·pat ro·da
automatic/ manual	transmisi otomatis/ manual	trans·mi·si o·to·ma·tis/ ma·noo·al
motorbike	sepeda motor	se·pe·da mo·tor

with ...	dengan ...	deng·an ...
air conditioning	AC	a·se
a driver	sopir	so·pir

How much for daily/weekly hire?
Berapa sewanya sehari/   be·ra·pa se·wa·nya se·ha·ri/
seminggu?   se·ming·goo

Does that include insurance?
Itu termasuk asuransi?   i·too ter·ma·sook a·soo·ran·si

Do you have a guide to the road rules (in English)?
Anda punya buku   an·da poo·nya boo·koo
peraturan jalan (dalam   pe·ra·too·ran ja·lan (da·lam
Bahasa Inggris)?   ba·ha·sa ing·gris)

Do you have a road map?
Anda punya peta jalan?   an·da poo·nya pe·ta ja·lan

---

signs

BERHENTI	ber·hen·ti	Stop
BERI JALAN	be·ri ja·lan	Give Way
DILARANG MASUK	di·la·rang ma·sook	No Entry
KELUAR	ke·loo·ar	Exit
MASUK	ma·sook	Entrance
SATU ARAH	sa·too a·rah	One-way

on the road

What's the speed limit?
Berapa batas kecepatan di sini?
be·ra·pa ba·tas ke·che·pa·tan di si·ni

Is this the road to (Banten)?
Ini jalan ke (Banten)?
i·ni ja·lan ke (ban·ten)

Where's a petrol station?
Di mana ada pompa bensin?
di ma·na a·da pom·pa ben·sin

Please fill it up.
Tolong, diisi sampai penuh.
to·long di·i·si sam·pai pe·nooh

I'd like (20) litres.
Saya mau (duapuluh) liter.
sa·ya mow (doo·a·poo·looh) li·ter

diesel n	*solar*	so·lar
leaded n	*bensin biasa*	ben·sin bi·a·sa
LPG n	*gas LPG*	gas el·pi·ji
premium unleaded n	*premix*	pre·miks
regular n	*bensin*	ben·sin
unleaded n	*premium*	pre·mi·oom

Can you check the ...?
Anda bisa cek ...?
an·da bi·sa chek ...

oil	*minyak*	mi·nyak
tyre pressure	*tekanan ban*	te·ka·nan ban
water	*air*	a·ir

(How long) Can I park here?
(Berapa lama) Boleh saya parkir di sini?
(be·ra·pa la·ma) bo·leh sa·ya par·kir di si·ni

Do I have to pay?
Saya harus bayar?
sa·ya ha·roos ba·yar

---

listen for ...

If you're hiring a car or the police have pulled you over, listen for the two ways people can say 'drivers license':

SIM
sim
Surat Ijin Mengemudi
soo·rat i·jin meng·e·moo·di

problems

I need a mechanic.
Saya perlu montir.   sa·ya per·loo mon·tir

I've had an accident.
Saya mengalami   sa·ya meng·a·la·mi
kecelekaan.   ke·che·le·ka·an

The car has broken down (at Ngade).
Mobil saya mogok   mo·bil sa·ya mo·gok
(di Ngade).   (di nga·de)

The motorbike has broken down (at Cibodas).
Sepeda motor saya   se·pe·da mo·tor sa·ya
mogok (di Cibodas).   mo·gok (di chi·bo·das)

The car won't start.
Mobil ini tidak mau   mo·bil i·ni ti·dak mow
hidup mesinnya.   hi·doop me·sin·nya

The motorbike won't start.
Sepeda motor ini   se·pe·da mo·tor i·ni
tidak mau hidup mesinnya.   ti·dak mow hi·doop me·sin·nya

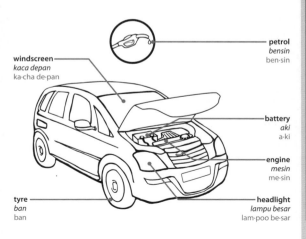

petrol
bensin
ben·sin

windscreen
kaca depan
ka·cha de·pan

battery
aki
a·ki

engine
mesin
me·sin

tyre
ban
ban

headlight
lampu besar
lam·poo be·sar

I have a flat tyre.
Bannya kempes.   ban·nya kem·pes

I've lost my car keys.
Kunci mobil saya hilang.   koon·chi mo·bil sa·ya hi·lang

I've locked the keys inside.
Kuncinya tertinggal   koon·chi·nya ter·ting·gal
di dalam.   di da·lam

I've run out of petrol.
Bensinnya habis.   ben·sin·nya ha·bis

Can you fix it (today)?
Bisa diperbaiki (hari ini)?   bi·sa di·per·bai·ki (ha·ri i·ni)

How long will it take?
Berapa lama selesainya?   be·ra·pa la·ma se·le·sai·nya

bicycle

sepeda

I'd like to buy/ hire a bicycle.	*Saya mau beli/ sewa sepeda.*	sa·ya mow be·li/ se·wa se·pe·da
I'd like a … bike.	*Saya mau sepeda …*	sa·ya mow se·pe·da …
mountain	*gunung*	goo·noong
racing	*balap*	ba·lap
second-hand	*bekas*	be·kas
How much is it per …?	*Berapa sewanya …?*	be·ra·pa se·wa·nya …
day	*sehari*	se·ha·ri
hour	*satu jam*	sa·too jam

Do I need a helmet?
Saya harus pakai helem?   sa·ya ha·roos pa·kai he·lem

I have a puncture.
Bannya bocor.   ban·nya bo·chor

I'd like my bicycle repaired.
Saya mau sepeda   sa·ya mow se·pe·da
saya diperbaiki.   sa·ya di·per·bai·ki

border crossing

imigrasi

I'm here …	*Saya di sini untuk …*	sa·ya di si·ni oon·took …
in transit	*singgah saja*	sing·gah sa·ja
on business	*urusan bisnis*	oo·roo·san bis·nis
on holiday	*berlibur*	ber·li·boor

I'm here for …	*Saya di sini selama …*	sa·ya di si·ni se·la·ma …
(10) days	*(sepuluh) hari*	(se·poo·looh) ha·ri
(two) months	*(dua) bulan*	(doo·a) boo·lan
(three) weeks	*(tiga) minggu*	(ti·ga) ming·goo

I'm going to (Bogor).
Saya mau ke (Bogor). sa·ya mow ke (bo·gor)

Do I need a travel permit to go to (Papua)?
Saya harus pakai surat sa·ya ha·roos pa·kai soo·rat
jalan kalau mau ke (Papua)? ja·lan ka·low mow ke (pa·poo·a)

I'm staying at (Wisma Firman).
Saya tinggal di sa·ya ting·gal di
(Wisma Firman). (wis·ma fir·man)

---

on your way in

look for …

Bea Cukai	be·a choo·kai	**Customs**
Pemeriksaan	pe·me·rik·sa·an	**Passport Control**
Paspor	pas·por	

listen for …

kelompok	ke·lom·pok	**group**
keluarga	ke·loo·ar·ga	**family**
sendiri	sen·di·ri	**alone**

at customs

Do I have to declare this?
Ini harus dilaporkan? · · · · · i·ni ha·roos di·la·por·kan

I have nothing to declare.
Tidak ada yang · · · · · ti·dak a·da yang
harus dilaporkan. · · · · · ha·roos di·la·por·kan

I have something to declare.
Ada barang saya · · · · · a·da ba·rang sa·ya
yang harus dilaporkan. · · · · · yang ha·roos di·la·por·kan

I didn't know I had to declare it.
Saya tidak tahu · · · · · sa·ya ti·dak ta·hoo
itu harus dilaporkan. · · · · · i·too ha·roos di·la·por·kan

That's (not) mine.
Itu (bukan) milik saya. · · · · · i·too (boo·kan) mi·lik sa·ya

Terima Kasih

Where's a/the ...?	Di mana ...?	di ma·na ...
bank	bank	bank
market	pasar	pa·sar
public toilet	WC umum	we·se oo·moom
tourist office	kantor	kan·tor
	pariwisata	pa·ri·wi·sa·ta

How do I get there?
Bagaimana cara ke sana?   ba·gai·ma·na cha·ra ke sa·na

How far is it?
Berapa jauh dari sini?   be·ra·pa ja·ooh da·ri si·ni

What's the address?
Apa alamatnya?   a·pa a·la·mat·nya

Can you show me (on the map)?
Bisa tunjukkan kepada   bi·sa toon·joo·kan ke·pa·da
saya (di peta)?   sa·ya (di pe·ta)

What street/village is this?
Ini jalan/kampung apa?   i·ni ja·lan/kam·poong a·pa

It's ...	Itu ...	i·too ...
behind ...	di belakang ...	di be·la·kang ...
close	dekat	de·kat
far	jauh	ja·ooh
here	di sini	di si·ni
in front of ...	di depan ...	di de·pan ...
near ...	dekat ...	de·kat ...
next to ...	di samping ...	di sam·ping ...
on the corner	di tikungan	di ti·koong·an
opposite ...	di seberang ...	di se·be·rang ...
straight ahead	lurus	loo·roos
there	di sana	di sa·na

For words used in addresses, see **transport**, page 57.

Turn (at the) ...	Belok ...	be·lok ...
corner	di tikungan	di ti·koong·an
left	kiri	ki·ri
right	kanan	ka·nan
traffic lights	di lampu	di lam·poo
	lalu-lintas	la·loolin·tas
by ...	naik ...	na·ik ...
bus	bis	bis
foot	jalan kaki	ja·lan ka·ki
minibus	bemo	be·mo
rickshaw	becak	be·chak
taxi	taksi	tak·si
train	kereta api	ke·re·ta a·pi
north	utara	oo·ta·ra
south	selatan	se·la·tan
east	timur	ti·moor
west	barat	ba·rat

traffic lights
*lampu
lalu-lintas*
lam·poo
la·loo lin·tas

shop
toko
to·ko

pedestrian
crossing
*penyeberangan
di jalan*
pe·nye·be·rang·an
di ja·lan

bus
bis
bis

intersection
simpang jalan
sim·pang ja·lan

corner
tikungan
ti·koong·an

taxi
taksi
tak·si

finding accommodation

Where's a …?	*Di mana ada …?*	di ma·na a·da …
guesthouse	*losmen*	los·men
hotel	*hotel*	ho·tel
inn	*wisma*	wis·ma
lodging house	*penginapan*	peng·i·na·pan
room for rent	*kamar yang*	ka·mar yang
	disewakan	di·se·wa·kan
Can you	*Anda bisa*	an·da bi·sa
recommend	*rekomendasikan*	re·ko·men·da·si·kan
somewhere …?	*tempat yang …?*	tem·pat yang …
cheap	*murah*	moo·rah
clean	*bersih*	ber·sih
good	*bagus*	ba·goos
luxurious	*mewah*	me·wah
nearby	*dekat*	de·kat
romantic	*romantis*	ro·man·tis

What's the address?
   Alamatnya apa?   a·la·mat·nya a·pa

For responses, see **directions**, page 73.

---

camp out

Indonesia doesn't usually offer youth hostels or camping grounds, but you can always ask …

Where's a …?	*Di mana ada …*	di ma·na a·da …
youth hostel	*losmen pemuda*	los·men pe·moo·da
camping	*kemping*	kem·ping
ground		

booking ahead & checking in

pesan di muka dan check-in

I'd like to book a room, please.
Tolong, saya mau — to·long sa·ya mow
pesan satu kamar. — pe·san sa·too ka·mar

I have a reservation.
Saya sudah punya booking. — sa·ya soo·dah poo·nya boo·king

My name's …
Nama saya … — na·ma sa·ya …

For (three) nights/weeks.
Selama (tiga) malam/ — se·la·ma (ti·ga) ma·lam/
minggu. — ming·goo

From (2 July) to (6 July).
Dari (dua Juli) — da·ri (doo·a joo·li)
sampai (enam Juli). — sam·pai (e·nam joo·li)

Do I need to pay upfront?
Saya harus bayar langsung? — sa·ya ha·roos ba·yar lang·soong

Do you have a … room?	*Ada kamar …?*	a·da ka·mar …
single	*untuk satu orang*	oon·took sa·too o·rang
double	*untuk dua orang*	oon·took doo·a o·rang
twin	*dengan dua tempat tidur*	deng·an doo·a tem·pat ti·door

How much per …?	Berapa satu …?	be·ra·pa sa·too …
night	malam	ma·lam
person	orang	o·rang
week	minggu	ming·goo

Can I see it?	Boleh saya lihat?	bo·leh sa·ya li·hat
I'll take it.	Saya ambil.	sa·ya am·bil

Can I pay by …?	Boleh saya bayar dengan …?	bo·leh sa·ya ba·yar deng·an …
credit card	kartu kredit	kar·too kre·dit
travellers cheque	cek perjalanan	chek per·ja·la·nan

Does that price include tax?
Tarifnya sudah termasuk pajak? — ta·rif·nya soo·dah ter·ma·sook pa·jak

Is hot water available 24 hours?
Air panasnya mengalir duapuluh empat jam? — air pa·nas·nya meng·a·lir doo·a·poo·looh em·pat jam

For other methods of payment, see **money**, page 41, and **banking**, page 101.

requests & queries

permintaan dan pertanyaan

When's breakfast served?
Jam berapa ada sarapan pagi? — jam be·ra·pa a·da sa·ra·pan pa·gi

Where's breakfast served?
Di mana ada sarapan pagi? — di ma·na a·da sa·ra·pan pa·gi

Please wake me at (seven).
Tolong, bangunkan saya pada jam (tujuh). — to·long bang·oon·kan sa·ya pa·da jam (too·jooh)

signs		
Kamar Mandi	ka·mar man·di	**Bathroom**
Masih Menerima Tamu	ma·sih me·ne·ri·ma ta·moo	**Vacancy**
Penuh	pe·nooh	**No Vacancy**

Can I use the ...?	Boleh saya pakai ...?	bo·leh sa·ya pa·kai ...
kitchen	dapur	da·poor
laundry	tempat cuci baju	tem·pat choo·chi ba·joo
telephone	telpon	tel·pon

Do you have a/an ...?	Ada ...?	a·da ...
elevator	lift	lift
laundry service	tukang cuci	too·kang choo·chi
message board	papan pencatat pesan	pa·pan pen·cha·tat pe·san
safe	kotak deposit	ko·tak de·po·sit
swimming pool	kolam renang	ko·lam re·nang

Do you ... here?	Anda bisa ... di sini?	an·da bi·sa ... di si·ni
arrange tours	merencanakan tour	me·ren·cha·na·kan toor
change money	tukar uang	too·kar oo·ang

Could I have (a) ... please?	Tolong, saya minta ...	to·long sa·ya min·ta ...
my key	kunci saya	koon·chi sa·ya
mosquito net	kelambu	ke·lam·boo
receipt	kuitansi	koo·i·tan·si

that kind of place

As you trawl through the city streets looking for a place to lay your head, there's one kind of hotel where you probably don't want to end up. Indonesians call these places either *hotel jam-jaman* ho·tel jam ja·man (lit: by-the-hour hotel) or *tempat begituan* tem·pat be·gi·too·an (lit: that kind of place). As you might guess, both cater mostly to prostitution.

Is there a message for me?
Ada pesan untuk saya?
a·da pe·san oon·took sa·ya

Can I leave a message for someone?
Boleh saya titip pesan
buat seseorang?
bo·leh sa·ya ti·tip pe·san
boo·at se·se·o·rang

I'm locked out of my room.
Kunci saya tertinggal
di dalam.
koon·chi sa·ya ter·ting·gal
di da·lam

Can I get another (blanket)?
Boleh saya minta satu
(selimut) lagi?
bo·leh sa·ya min·ta sa·too
(se·li·moot) la·gi

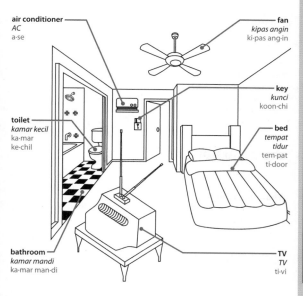

air conditioner
AC
a·se

fan
kipas angin
ki·pas ang·in

key
kunci
koon·chi

toilet
kamar kecil
ka·mar
ke·chil

bed
tempat
tidur
tem·pat
ti·door

bathroom
kamar mandi
ka·mar man·di

TV
TV
ti·vi

Who is it?	*Siapa itu?*	si·a·pa i·too
Just a moment.	*Sebentar.*	se·ben·tar
Come in.	*Masuk.*	ma·sook
Come back later, please.	*Tolong, datang nanti.*	to·long da·tang nan·ti

complaints

keluhan

It's (too) ...	*Ini (terlalu) ...*	i·ni (ter·la·loo) ...
bright	*terang*	te·rang
cold	*dingin*	ding·in
dark	*gelap*	ge·lap
expensive	*mahal*	ma·hal
noisy	*ribut*	ri·boot
small	*kecil*	ke·chil

The (fan) doesn't work.
(Kipas angin) tidak berfungsi. (ki·pas ang·in) ti·dak ber·foong·si

This (pillow) isn't clean.
(Bantal) ini tidak bersih. (ban·tal) i·ni ti·dak ber·sih

checking out

check out

What time is checkout?
Jam berapa harus check-out? jam be·ra·pa ha·roos chek owt

Can I have a late checkout?
Boleh saya terlambat check-out? bo·leh sa·ya ter·lam·bat chek owt

Can you call a taxi for me (for 11 o'clock)?
Bisa pesan taksi untuk saya pada (jam sebelas)? bi·sa pe·san tak·si oon·took sa·ya pa·da (jam se·be·las)

I'm leaving now.
Saya berangkat.   sa·ya be·rang·kat

Can I leave my bags here?
Boleh saya titip tas di sini?   bo·leh sa·ya ti·tip tas di si·ni

There's a mistake in the bill.
Ada kesalahan dalam   a·da ke·sa·la·han da·lam
kuitansi ini.   koo·i·tan·si i·ni

Could I have my ..., please?	*Saya minta ...*	sa·ya min·ta ...
	saya.	sa·ya
deposit	*deposit*	de·po·sit
passport	*paspor*	pas·por
valuables	*barang berharga*	ba·rang ber·har·ga

I'll be back ...	*Saya akan*	sa·ya a·kan
	kembali ...	kem·ba·li ...
in (three) days	*dalam (tiga) hari*	da·lam (ti·ga) ha·ri
on (Tuesday)	*hari (Selasa)*	ha·ri (se·la·sa)

I had a great stay, thank you.
Saya sangat senang   sa·ya sang·at se·nang
tinggal di sini, terima kasih!   ting·gal di si·ni te·ri·ma ka·sih

I'll recommend it to my friends.
Saya akan rekomendasikan   sa·ya a·kan re·ko·men·da·si·kan
kepada teman-teman saya.   ke·pa·da te·man te·man sa·ya

---

kost-effective accommodation

If you plan to stay for at least a month, think about book-ing into a *kost* kost. This is Indonesia's answer to a shared-house, and you'll normally find them near universities and colleges. Rules and regulations sometimes apply – such as *jam malam* jam ma·lam (curfew) – and many are segre-gated into *kost pria* kost pri·a (men's accommodation) and *kost wanita* kost wa·ni·ta (women's accommodation).

renting

I'm here about the ... for rent.	Saya ke sini ingin tanya ... yang disewakan.	sa·ya ke si·ni ing·in ta·nya ... yang di·se·wa·kan
Do you have a/an ... for rent?	Anda punya ... untuk disewakan?	an·da poo·nya ... oon·took di·se·wa·kan
apartment	apartemen	a·par·te·men
cabin	pondok	pon·dok
house	rumah	roo·mah
room	kamar	ka·mar
villa	vila	vi·la
furnished	dilengkapi perabotan	di·leng·ka·pi pe·ra·bo·tan
partly furnished	dengan sebagian perabotnya	deng·an se·ba·gi·an pe·ra·bot·nya
unfurnished	tanpa perabotan	tan·pa pe·ra·bo·tan

staying with locals

Can I stay at your place?
Boleh saya tinggal
di tempat Anda?
bo·leh sa·ya ting·gal
di tem·pat an·da

Is there anything I can do to help?
Ada yang saya bisa
bantu?
a·da yang sa·ya bi·sa
ban·too

I have my own (mattress).
Saya punya (kasur)
sendiri.
sa·ya poo·nya (ka·soor)
sen·di·ri

Can I …?	Boleh saya …?	bo·leh sa·ya …
bring anything for the meal	bawa sesuatu untuk dimasak	ba·wa se·soo·a·too oon·took di·ma·sak
do the dishes	bantu mencuci	ban·too men·choo·chi
set/clear the table	mengatur meja	meng·a·toor me·ja
take out the rubbish	keluarkan sampah	ke·loo·ar·kan sam·pah

Delicious!	*Enak!*	e·nak

Thanks for your hospitality.
Terima kasih atas   te·ri·ma ka·sih a·tas
keramahtamahannya.   ke·ra·mah·ta·ma·han·nya

To compliment your hosts' cooking, see **eating out**, page 167.

accommodation

Indonesians are quick to offer travellers an invitation to their house, and it's customary to swap addresses or business cards. The home is where formalities really kick in, and the casual friendliness you may have experienced on the street will often be replaced with an almost uncomfortable reverence. Once you take off your shoes and walk in, you're a respected guest who's expected to do absolutely nothing.

If there are older people in the room as you enter, it's polite to approach and greet them with your head slightly bowed. Your host will bustle around, shooing away children and preparing small snacks plus tea, coffee or sweet drinks. Wait until these are offered to you before eating, and if something's not to your liking, it's fine to just have a bit. If you don't want the snack, say:

Sorry, I've just eaten.
Maaf, saya baru makan.　　　ma·af sa·ya ba·roo ma·kan

Once you feel it's time to move on, your phrase of choice will be:

Excuse me, I should go home now.
Permisi, pulang dulu.　　　per·mi·si poo·lang doo·loo

looking for ...

Where's a ...?	*Di mana ...?*	di ma·na ...
corner store	*kios*	ki·os
department store	*toko serbaada*	to·ko ser·ba·a·da
market	*pasar*	pa·sar
shop	*toko*	to·ko
supermarket	*supermarket*	soo·per·mar·ket

When do the markets run?
Jam berapa pasar buka? jam be·ra·pa pa·sar boo·ka

Where can I buy (a padlock)?
Di mana saya bisa di ma·na sa·ya bi·sa
beli (gembok)? be·li (gem·bok)

For more items and shopping locations, see the **dictionary**.

Boleh saya tolong?	
bo·leh sa·ya to·long	**Can I help you?**
Anda cari apa?	
an·da cha·ri a·pa	**What would you like?**
Ada lagi?	
a·da la·gi	**Anything else?**
Kami tidak punya.	
ka·mi ti·dak poo·nya	**No, we don't have any.**

making a purchase

I'm just looking.
Saya lihat-lihat saja.   sa·ya li·hat li·hat sa·ja

I'd like to buy (an adaptor plug).
Saya mau beli (adaptor).   sa·ya mow be·li (a·dap·tor)

How much is it?
Berapa harganya?   be·ra·pa har·ga·nya

Can you write down the price?
Bisa tulis berapa harganya?   bi·sa too·lis be·ra·pa har·ga·nya

Do you have any others?
Ada yang lain?   a·da yang la·in

Can I look at it?
Boleh saya lihat?   bo·leh sa·ya li·hat

Do you accept …?   *Anda menerima …?*   an·da me·ne·ri·ma …
credit cards	*kartu kredit*	kar·too kre·dit
debit cards	*debit card*	de·bit kard
travellers	*cek*	chek
cheques	*perjalanan*	per·ja·la·nan

Could I have a bag/receipt, please?
Tolong, saya   to·long sa·ya
minta tas/kuitansi.   min·ta tas/koo·i·tan·si

I don't need a bag, thanks.
Saya tidak perlu tas,   sa·ya ti·dak per·loo tas
terima kasih.   te·ri·ma ka·sih

Does it have a guarantee?
Ada garansinya?   a·da ga·ran·si·nya

---

local talk

bargain a	*murah banget*	moo·rah bang·et
rip off	*bikin kantong kempes*	bi·kin kan·tong kem·pes
sale n	*diskon*	dis·kon
specials	*penawaran khusus*	pe·na·wa·ran khoo·soos

Could I have it wrapped?
 Boleh saya minta dibungkuskan?   bo·leh sa·ya min·ta di·boong·koos·kan

Can I have it sent overseas?
 Bisa dikirimkan ke luar negeri?   bi·sa di·ki·rim·kan ke loo·ar ne·ge·ri

Can you order it for me?
 Bisa Anda pesankan untuk saya?   bi·sa an·da pe·san·kan oon·took sa·ya

Can I pick it up later?
 Boleh saya ambil nanti?   bo·leh sa·ya am·bil nan·ti

It's faulty.
 Ini rusak.   i·ni roo·sak

I'd like …, please.	*Saya mau …*	sa·ya mow …
a refund	*uang saya kembali*	oo·ang sa·ya kem·ba·li
my change	*uang kembalian saya*	oo·ang kem·ba·li·an sa·ya
to return this	*kembalikan ini*	kem·ba·li·kan i·ni

bargaining

That's too expensive.
 Itu terlalu mahal!   i·too ter·la·loo ma·hal

Can you lower the price?
 Boleh kurang?   bo·leh koo·rang

Do you have anything cheaper?
 Ada yang lebih murah?   a·da yang le·bih moo·rah

How much would you sell that to an Indonesian for?
 Untuk orang Indonesia dijual dengan harga berapa?   oon·took o·rang in·do·ne·si·a di·joo·al deng·an har·ga be·ra·pa

No more than (70,000) rupiah.
Tidak lebih dari (tujuh-   ti·dak le·bih da·ri (too·jooh-
puluh ribu) rupiah.   poo·looh ri·boo) roo·pi·ah

I'll give you (50,000).
Saya kasih (limapuluh ribu).   sa·ya ka·sih (li·ma·poo·looh ri·boo)

This is my final offer.
Ini tawaran terakhir saya.   i·ni ta·wa·ran te·ra·khir sa·ya

books & reading

buku dan pembacaan

Do you have a/an …?	*Ada …?*	a·da …
book by (Ananta Toer)	*buku karangan (Ananta Toer)*	boo·koo ka·rang·an (a·nan·ta toor)
entertainment guide	*panduan hiburan*	pan·doo·an hi·boo·ran
Is there an (English)-language …?	*Ada … Bahasa (Inggris)?*	a·da … ba·ha·sa (ing·gris)
bookshop	*toko buku*	to·ko boo·koo
section	*bagian*	ba·gi·an
I'd like a …	*Saya mau …*	sa·ya mow …
dictionary	*kamus*	ka·moos
newspaper (in English)	*koran (Bahasa Inggris)*	ko·ran (ba·ha·sa ing·gris)
notepad	*buku catatan*	boo·koo cha·ta·tan

---

got the goods

Remember to always say the g in the pronunciation guides like the 'g' in 'good', not the 'g' in 'gist'.

Can you recommend a book for me?
Bisa Anda rekomendasikan — bi·sa an·da re·ko·men·da·si·kan
buku kepada saya? — boo·koo ke·pa·da sa·ya

Do you have Lonely Planet guidebooks?
Ada panduan perjalanan — a·da pan·doo·an per·ja·la·nan
terbitan Lonely Planet? — ter·bi·tan lon·li ple·net

clothes

pakaian

My size is ...	*Ukuran saya ...*	oo·koo·ran sa·ya ...
(40)	*(empatpuluh)*	(em·pat·poo·looh)
small	*kecil*	ke·chil
medium	*sedang*	se·dang
large	*besar*	be·sar

| **Can I try it on?** | *Boleh saya coba?* | bo·leh sa·ya cho·ba |
| **It doesn't fit.** | *Tidak pas.* | ti·dak pas |

For different types of clothing, see the **dictionary**, and for sizes, see **numbers & amounts**, page 31.

electronic goods

barang-barang elektronik

Where can I buy duty-free electronic goods?
Di mana saya bisa beli — di ma·na sa·ya bi·sa be·li
barang-barang elektronik — ba·rang ba·rang e·lek·tro·nik
bebas bea? — be·bas be·a

Is this the latest model?
Ini model yang terbaru? — i·ni mo·del yang ter·ba·roo

Is this (240) volts?
Ini voltasenya — i·ni vol·ta·se·nya
(dua ratus empatpuluh)? — (doo·a·ra·toos em·pat·poo·looh)

hairdressing

I'd like (a) ...	Saya mau ...	sa·ya mow ...
blow wave	di-blow	di blo
colour	rambut saya dicat	ram·boot sa·ya di·chat
haircut	rambut saya	ram·boot sa·ya
	digunting	di·goon·ting
my beard	jenggot saya	jeng·got sa·ya
trimmed	dirapikan	di·ra·pi·kan
shave	dicukur	di·choo·koor
trim	pangkas	pang·kas

Don't cut it too short.
Jangan terlalu pendek! jan·gan ter·la·loo pen·dek

Please use a new blade.
Tolong, pakai silet to·long pa·kai si·let
yang baru. yang ba·roo

Shave it all off!
Cukur semua! choo·koor se·moo·a

I should never have let you near me!
Rambutku jadi jelek benar! ram·boot·koo ja·di je·lek be·nar

music & DVD

I'd like a ...	Saya mau ...	sa·ya mow ...
blank tape	tape kosong	tep ko·song
CD	CD	see·dee
DVD	DVD	dee·vee·dee
video	video	vi·de·o

I'm looking for something by (Yopie Latul).
Saya cari lagunya   sa·ya cha·ri la·goo·nya
(Yopie Latul).   (yo·pi la·tool)

What's their best recording?
Rekamannya yang   re·ka·man·nya yang
terbaik mana?   ter·ba·ik ma·na

Can I listen to this?
Bisa dites di sini?   bi·sa di·tes di si·ni

Will this work on any DVD player?
Apa DVD ini bisa buat   a·pa dee·vee·dee i·ni bi·sa boo·at
semua player?   se·moo·a ple·yer

Is this for a (PAL/NTSC) system?
Ini untuk sistem   i·ni oon·took si·stem
(PAL/NTSC)?   (pal/en·te·es·che)

souvenirs

basket	*keranjang*	ke·ran·jang
bracelet	*gelang*	ge·lang
caneware	*rotan*	ro·tan
earrings	*anting-anting*	an·ting an·ting
handicrafts	*kerajinan tangan*	ke·ra·ji·nan tang·an
jewellery	*perhiasan*	per·hi·a·san
machete	*parang*	pa·rang
mask	*topeng*	to·peng
necklace	*kalung*	ka·loong
ornamental dagger	*kris*	kris
painting	*lukisan*	loo·ki·san
pottery	*keramik*	ke·ra·mik
ring	*cincin*	chin·chin
sarong	*sarung*	sa·roong
shadow puppet	*wayang kulit*	wa·yang koo·lit
shell	*kerang*	ke·rang
statue	*patung*	pa·toong
stone carving	*ukiran batu*	oo·ki·ran ba·too
wood carving	*ukiran kayu*	oo·ki·ran ka·yoo
wooden puppet	*wayang golek*	wa·yang go·lek

video & photography

Do you have …	*Ada … buat*	a·da … boo·at
for this camera?	*tustel ini?*	too·stel i·ni
batteries	*batere*	ba·te·re
memory cards	*memory card*	me·mo·ri kard
Can you …?	*Bisa …?*	bi·sa …
develop digital	*cetak foto*	che·tak fo·to
photos	*digital*	di·gi·tal
develop this film	*cuci roll ini*	choo·chi rol i·ni
load my film	*isikan film ke*	i·si·kan film ke
	tustel saya	too·stel sa·ya
recharge the	*batere tustel*	ba·te·re too·stel
battery for my	*digital*	di·gi·tal
digital camera	*saya diisi ulang*	sa·ya di·i·si oo·lang
transfer photos	*ditransfer gambar-*	di·trans·fer gam·bar
from my	*gambar ini dari*	gam·bar i·ni da·ri
camera to CD	*tustel ke CD*	too·stel ke see·dee

I need a cable to connect my camera to a computer.
Saya perlu kabel   sa·ya per·loo ka·bel
menghubung dari   meng·hoo·boong da·ri
komputer ke tustel.   kom·poo·ter ke too·stel

I need a cable to recharge this battery.
Saya perlu kabel buat   sa·ya per·loo ka·bel boo·at
mengisi ulang tustel ini.   meng·i·si oo·lang too·stel i·ni

I need a video cassette for this camera.
Saya perlu kaset video   sa·ya per·loo ka·set vi·de·o
buat kamera ini.   boo·at ka·me·ra i·ni

When will it be ready?
Kapan selesai?   ka·pan se·le·sai

I need ... film for this camera.	Saya perlu film ... buat tustel ini.	sa·ya per·loo film ... boo·at too·stel i·ni
APS	APS	a·pe·es
B&W	hitam-putih	hi·tam poo·tih
colour	berwarna	ber·war·na
slide	slide	slaid
(200) speed	kecepatan (dua ratus)	ke·che·pa·tan (doo·a ra·toos)

I need a passport photo taken.
Saya mau bikin pasfoto.   sa·ya mow bi·kin pas·fo·to

How much is it?
Ongkosnya berapa?   ong·kos·nya be·ra·pa

I'm not happy with these photos.
Saya tidak puas dengan   sa·ya ti·dak poo·as deng·an
hasil foto-foto ini.   ha·sil fo·to fo·to i·ni

I don't want to pay the full price.
Saya tidak mau   sa·ya ti·dak mow
bayar penuh.   ba·yar pe·nooh

repairs

Can I have my ... repaired here? When will my ... be ready?	Bisa ... saya diperbaiki di sini? Kapan selesai ... saya?	bi·sa ... sa·ya di·per·ba·i·ki di si·ni ka·pan se·le·sai ... sa·ya
backpack	ransel	ran·sel
camera	tustel	too·stel
glasses	kacamata	ka·cha·ma·ta
shoes	sepatu	se·pa·too
sunglasses	kacamata hitam	ka·cha·ma·ta hi·tam

textiles

Did you weave this?
Anda yang tenun ini?   an·da yang te·noon i·ni

How long did that take to make?
Berapa lama waktu   be·ra·pa la·ma wak·too
membuatannya?   mem·boo·a·tan·nya

That's a beautiful colour!
Warnanya indah!   war·na·nya in·dah

How did you get that colour?
Bagaimana bisa   ba·gai·ma·na bi·sa
mendapatkan warna ini?   men·da·pat·kan war·na i·ni

Was this made locally?
Ini buatan asli di sini?   i·ni boo·a·tan as·li di si·ni

Is this handmade?
Ini buatan tangan?   i·ni boo·a·tan tang·an

How old is this fabric?
Seberapa tua usia kain ini?   se·be·ra·pa too·a oo·si·a ka·in i·ni

What's this type of fabric called?
Sebutannya apa buat   se·boo·tan·nya a·pa boo·at
kain ini?   ka·in i·ni

Is this piece for sale?
Kain ini dijual?   ka·in i·ni di·joo·al

Do you have another style?
Ada corak mode yang lain?   a·da cho·rak mo·de yang la·in

Do you have another colour?
Ada warna yang lain?   a·da war·na yang la·in

handmade *batik*	*batik tulis*	ba·tik too·lis
printed *batik*	*batik cap*	ba·tik chap
ceremonial garment	*pakaian adat*	pa·kai·an a·dat
damaged	*rusak*	roo·sak
loom	*alat tenun*	a·lat te·noon
needles	*jarum*	ja·room
pattern	*pola*	po·la
print n	*cap-capan*	chap cha·pan
thread n	*benang*	be·nang
tie-dye n	*ikat*	i·kat
weave v	*tenun*	te·noon

the internet

Where's the local Internet café?
Di mana warnet yang terdekat?
di ma·na war·net yang ter·de·kat

I'd like to … *Saya mau …* sa·ya mow …
  check my email *cek email* chek i·mel
  get Internet access *pakai internet* pa·kai in·ter·net
  use a printer *pakai printer* pa·kai prin·ter
  use a scanner *pakai scanner* pa·kai ske·ner

Do you have …? *Ada …?* a·da …
  Macs *Mac* mak
  PCs *komputer* kom·poo·ter
  a Zip drive *Zip* zip

How much per …? *Berapa …?* be·ra·pa …
  hour *satu jam* sa·too jam
  (five) minutes *(lima) menit* (li·ma) me·nit
  page *satu lembar* sa·too lem·bar

say what you mean

Keep your wits about you when you're chatting or flirting –
the word *burung* boo·roong means 'bird' and 'dick', while
main ma·in can mean both 'play' and 'have sex'.

How do I log on?
Bagaimana cara log in-nya?   ba·gai·ma·na cha·ra log in·nya

Please change it to the (English)-language setting.
Tolong, ganti setting   to·long gan·ti se·ting
ke Bahasa (Inggris).   ke ba·ha·sa (ing·gris)

It's crashed.
Ini crash.   i·ni kresh

I've finished.
Saya selesai.   sa·ya se·le·sai

mobile/cell phone

HP

I'd like a …   *Saya mau …*   sa·ya mow …
  charger for   *charger buat*   char·jer boo·at
  my phone   *HP saya*   ha·pe sa·ya
  mobile/cell   *sewa HP*   se·wa ha·pe
  phone for hire
  prepaid mobile/   *HP prabayar*   ha·pe pra·ba·yar
  cell phone
  SIM card for   *SIM kard untuk*   sim kard oon·took
  your network   *network Anda*   net·work an·da

What are the rates?
Tarifnya berapa?   ta·rif·nya be·ra·pa

(1000) rupiah per (30) seconds.
(Seribu) rupiah per   (se·ri·boo) roo·pi·ah per
(tigapuluh) detik.   (ti·ga·poo·looh) de·tik

---

get your hand off it

Try this handy hint to remember how to say 'mobile phone'
or 'cell phone' in Indonesian. The word is *HP* ha·pe, an
abbreviation of *hanpon* han·pon – which as you could
guess, it comes from the English 'hand phone'.

Dengan siapa ini?	deng·an si·a·pa i·ni	**Who's calling?**
Mau bicara	mow bi·cha·ra	**Who do you want**
dengan siapa?	deng·an si·a·pa	**to speak to?**
Sebentar.	se·ben·tar	**One moment.**
Dia tidak ada.	di·a ti·dak a·da	**He/She isn't here.**
Salah nomor.	sa·lah no·mor	**Wrong number.**

phone

telpon

What's your phone number?
Apa nomor telpon Anda?　　a·pa no·mor tel·pon an·da

Where's the nearest public phone?
Di mana boks telpon　　di ma·na boks tel·pon
umum yang terdekat?　　oo·moom yang ter·de·kat

Can I look at a phone book?
Boleh saya pinjam　　bo·leh sa·ya pin·jam
buku telpon?　　boo·koo tel·pon

I want to ...	*Saya mau ...*	sa·ya mow ...
buy a	*beli kartu*	be·li kar·too
phonecard	*telpon*	tel·pon
call	*menelpon*	me·nel·pon
(Singapore)	*(ke Singapura)*	(ke sin·ga·poo·ra)
make a	*menelpon*	me·nel·pon
(local) call	*nomor (lokal)*	no·mor (lo·kal)
reverse	*menelpon dengan*	me·nel·pon deng·an
the charges	*pembayaran*	pem·ba·ya·ran
	dibebankan si	di·be·ban·kan si
	penerima	pe·ne·ri·ma
speak for	*bicara selama*	bi·cha·ra se·la·ma
(three)	*(tiga) menit*	(ti·ga) me·nit
minutes		

communications

How much	Berapa	be·ra·pa
does ... cost?	biayanya ...?	bi·a·ya·nya ...
a (three)-	telpon per	tel·pon per
minute call	(tiga) menit	(ti·ga) me·nit
each extra	tiap menit	ti·ap me·nit
minute	seterusnya	se·te·roos·nya

What's the code for (New Zealand)?
Berapa kode   be·ra·pa ko·de
(Selandia Baru)?   (se·lan·di·a ba·roo)

The number is ...
Nomornya ...   no·mor·nya ...

It's engaged.
Sibuk.   si·book

I've been cut off.
Terputus.   ter·poo·toos

The connection's bad.
Konneksinya buruk.   ko·nek·si·nya boo·rook

Hello.
Halo.   ha·lo

Can I speak to ...?
Boleh saya bicara   bo·leh sa·ya bi·cha·ra
dengan ...?   deng·an ...

It's ...
Ini ...   i·ni ...

Is ... there?
... ada di sana?   ... a·da di sa·na

Please tell him/her I called.
Tolong sampaikan bahwa   to·long sam·pai·kan bah·wa
tadi saya menelpon.   ta·di sa·ya me·nel·pon

'allo 'allo

To say 'hello' on the telephone, use *halo* ha·lo instead of *salam* sa·lam. Some Muslims will say *assalaamualaikum* a·sa·la·a·moo·a·lai·koom (lit: peace be on you) when they pick up the phone.

Can I leave a message?
Boleh titip pesan?   bo·leh ti·tip pe·san

My number is …
Nomor saya …   no·mor sa·ya …

I don't have a contact number.
Saya tidak punya   sa·ya ti·dak poo·nya
nomor telpon.   no·mor tel·pon

I'll call back later.
Nanti saya menelpon lagi.   nan·ti sa·ya me·nel·pon la·gi

post office

I want to send a …	*Saya mau kirim …*	sa·ya mow ki·rim …
fax	*faks*	faks
letter	*surat*	soo·rat
parcel	*paket*	pa·ket
postcard	*kartu pos*	kar·too pos
I want to buy …	*Saya mau beli …*	sa·ya mow be·li …
an aerogram	*warkat pos*	war·kat pos
an envelope	*amplop*	am·plop
a stamp	*perangko*	pe·rang·ko
customs	*deklarasi bea*	de·kla·ra·si be·a
declaration	*cukai*	choo·kai
domestic a	*dalam negeri*	da·lam ne·ge·ri
fragile a	*gampang pecah*	gam·pang pe·chah
international a	*internasional*	in·ter·na·si·o·nal
mail n	*pos*	pos
mailbox	*kotak pos*	ko·tak pos
PO box	*kotak pos*	ko·tak pos
postcode	*kode pos*	ko·de pos

snail mail		
express a	*kilat*	ki·lat
registered	*tercatat*	ter·cha·tat
sea a	*biasa*	bi·a·sa

communications

99

Please send it by air/surface mail to (Australia).
Tolong, kirim dengan pos   to·long ki·rim deng·an pos
udara/biasa ke (Australia).   oo·da·ra/bi·a·sa ke (a·oo·stra·li·a)

It contains (souvenirs).
Isinya (oleh-oleh).   i·si·nya (o·leh o·leh)

Where's the poste restante section?
Di mana bagian   di ma·na ba·gi·an
poste restante?   po·ste re·stan·te

Is there any mail for me?
Ada kiriman untuk saya?   a·da ki·ri·man oon·took sa·ya

body talk

• If you're crossing the path of someone who's seated, or interrupting people who are speaking, it's polite to say *permisi* per·mi·si (excuse me) and make a slight bow.

• Get into the habit of using your right hand for eating and passing things – left-handedness is considered an anomaly in Indonesia, and children are forced to use their right hand from an early age (Indonesians use their left hand to clean themselves). If you're lucky enough to be left-handed, expect to be called *kidal* ki·dal (lefty).

• Physical contact between men and women in public is minimal in Indonesian society – it's polite, especially in traditional areas, to rather approach strangers of your own gender whenever you can. Contact between those of the same sex, however, is considered normal behaviour and not at all sexual. You'll see boys hanging out with their arms around each other's shoulders, and women can be very affectionate with their close friends.

• Touching the top of someone's head is generally unacceptable, as it's believed that this is where the soul resides. There are some exceptions you'll probably see, children are frequently caressed on the head, and friends of the same age often stroke each others' hair affectionately.

banking
perbankan

Large cities in Indonesia will all offer the usual foreign exchange services. Once you head off into the more remote areas, however, your chances of even changing money are quite slim – make sure you've changed enough *rupiah* before getting off the beaten track.

What time does the bank open/close?
Bank ini buka/tutup   bank i·ni boo·ka/too·toop
jam berapa?   jam be·ra·pa

I'd like to ...	*Saya mau ...*	sa·ya mow ...
Where can I ...?	*Di mana saya bisa ...?*	di ma·na sa·ya bi·sa ...
cash a cheque	*menguangkan cek*	meng·oo·ang·kan chek
change a travellers cheque	*tukar cek perjalanan*	too·kar chek per·ja·la·nan
change money	*tukar uang*	too·kar oo·ang
get a cash advance	*minta cash advance*	min·ta kesh ad·vans
withdraw money	*menarik uang*	me·na·rik oo·ang

listen for ...

Tanda tangan di sini. tan·da tang·an di si·ni	**Sign here.**
Ada masalah. a·da ma·sa·lah	**There's a problem.**
Kami tidak bisa. ka·mi ti·dak bi·sa	**We can't do that.**
Tidak ada uang tersisa lagi. ti·dak a·da oo·ang ter·si·sa la·gi	**You have no funds left.**

What's the ...?	Berapa ...?	be·ra·pa ...
exchange rate	kursnya	koors·nya
charge for that	beayanya itu	be·a·ya·nya i·too
Where's a/an ...?	Di mana ...?	di ma·na ...
automated teller machine	ATM	a·te·em
foreign exchange office	kantor penukaran mata uang asing	kan·tor pe·noo·ka·ran ma·ta oo·ang a·sing

The automated teller machine took my card.
ATM menelan kartu saya.   a·te·em me·ne·lan kar·too sa·ya

I've forgotten my PIN.
Saya lupa kode PIN saya.   sa·ya loo·pa ko·de pin sa·ya

Can I use my credit card to withdraw money?
Bisa saya ambil uang   bi·sa sa·ya am·bil oo·ang
dengan kartu kredit saya?   deng·an kar·too kre·dit sa·ya

Has my money arrived yet?
Uang saya sudah masuk?   oo·ang sa·ya soo·dah ma·sook

How long will it take to arrive?
Perlu berapa lama   per·loo be·ra·pa la·ma
sampai uangnya masuk?   sam·pai oo·ang·nya ma·sook

For other useful phrases, see **money**, page 41.

---

on the money

The currency of Indonesia is the *rupiah* roo·pi·ah (rupiah), which you'll also see abbreviated to '*Rp*'. Coins come in denominations of 25, 50, 100 and 500 *rupiah*, while notes are available in 500, 1000, 5000, 10,000, 20,000, 50,000 and 100,000 *rupiah*.

A common slang term for *uang* oo·ang (money) is *duit* doo·it, but you probably shouldn't be using it in a bank ...

I'd like a ...	*Saya minta ...*	sa·ya min·ta ...
catalogue	*katalog*	ka·ta·log
guide	*pemandu*	pe·man·doo
guidebook	*buku petunjuk*	boo·koo pe·toon·jook
(in English)	*pariwisata (dalam Bahasa Inggris)*	pa·ri·wi·sa·ta (da·lam ba·ha·sa ing·gris)
(local) map	*peta (daerah)*	pe·ta (da·e·rah)

Do you have information on ... sights?	*Anda punya informasi tentang obyek wisata ...?*	an·da poo·nya in·for·ma·si ten·tang ob·yek wi·sa·ta ...
cultural	*budaya*	boo·da·ya
historical	*sejarah*	se·ja·rah
natural	*alam*	a·lam
religious	*agama*	a·ga·ma

I'd like to see ...
Saya mau lihat ... — sa·ya mow li·hat ...

What's that?
Apa itu? — a·pa i·too

Who made it?
Dibuat oleh siapa? — di·boo·at o·leh si·a·pa

How old is it?
Berapa umurnya? — be·ra·pa oo·moor·nya

Could you take a photo of me?
Bisa saya minta tolong dipotretkan? — bi·sa sa·ya min·ta to·long di·po·tret·kan

Can I take a photo (of you)?
Boleh saya potret (Anda)? — bo·leh sa·ya po·tret (an·da)

I'll send you the photo.
Saya akan kirim fotonya. — sa·ya a·kan ki·rim fo·to·nya

getting in

What time does it open/close?
Jam berapa buka/tutup?   jam be·ra·pa boo·ka/too·toop

What's the admission charge?
Ongkos masuk berapa?   ong·kos ma·sook be·ra·pa

Is there a	*Ada diskon*	a·da dis·kon
discount for …?	*untuk …?*	oon·took …
children	*anak*	a·nak
older	*orang berusia*	o·rang be·roo·si·a
people	*lanjut*	lan·joot
students	*mahasiswa*	ma·ha·sis·wa

tours

Can you	*Anda bisa*	an·da bi·sa
suggest a …?	*rekomendasikan …?*	re·ko·men·da·si·kan …
When's the	*Kapan … yang*	ka·pan … yang
next …?	*berikutnya?*	be·ri·koot·nya
boat trip	*tour pakai kapal*	toor pa·kai ka·pal
day trip	*tour sehari*	toor se·ha·ri
tour	*tour*	toor

Is … included?	*Termasuk …?*	ter·ma·sook …
accom-	*ongkos*	ong·kos
modation	*menginap*	meng·i·nap
food	*makanan*	ma·ka·nan
transport	*transportasi*	tran·spor·ta·si

The guide will pay.
Pemandu yang bayar.   pe·man·doo yang ba·yar

How long is the tour?
Berapa lama tournya?   be·ra·pa la·ma toor·nya

What time should we be back?
Jam berapa kami   jam be·ra·pa ka·mi
harus kembali?   ha·roos kem·ba·li

Where's the …?	Di mana …?	di ma·na …
I'm attending a …	Saya menghadiri …	sa·ya meng·ha·di·ri …
conference	konferensi	kon·fe·ren·si
course	kursus	koor·soos
meeting	rapat	ra·pat
trade fair	pekan raya	pe·kan ra·ya
	dagang	da·gang

I'm with …	Saya dengan …	sa·ya deng·an …
(Gramedia)	(Gramedia)	(gra·me·di·a)
my colleague(s)	teman sekerja	te·man se·ker·ja
	saya	sa·ya
(two) others	(dua) orang lain	(doo·a) o·rang la·in

I'm alone.
Saya sendiri.   sa·ya sen·di·ri

I have an appointment with …
Saya ada janji dengan …   sa·ya a·da jan·ji deng·an …

I'm staying at (the Hotel Ayu), room (14).
Saya tinggal di (Hotel Ayu),   sa·ya ting·gal di (ho·tel a·yoo)
kamar nomor (empatbelas).   ka·mar no·mor (em·pat·be·las)

I'm here for (two) days/weeks.
Saya di sini selama   sa·ya di si·ni se·la·ma
(dua) hari/minggu.   (doo·a) ha·ri/ming·goo

Here's my business card.
Ini kartu nama saya.   i·ni kar·too na·ma sa·ya

Here's my …	Ini … saya.	i·ni … sa·ya
What's your …?	Apa … Anda?	a·pa … an·da
(email) address	alamat (email)	a·la·mat (i·mel)
fax number	nomor faks	no·mor faks
mobile number	nomor HP	no·mor ha·pe
pager number	nomor pager	no·mor pe·jer
work number	nomor telpon	no·mor tel·pon
	kantor	kan·tor

I need (a/an) ...	Saya perlu ...	sa·ya per·loo ...
computer	komputer	kom·poo·ter
Internet connection	koneksi internet	ko·nek·si in·ter·net
interpreter	juru bahasa	joo·roo ba·ha·sa
more business cards	kartu nama lagi	kar·too na·ma lagi
some space to set up	tempat untuk mengeset	tem·pat oon·took meng·e·set
to send a fax	kirim faks	ki·rim faks

That went very well.
Itu berjalan baik.
i·too ber·ja·lan ba·ik

Thank you for your time.
Terima kasih atas waktunya.
te·ri·ma ka·sih a·tas wak·too·nya

Shall we go for a drink/meal?
Mau pergi minum/ makan bersama?
mow per·gi mi·noom/ makan ber·sa·ma

It's on me.
Saya traktir.
sa·ya trak·tir

---

when in java ...

... speak as the Javanese do. Here are some terms which are specific to Indonesia's capital-island.

mas	mas	Literally 'older brother', *mas* is a polite term used to address younger men.
mbak	mbak	The female equivalent of *mas* (so, 'older sister') used to address younger women.
tambul	tam·bool	A term for food that goes well with drinks.
wedang	we·dang	The island word for 'a drink'.

senior & disabled travellers
keperulan khusus

Offering special services to seniors and disabled people is generally unknown in Indonesia – you may be lucky in the larger airports and hotels, where English is spoken.

The good news, however, is that older people are highly respected and disabled travellers will usually find locals very helpful. Consider hiring a guide to assist you.

I have a disability.
   Saya penyandang cacat.   sa·ya pe·nyan·dang cha·chat

I need assistance.
   Saya perlu dibantu.   sa·ya per·loo di·ban·too

Can I hire a guide to help me?
   Bisa saya sewa seorang   bi·sa sa·ya se·wa se·o·rang
   pengantar untuk   peng·an·tar oon·took
   membantu saya?   mem·ban·too sa·ya

What services do you have for people with a disability?
   Anda punya pelayanan   an·da poo·nya pe·la·ya·nan
   khusus apa untuk   khoo·soos a·pa oon·took
   orang cacat?   o·rang cha·chat

I'm deaf.
   Saya tuli.   sa·ya too·li

I have a hearing aid.
   Saya pakai alat bantu   sa·ya pa·kai a·lat ban·too
   dengar.   deng·ar

Are guide dogs permitted?
   Anjing penuntun   an·jing pe·noon·toon
   boleh masuk?   bo·leh ma·sook

My companion is blind/deaf.
   Teman saya buta/tuli.   te·man sa·ya boo·ta/too·li

Can I reach/enter it by wheelchair?
   Bisa saya sampai/masuk   bi·sa sa·ya sam·pai/ma·sook
   di sana dengan kursi-roda?   di sa·na deng·an koor·si ro·da

Is there a lift/elevator?
    Ada lift?   a·da lift

How many steps are there?
    Ada berapa anak tangga?   a·da be·ra·pa a·nak tang·ga

How wide is the entrance?
    Berapa lebar pintu   be·ra·pa le·bar pin·too
    masuknya?   ma·sook·nya

Could you help me (cross the street safely)?
    Bisa Anda bantu saya   bi·sa an·da ban·too sa·ya
    (menyeberang jalan   (me·nye·be·rang ja·lan
    secara aman)?   se·cha·ra a·man)

Is there somewhere I can sit down?
    Ada tempat agar   a·da tem·pat a·gar
    saya bisa duduk?   sa·ya bi·sa doo·dook

guide dog	*anjing penuntun*	an·jing pe·noon·toon
older person	*orang usia lanjut*	o·rang oo·si·a lan·joot
person with	*orang penyandang*	o·rang pe·nyan·dang
a disability	*cacat*	cha·chat
ramp	*jalan melandai*	ja·lan me·lan·dai
walking frame	*penyangga jalan*	pe·nyang·ga ja·lan
walking stick	*tongkat*	tong·kat
wheelchair	*kursi-roda*	koor·si ro·da

it's all about you

There are several forms of the word 'you' in Indonesian, with varying levels of politeness. The word you can use politely with any individual is *Anda* an·da – this is used in most of this book. Make sure you use *Anda* or *saudara* sow·da·ra (lit: sibling) for strangers. Use *kalian* ka·li·an or its more polite version *Anda sekalian* an·da se·ka·li·an if you're talking to more than one person. With peers of your own age, use *engkau* eng·kow (*kau* kow for short), and for children and close friends you can use *kamu* ka·moo (or *mu* moo). To show extra respect, use the word *Bapak* ba·pak (lit: Father) or *Ibu* i·boo (lit: Mother). For more on how to address people, see **meeting people**, page 115, and **personal pronouns** in the **phrasebuilder**, page 23.

travelling with children

perjalanan dengan anak-anak

Services for *anak-anak* (children) aren't readily available in Indonesia, unless you're using facilities which cater especially to Westerners. If you're travelling in rural areas, you'll find this particularly challenging. A saving grace is that Indonesians love children, and are very tolerant of them in most situations.

Is there a ...?	*Ada ... anak?*	a·da ... a·nak
child-minding service	*servis penjagaan*	ser·vis pen·ja·ga·an
discount for children	*diskon khusus*	dis·kon khoo·soos

I need a/an ...	*Saya perlu ...*	sa·ya per·loo ...
baby seat	*jok bayi*	jok ba·yi
(English-speaking) babysitter	*pengasuh anak (yang bisa berbahasa Inggris)*	peng·a·sooh a·nak (yang bi·sa ber·ba·ha·sa ing·gris)
booster seat	*jok anak*	jok a·nak
cot	*velbet*	vel·bet
highchair	*kursi tinggi*	koor·si ting·gi
	buat balita	boo·at ba·li·ta
plastic bag	*kantong plastik*	kan·tong pla·stik
plastic sheet	*alas tidur plastik*	a·las ti·door pla·stik
potty	*pispot anak-anak*	pis·pot a·nak a·nak
pram/stroller	*kereta dorong bayi*	ke·re·ta do·rong ba·yi
sick bag	*kantong muntah*	kan·tong moon·tah

Do you sell ...?	Anda jual ...?	an·da joo·al ...
baby wipes	tisu bayi	ti·soo ba·yi
disposable nappies/diapers	popok sekali pakai	po·pok se·ka·li pa·kai
painkillers for infants	obat penawar sakit untuk bayi	o·bat pe·na·war sa·kit oon·took ba·yi
tissues	tisu	ti·soo

Where's the nearest ...?	Di mana ... yang terdekat?	di ma·na ... yang ter·de·kat
park	taman	ta·man
playground	tempat bermain	tem·pat ber·ma·in
swimming pool	kolam renang	ko·lam re·nang
tap/faucet	keran	ke·ran
toyshop	toko mainan	to·ko ma·i·nan

Are there any good places to take children around here?

Ada tempat yang cocok
untuk anak-anak di
sekitar sini?

a·da tem·pat yang cho·chok
oon·took a·nak a·nak di
se·ki·tar si·ni

Is there space for a pram?

Ada tempat khusus
kereta bayi?

a·da tem·pat khoo·soos
ke·re·ta ba·yi

Are children allowed?

Anak-anak boleh masuk?   a·nak a·nak bo·leh ma·sook

Where can I change a nappy?

Di mana tempat untuk
menganti popok bayi?

di ma·na tem·pat oon·took
men·gan·ti po·pok ba·yi

Can I breast-feed here?

Boleh saya menyusui
bayi di sini?

bo·leh sa·ya me·nyoo·soo·i
ba·yi di si·ni

Could I have some paper and pencils, please?

Boleh saya minta
kertas dan pensil?

bo·leh sa·ya min·ta
ker·tas dan pen·sil

Is this suitable for (five)-year-old children?

Ini sesuai untuk anak
usia (lima) tahun?

i·ni se·soo·ai oon·took a·nak
oo·si·a (li·ma) ta·hoon

Do you know a …	*Anda tahu …*	an·da ta·hoo …
who's good with	*yang cocok buat*	yang cho·chok boo·at
children?	*anak-anak?*	a·nak a·nak
dentist	* dokter gigi*	dok·ter gi·gi
doctor	* dokter*	dok·ter

If your child is sick, see **health**, page 193.

talking with children

In this section, phrases are in the informal *kamu* (you) form only.
If you're not sure what this means, see the box on page 108.

What's your name?
Siapa namamu?   si·apa na·ma·moo

How old are you?
Berapa umurmu?   be·ra·pa oo·moor·moo

When's your birthday?
Ulang tahunmu kapan?   oo·lang ta·hoon·moo ka·pan

Do you go to …?	*Kamu sudah …?*	ka·moo soo·dah …
kindergarten	* taman*	ta·man
	* kanak-kanak*	ka·nak ka·nak
school	* sekolah*	se·ko·lah

Do you like your …?	*Kamu suka …?*	ka·moo soo·ka …
school	* sekolah*	se·ko·lah
sport	* olahraga*	o·lah·ra·ga
teacher (male)	* Bapak gurumu*	ba·pak goo·roo·moo
teacher (female)	* Ibu gurumu*	i·boo goo·roo·moo

What grade are you in?
Kamu sudah kelas berapa?   ka·moo soo·dah ke·las be·ra·pa

What do you do after school?
Setelah pulang sekolah   se·te·lah poo·lang se·ko·lah
biasanya melakukan apa?   bi·a·sa·nya me·la·koo·kan a·pa

Do you learn (English)?
Kamu belajar   ka·moo be·la·jar
(Bahasa Inggris)?   (ba·ha·sa ing·gris)

children

111

talking about children

Do you have any children (yet)?
Sudah punya anak?   soo·dah poo·nya a·nak

Yes. (lit: already)
Sudah.   soo·dah

Not yet.
Belum.   be·loom

How many children do you have?
Putranya berapa?   poo·tra·nya be·ra·pa

Is this your first child?
Ini anak yang pertama?   i·ni a·nak yang per·ta·ma

When's the baby due?
Kapan bayinya lahir?   ka·pan ba·yi·nya la·hir

What are you going to call the baby?
Anaknya mau   a·nak·nya mow
dinamai siapa?   di·na·ma·i si·a·pa

What a beautiful child!
Anaknya cantik sekali!   a·nak·nya chan·tik se·ka·li

Is it a boy or a girl?
Laki-laki atau perempuan?   la·ki la·ki a·tow pe·rem·poo·an

How old is he/she?
Berapa umurnya?   be·ra·pa oo·moor·nya

Does he/she go to school?
Sudah sekolah?   soo·dah se·ko·lah

What's his/her name?
Namanya siapa?   na·ma·nya si·a·pa

He/She looks like you.
Dia wajahnya mirip   di·a wa·jah·nya mi·rip
dengan Anda.   deng·an an·da

all in the family

You can use the word *adik* a·dik (lit: little sibling) instead of *kamu* ka·moo (you) when talking to children.

basics

Yes.	*Ya.*	ya
No.	*Tidak.*	ti·dak
Please.	*Silakan.*	si·la·kan
Thank you	*Terima kasih*	te·ri·ma ka·sih
(very much).	*(banyak).*	(ba·nyak)
You're welcome.	*Kembali.*	kem·ba·li
Excuse me.	*Permisi.*	per·mi·si
Sorry.	*Maaf.*	ma·af

coming through

Permisi (excuse me) may just become your favourite Indonesian word – use it to get attention in a shop, find a path through a crowded market, or as you enter or leave a room. It's a polite and effective way to make yourself heard.

greetings & goodbyes

Shaking hands is appropriate for both men and women when meeting someone, but it's a gentle squeeze rather than a firm grip. At a first meeting, Indonesians often shake hands while telling you their name. To show warmth and sincerity, many people follow the handshake by touching their heart. In some areas, especially in Java, the locals greet each other by pressing their palms together with the right hand slightly forward, and lightly touch the fingertips of the other person's right hand.

In cases which warrant extreme respect, such as when a young child greets an elder, the child will kiss the elder's hand then touch it to their own forehead.

| Hello. | Salam. | sa·lam |
| Hi. | Halo. | ha·lo |

Good ...	Selamat ...	se·la·mat ...
day	siang	si·ang
morning	pagi	pa·gi
afternoon	sore	so·re
evening	malam	ma·lam

hello in arabic

In Muslim areas people will use Arabic greetings – the first speaker will say *assalaamualaikum* a·sa·la·a·moo·a·lai·koom (peace be on you), to which the response is *alaikumsalam* a·lai·koom·sa·lam (on you be peace).

How are you?	Apa kabar?	a·pa ka·bar
Fine.	Kabar baik.	ka·bar ba·ik
And you?	Anda bagaimana?	an·da ba·gai·ma·na
What's your name?	Siapa namanya?	si·a·pa na·ma·nya
My name is ...	Nama saya ...	na·ma sa·ya ...

This is my ...	Ini ... saya.	i·ni ... sa·ya
I'd like to introduce	Saya mau	sa·ya mow
you to my ...	memperkenalkan	mem·per·ke·nal·kan
	Anda dengan ...	an·da deng·an ...
child	anak	a·nak
colleague	teman sekerja	te·man se·ker·ja
friend	teman	te·man
husband	suami	soo·a·mi
partner (intimate)	jodoh	jo·doh
wife	istri	ist·ri

For other family members, see **family**, page 121.

I'm pleased to meet you.
Saya senang bertemu
dengan Anda.
sa·ya se·nang ber·te·moo
deng·an an·da

See you later.
Sampai jumpa lagi.
sam·pai joom·pa la·gi

Goodbye. (to those leaving)
Selamat jalan.
se·la·mat ja·lan

Goodbye. (to those staying)
Selamat tinggal.
se·la·mat ting·gal

Good night.
Selamat malam.
se·la·mat ma·lam

addressing people

Titles and polite forms of address are crucial in Indonesian as they acknowledge the age and status of those participating in the conversation. Using the incorrect form of address can be seen as a sign of disrespect and result in poor communication – especially with officials.

To show respect to elders or 'superiors', use the words *Bapak* (lit: Father) or *Ibu* (lit: Mother). If you know the person's name (eg Anungseto or Ninik), you can address them as *Bapak Anungseto* (lit: Father Anungseto) or *Ibu Ninik* (lit: Mother Ninik). Those of similar age and status to you can politely be addressed as *Saudara/Saudari* (lit: Brother/Sister). If you're a young woman, expect to be called *Nona* (Miss) by your elders.

For more on politeness, see the box on page 108.

Mr/Sir	*Bapak*	ba·pak
Ms/Mrs/Madam	*Ibu*	i·boo
Miss	*Nona*	no·na
'Brother'	*Saudara*	sow·da·ra
'Sister'	*Saudari*	sow·da·ri

making conversation

Conversation starters in Indonesia are probably quite different from what you're used to. Indonesians will often begin by asking you about your age, marital status and religion, as well as your children, your travel plans, and your thoughts on Indonesia. If you'd rather not share your secrets, evasive or joking replies are much more polite than refusing to answer.

We've given typical conversation starters throughout this chapter, and you'll find more in **children**, pages 111 and 112.

Where are you going?
  Mau kemana?   mow ke·ma·na

I am going to …
  Saya ke …   sa·ya ke …

Where are you staying?
  Tinggal di mana?   ting·gal di ma·na

I am staying at (the Hotel Pangrango).
  Saya tinggal di   sa·ya ting·gal di
  (Hotel Pangrango) .   (ho·tel pang·rang·o)

Can I take a photo (of you)?
  Boleh saya potret (Anda)?   bo·leh sa·ya po·tret (an·da)

Of course, no problem!
  Tentu, tidak apa-apa!   ten·too ti·dak a·pa a·pa

What are you here for?
  Dalam rangka apa ke sini?   da·lam rang·ka a·pa ke si·ni

---

where are you going with that?

Remember that the phrase *Mau kemana?* (Where are you going?) is just a conversation starter. Easy answers include:

To (Denpasar).   *Ke (Denpasar).*   ke (den·pa·sar)
Travelling/Sightseeing.   *Jalan-jalan.*   ja·lan ja·lan
Out and about.   *Makan angin.*   ma·kan ang·in
  (lit: eating the breeze)

There are a few topics you should steer clear of as you chit-chat. The concept of 'face' is important in Indonesia, and refers to correct and appropriate conduct according to your social status, the social context and your relationship with those you're speaking to. The main rule is to be tactful – it's best to only hint at negative experiences or tell small lies to avoid an uncomfortable truth. Don't openly criticise the religion, gender roles or politics of those you're speaking with, and avoid talk of health problems or money worries.

I'm here ...	*Saya di sini ...*	sa·ya di si·ni ...
for a holiday	*untuk liburan*	oon·took li·boo·ran
on business	*untuk urusan bisnis*	oon·took oo·roo·san bis·nis
to study	*belajar*	be·la·jar

How long are you here for?
Rencana berapa lama di sini? ren·cha·na be·ra·pa la·ma di si·ni

I'm here for (four) weeks/days.
Saya di sini selama (empat) minggu/hari. sa·ya di si·ni se·la·ma (em·pat) ming·goo/ha·ri

How long have you been here?
Sudah berapa lama di sini? soo·dah be·ra·pa la·ma di si·ni

Where have you been so far?
Sudah ke mana? soo·dah ke ma·na

Have you been to (Bali)?
Sudah ke (Bali)? soo·dah ke (ba·li)

Do you like it in (Indonesia)?
Anda senang di (Indonesia)? an·da se·nang di (in·do·ne·si·a)

It's very nice here.
Enak sekali di sini. e·nak se·ka·li di si·ni

We love it here.
Kami senang di sini. ka·mi se·nang di si·ni

nationalities

Where are you from?
Anda dari mana?   an·da da·ri ma·na

I'm from …	*Saya dari …*	sa·ya da·ri …
Australia	*Australia*	a·oo·stra·li·a
Canada	*Kanada*	ka·na·da
Singapore	*Singapura*	sin·ga·poo·ra

but where exactly are you from?

When asking someone where they're from, use these questions to get right down to the specifics:

Where have you just come from?
Baru dari mana?   ba·roo da·ri ma·na

Where are you originally from?
Anda berasal dari mana?   an·da be·ra·sal da·ri ma·na

Where do you live?
Anda tinggal di mana?   an·da ting·gal di ma·na

Where do your parents live?
Orang tuanya tinggal   o·rang too·a·nya ting·gal
di mana?   di ma·na

age

How old …?	*Berapa … Anda?*	be·ra·pa … an·da
are you	*umur*	oo·moor
is your	*umur anak*	oo·moor a·nak
son	*laki-laki*	la·ki la·ki
is your	*umur anak*	oo·moor a·nak
daughter	*perempuan*	pe·rem·poo·an

I'm ... years old.
Umur saya ... tahun.   oo·moor sa·ya ... ta·hoon

He/She is ... years old.
Umurnya ... tahun.   ooo·moor·nya ... ta·hoon

Too old!
Terlalu tua!   ter·la·loo too·a

I'm younger than I look.
Saya lebih muda dari   sa·ya le·bih moo·da da·ri
usia sebenarnya.   oo·si·a se·be·nar·nya

For your age, see **numbers & amounts**, page 31.

occupations & studies

pekerjaan dan studi

What's your occupation?
Pekerjaan Anda apa?   pe·ker·ja·an an·da a·pa

I work in ...	*Saya kerja di ...*	sa·ya ker·ja di ...
administration	*administrasi*	ad·mi·ni·stra·si
health	*kesehatan*	ke·se·ha·tan
sales &	*bidang*	bi·dang
marketing	*penjualan dan*	pen·joo·a·lan dan
	pemasaran	pe·ma·sa·ran

local talk		
Hey!	*Hai!*	hai
How are things?	*Bagaimana?*	ba·gai·ma·na
Great!	*Asyik!*	a·sik
OK!	*Baik!*	ba·ik
Sure.	*Pasti.*	pa·sti
Maybe.	*Mungkin.*	moong·kin
No way!	*Tidak mungkin!*	ti·dak moong·kin
Just joking.	*Cuma bercanda!*	choo·ma ber·chan·da
Just a minute.	*Sebentar lagi.*	se·ben·tar la·gi
It's OK.	*Tidak masalah.*	ti·dak ma·sa·lah
No problem.	*Tidak apa-apa.*	ti·dak a·pa a·pa

I'm (a) ...	Saya ...	sa·ya ...
chef	*juru masak*	joo·roo ma·sak
driver	*sopir*	so·pir
farmer	*petani*	pe·ta·ni
fisherman	*nelayan*	ne·la·yan
journalist	*wartawan*	war·ta·wan
manual worker	*buruh kasar*	boo·rooh ka·sar
policeman	*polisi*	po·li·si
retired	*pensiunan*	pen·si·oo·nan
sailor	*pelaut*	pe·la·oot
self-employed	*swasta*	swa·sta
shopkeeper	*pemilik toko*	pe·mi·lik to·ko
teacher	*guru*	goo·roo
trader	*pedangang*	pe·da·gang
unemployed	*pengangguran*	peng·ang·goo·ran

What are you studying?
Anda belajar apa?   an·da be·la·jar apa

I'm studying ...	Saya belajar ...	sa·ya be·la·jar ...
humanities	*ilmu sastera*	il·moo sa·ste·ra
Indonesian	*Bahasa Indonesia*	ba·ha·sa in·do·ne·si·a
science	*ilmu*	il·moo
	pengetahuan	peng·e·ta·hoo·an

living in sin

Indonesia is a very religious country, and admitting that you live with your partner – but aren't married – is likely to bring disapproval. If you happen to be living 'in sin', you can claim to be married or say that you have a *pacar* pa·char (girlfriend/boyfriend):

I live with someone.
Saya tinggal serumah   sa·ya ting·gal se·roo·mah
dengan pacar saya.   deng·an pa·char sa·ya

family

Do you have (a) …?	*Anda punya …?*	an·da poo·nya …
I (don't) have (a) …	*Saya (tidak) punya …*	sa·ya (ti·dak) poo·nya …
brother	*saudara laki-laki*	sow·da·ra la·ki la·ki
children	*anak*	a·nak
daughter	*anak perempuan*	a·nak pe·rem·poo·an
grandchild	*cucu*	choo·choo
husband	*suami*	soo·a·mi
older brother	*kakak laki-laki*	ka·kak la·ki la·ki
older sister	*kakak perempuan*	ka·kak pe·rem·poo·an
partner (intimate)	*jodoh*	jo·doh
sister	*saudara perempuan*	sow·da·ra pe·rem·poo·an
son	*anak laki-laki*	a·nak la·ki la·ki
wife	*istri*	i·stri
younger brother	*adik laki-laki*	a·dik la·ki la·ki
younger sister	*adik perempuan*	a·dik pe·rem·poo·an

Are you married (yet)?	*Sudah kawin?*	soo·dah ka·win
Yes, I am.	*Sudah.*	soo·dah
Not yet.	*Belum.*	be·loom
I'm …	*Saya …*	sa·ya …
married	*sudah kawin*	soo·dah ka·win
divorced	*bercerai*	ber·che·rai
single	*bujang*	boo·jang

For more information on how to answer questions about status, see the box in **language difficulties**, page 29.

farewells

(Tomorrow) is my last day here.
(Besok) hari terakhir   (be·sok) ha·ri te·ra·khir
saya di sini.   sa·ya di si·ni

It's been great meeting you.
Saya senang bertemu   sa·ya se·nang ber·te·moo
dengan Anda.   deng·an an·da

If you come to (England) you can stay with me.
Kalau Anda ke (Inggris)   ka·low an·da ke (ing·gris)
silakan tinggal di rumah   si·la·kan ting·gal di roo·mah
saya.   sa·ya

Keep in touch!
Jangan lupa dengan saya!   jan·gan loo·pa deng·an sa·ya

Here's my ...	*Ini ... saya.*	i·ni ... sa·ya
What's your ...?	*Apa ... Anda?*	a·pa ... an·da
address	*alamat*	a·la·mat
email address	*alamat email*	a·la·mat i·mel
phone number	*nomor telpon*	no·mor tel·pon

well-wishing

Bon voyage!	*Selamat sampai di tujuan!*	se·la·mat sam·pai di too·joo·an
Congratulations!	*Selamat!*	se·la·mat
Good luck!	*Semoga berhasil!*	se·mo·ga ber·ha·sil
Happy Birthday!	*Selamat ulang tahun!*	se·la·mat oo·lang ta·hoon
Merry Christmas!	*Selamat hari Natal!*	se·la·mat ha·ri na·tal

common interests

minat bersama

What do you do in your spare time?
Apa yang Anda suka   a·pa yang an·da soo·ka
lakukan kalau lagi sengang?   la·koo·kan ka·low la·gi seng·ang

Do you like ...?	*Anda suka ...?*	an·da soo·ka ...
I (don't) like ...	*Saya (tidak)*	sa·ya (ti·dak)
	suka ...	soo·ka ...
batik	*batik*	ba·tik
computer games	*main komputer*	ma·in kom·poo·ter
cooking	*masak*	ma·sak
dancing	*menari*	me·na·ri
drawing	*menggambar*	meng·gam·bar
films	*film*	film
gamelan	*gamelan*	ga·me·lan
gardening	*berkebun*	ber·ke·boon
hiking	*naik gunung*	na·ik goo·noong
music	*musik*	moo·sik
painting	*lukis*	loo·kis
photography	*fotografi*	fo·to·gra·fi
reading	*membaca*	mem·ba·cha
shopping	*belanja*	be·lan·ja
socialising	*gaul*	ga·ool
sport	*olahraga*	o·lah·ra·ga
surfing	*main internet*	ma·in in·ter·net
the Internet		
travelling	*jalan-jalan*	ja·lan ja·lan
watching TV	*nonton TV*	non·ton tee·vee
weaving	*tenun*	te·noon

For types of sports, see **sport**, page 145, and the **dictionary**.

shadow puppets

Here's some terminology to help you understand the details of *wayang kulit* wa·yang koo·lit (shadow puppet) performances …

cempala	chem·pa·la	wooden mallet used in performance
dalang	da·lang	puppeteer
gamelan	ga·me·lan	orchestra which accompanies the show
kayon	ka·yon	leaf-shaped device used to end scenes or symbolise wind, mountains, obstacles, clouds or the sea
kendang	ken·dang	drum
lakon	la·kon	drama taken from legend & performed with *wayang kulit*

music

musik

Do you …?	*Anda biasa …?*	an·da bi·a·sa …
dance	*menari*	me·na·ri
go to concerts	*pergi ke konser*	per·gi ke kon·ser
listen to music	*mendengarkan lagu*	men·deng·ar·kan la·goo
play an instrument	*memainkan satu alat musik*	me·ma·in·kan sa·too a·lat moo·sik
sing	*menyanyi*	me·nya·nyi

What … do you like?	*Anda suka … apa?*	an·da soo·ka … a·pa
bands	*kelompok*	ke·lom·pok
music	*musik*	moo·sik
singers	*penyanyi*	pe·nya·nyi

Planning to go to a concert? See **tickets**, page 59, and **going out**, page 134.

cinema & theatre

I feel like going to a (film).
Saya ingin pergi ke (film).　　sa·ya ing·in per·gi ke (film)

Did you like the (play)?
Anda suka (drama)?　　an·da soo·ka (dra·ma)

What's showing at the cinema tonight?
Malam ini bioskop　　ma·lam i·ni bi·os·kop
putar apa?　　poo·tar a·pa

What's showing at the theatre tonight?
Malam ini teater　　ma·lam i·ni te·a·ter
pertunjukan apa?　　per·toon·joo·kan a·pa

Is it in (English)?
Apakah dalam Bahasa　　a·pa·kah da·lam ba·ha·sa
(Inggris)?　　(ing·gris)

Does it have (English) subtitles?
Ada teks di bawah　　a·da teks di ba·wah
dalam Bahasa (Inggris)?　　da·lam ba·ha·sa (ing·gris)

Have you seen (*Pasir Berbisik*)?
Anda sudah lihat　　an·da soo·dah li·hat
(Pasir Berbisik)?　　(pa·sir ber·bi·sik)

Who's in it?
Yang main siapa?　　yang ma·in si·a·pa

It stars (Rano Karno).
Dibintangi oleh (Rano Karno).　di·bin·tang·i o·leh (ra·no kar·no)

Is this seat available?
Tempat ini masih kosong?　　tem·pat i·ni ma·sih ko·song

I thought it was …	*Saya pikir itu …*	sa·ya pi·kir i·too …
excellent	*bagus sekali*	ba·goos se·ka·li
long	*lama*	la·ma
OK	*lumayan*	loo·ma·yan

I (don't) like ...	Saya (tidak) suka ...	sa·ya (ti·dak) soo·ka ...
action movies	film laga	film la·ga
animated films	film animasi	film a·ni·ma·si
comedies	komedi	ko·me·di
documentaries	film	film
	dokumenter	do·koo·men·ter
drama	film drama	film dra·ma
(Indonesian)	film	film
cinema	(Indonesia)	(in·do·ne·si·a)
horror movies	film horor	film ho·ror
sci-fi	film fiksi ilmiah	film fik·si il·mi·ah
short films	film pendek	film pen·dek
thrillers	thriller	sri·ler
war movies	film perang	film pe·rang

more than just *gamelan*

There's a huge range of local music in Indonesia, both traditional and modern. To talk about Western music styles,
just use the English words and you'll be understood, but
remember to check out some native rhythms:

dangdut   dang·doot
Passionate, sexy, pop sounds with Arabic and Hindu influ-
ences, all mixed Indonesian-style.

gamelan   ga·me·lan
An orchestra which consists mainly of percussion instruments (gongs, drums, xylophones) but can also include
vocals and flute.

jaipongan   jai·pong·an
A blend of traditional instruments and modern rhythm
incorporating strong and complex beats on the *kendang*
ken·dang (drum). Some consider *jaipongan* uncouth, which
makes it rather risqué.

kacapi suling   ka·cha·pi soo·ling
Serene music style which features the *kacapi* ka·cha·pi (a
harp-like instrument), *suling* soo·ling (flute) and singing.

feelings

Are you …?	*Anda …?*	an·da …
I'm (not) …	*Saya (tidak) …*	sa·ya (ti·dak) …
annoyed	*tergangu*	ter·gang·oo
cold	*dingin*	ding·in
disappointed	*kecewa*	ke·che·wa
embarrassed	*malu*	ma·loo
happy	*senang*	se·nang
homesick	*rindu kampung*	rin·doo kam·poong
	halaman	ha·la·man
hot	*panas*	pa·nas
hungry	*lapar*	la·par
in a hurry	*tergesa-gesa*	ter·ge·sa ge·sa
sad	*sedih*	se·dih
surprised	*heran*	he·ran
thirsty	*haus*	ha·oos
tired	*capek*	cha·pek
well	*sehat*	se·hat
worried	*cemas*	che·mas

If you're not feeling well, see **health**, page 193.

opinions

Did you like it?
Anda suka?   an·da soo·ka

What do you think of it?
Apa pendapat Anda?   a·pa pen·da·pat an·da

how do you feel?		
a little	*sedikit*	se·di·kit
I'm a little sad.	*Saya sedikit sedih.*	sa·ya se·di·kit se·dih
quite/enough	*cukup*	choo·koop
I'm quite full.	*Saya cukup kenyang.*	sa·ya choo·koop ke·nyang
very	*sekali*	se·ka·li
I feel very lucky.	*Saya merasa beruntung sekali.*	sa·ya me·ra·sa be·roon·toong se·ka·li
extremely	*luar biasa*	loo·ar bi·a·sa
I'm extremely happy.	*Saya luar biasa senang.*	sa·ya loo·ar bi·a·sa se·nang

It's ...	*Itu ...*	i·too ...
I thought it was ...	*Saya pikir itu ...*	sa·ya pi·kir i·too ...
awful	*mengerikan*	meng·e·ri·kan
beautiful	*indah*	in·dah
boring	*membosankan*	mem·bo·san·kan
(too) expensive	*(terlalu) mahal*	(ter·la·loo) ma·hal
great	*jago*	ja·go
interesting	*menarik*	me·na·rik
OK	*boleh*	bo·leh
strange	*aneh*	a·neh
wonderful	*bagus sekali*	ba·goos se·ka·li

politics & social issues

politik dan isu sosial

Indonesians are very sensitive to outright criticism, and they aren't very appreciative of foreigners telling them how their country should be run – you probably aren't either. Be tactful when commenting on potentially sensitive environmental and political issues especially when nationalist pride might be at stake.

Indonesians can be very complimentary, and very honest.

You're beautiful.	*Anda cantik.*	an·da chan·tik
You're handsome.	*Anda ganteng.*	an·da gan·teng
You're clever.	*Anda pandai.*	an·da pan·dai
Your hair is beautiful.	*Rambut anda cantik.*	ram·boot an·da chan·tik
You're fat.	*Anda gemuk.*	an·da ge·mook
You're skinny.	*Anda kurus.*	an·da koo·roos
So are you.	*Anda juga.*	an·da joo·ga

Who do you vote for?
Siapa yang Anda pilih?   si·a·pa yang an·da pi·lih

I support the … party.	*Saya mendukung partai …*	sa·ya men·doo·koong par·tai …
I'm a member of the … party.	*Saya anggota partai …*	sa·ya ang·go·ta par·tai …
communist	*kommunis*	ko·moo·nis
conservative	*konservatif*	kon·ser·va·tif
democratic	*demokrat*	de·mo·krat
green	*pecinta linkungan hidup*	pe·chin·ta lin·koong·an hi·doop
liberal (progressive)	*liberal*	li·be·ral
social democratic	*demokrat sosialis*	de·mo·krat so·si·a·lis
socialist	*sosialis*	so·si·a·lis

I'm (Australian) and I voted against (John Howard)!
Saya orang (Australia)   sa·ya o·rang (a·oo·stra·li·a)
tetapi tidak memilih   te·ta·pi ti·dak me·mi·lih
(John Howard)!   (jon hau·ward)

political games

Here are some of Indonesia's key political players:

Functional Groups Party
Partai Golongan Karya (Golkar) — par·tai go·long·an kar·ya (gol·kar)

Indonesian Democratic Party-Struggle
Partai Demokrasi Indonesia-Perjuangan (PDI-P) — par·tai de·mo·kra·si in·do·ne·si·a per·joo·ang·an (pe·de·ee·pe)

Indonesian National Army
Tentara Nasional Indonesia (TNI) — ten·ta·ra na·si·o·nal in·do·ne·si·a (te·en·i)

National Awakening Party
Partai Kebangkitan Bangsa (PKB) — par·tai ke·bang·ki·tan bang·sa (pe·ka·be)

National Mandate Party
Partai Amanat Nasional (PAN) — par·tai a·ma·nat na·si·o·nal (pan)

United Development Party
Partai Persatuan Pembangunan (PPP) — par·tai per·sa·too·an pem·bang·oo·nan (pe ti·ga)

Did you hear about …?
Anda sudah dengar tentang …? — an·da soo·dah deng·ar ten·tang …

Do you agree with it?
Anda setuju? — an·da se·too·joo

I (don't) agree with …
Saya (tidak) setuju … — sa·ya (ti·dak) se·too·joo …

How do people feel about …?
Bagaimana perasaan masyarakat tentang …? — ba·gai·ma·na pe·ra·sa·an ma·sa·ra·kat ten·tang …

How can we protest against …?
Bagaimana kita bisa memprotes …? — ba·gai·ma·na ki·ta bi·sa mem·pro·tes …

abortion	abortus	a·bor·toos
crime	kriminalitas	kri·mi·na·li·tas
discrimination	diskriminasi	dis·kri·mi·na·si
drugs	narkoba	nar·ko·ba
the economy	ekonomi	e·ko·no·mi
education	pendidikan	pen·di·di·kan
equal	kesempatan	ke·sem·pa·tan
opportunity	yang sama	yang sa·ma
family planning	keluarga	ke·loo·ar·ga
	berencana	be·ren·cha·na
globalisation	globalisasi	glo·ba·li·sa·si
human rights	hak asasi	hak a·sa·si
	manusia	ma·noo·si·a
immigration	imigrasi	i·mi·gra·si
inequality	ketidaksamaan	ke·ti·dak·sa·ma·an
party politics	politik dari partai	po·li·tik da·ri par·tai
poverty	kemiskinan	ke·mi·ski·nan
privatisation	privatisasi	pri·va·ti·sa·si
racism	rasisme	ra·sis·me
refugees	penungsi	pe·noong·si
separatist	gerakan	ge·ra·kan
movements	separatis	se·pa·ra·tis
social unrest	kerusuhan	ke·roo·soo·han
(riots/violence)		
social welfare	kesejahteraan	ke·se·jah·te·ra·an
	sosial	so·si·al
terrorism	terrorisme	te·ro·ris·me
transmigration	transmigrasi	trans·mi·gra·si
the UN	PBB	pe·be·be
unemployment	pengangguran	peng·ang·goo·ran
the war in …	perang di …	pe·rang di …

goodness & greatness

The word *bagus* ba·goos (good) is indeed good, but you can't use *bagus* to describe people. A person can be *baik hati* ba·ik ha·ti (good-hearted), *murah hati* moo·rah ha·ti (generous) or simply *baik* ba·ik (good).

the environment

Is there a … problem here?
Ada persoalan … di sini?
a·da per·so·a·lan … di si·ni

What should be done about …?
Apa yang bisa dilakukan untuk mengatasi …?
a·pa yang bi·sa di·la·koo·kan oon·took meng·a·ta·si …

How can we support …?
Bagaimana kita bisa mendukung …?
ba·gai·ma·na ki·ta bi·sa men·doo·koong …

conservation	konservasi	kon·ser·va·si
deforestation	penebangan hutan	pe·ne·bang·an hoo·tan
drought	kemarau	ke·ma·row
earthquake	gempa bumi	gem·pa boo·mi
ecosystem	ekosistem	e·ko·si·stem
endangered species	jenis terancam punah	je·nis te·ran·cham poo·nah
fishing	perikanan	per·i·ka·nan
genetically modified food	makanan yang dimodifikasi secara genetis	ma·ka·nan yang di·mo·di·fi·ka·si se·cha·ra ge·ne·tis
hunting	pemburuan	pem·boo·roo·an
hydroelectricity	tenaga hydrolisterik	te·na·ga hid·ro·li·ste·rik
illegal logging	penebangan liar	pe·ne·bang·an li·ar
irrigation	irigasi	i·ri·ga·si
nuclear energy	tenaga nuklir	te·na·ga noo·klir
ozone layer	lapisan ozon	la·pi·san o·zon
pesticides	pestisida	pe·sti·si·da
pollution	pollusi	po·loo·si
recycling program	program daur ulang sampah	pro·gram da·oor oo·lang sam·pah
salination	salinitas	sa·li·ni·tas
toxic waste	sampah beracun	sam·pah be·ra·choon
tsunami	tsunami	tsoo·na·mi
volcanic eruption	letusan gunung api	le·too·san goo·noong a·pi
water supply	persediaan air	per·se·di·a·an a·ir

where to go

What's on …?	*Ada apa saja …?*	a·da a·pa sa·ja …
locally	*di sekitar sini*	di se·ki·tar si·ni
today	*hari ini*	ha·ri i·ni
tonight	*malam ini*	ma·lam i·ni
this weekend	*akhir minggu ini*	a·khir ming·goo i·ni
Is there a local	*Ada panduan …*	a·da pan·doo·an …
… guide?	*buat daerah ini?*	boo·at da·e·rah i·ni
entertainment	*hiburan*	hi·boo·ran
film	*film*	film
music	*musik*	moo·sik
Where can I	*Di mana saya*	di ma·na sa·ya
find …?	*dapat …?*	da·pat …
gay venues	*tempat gay*	tem·pat gey
	mangkal	mang·kal
nightclubs	*klub malam*	kloob ma·lam
places to eat	*tempat makan*	tem·pat ma·kan
pubs	*tempat minum*	tem·pat mi·noom
I feel like	*Saya ingin ke …*	sa·ya ing·in ke …
going to a …		
bar	*bar*	bar
café	*kafe*	ka·fe
concert	*konser*	kon·ser
film	*film*	film
karaoke bar	*karaoke*	ka·ra·o·ke
party	*pesta*	pe·sta
performance	*pertunjukan*	per·toon·joo·kan

For more on bars, drinks and partying, see **romance**, page 137, and **eating out**, page 171.

invitations

What are you doing …?	Apa rencana Anda buat …?	a·pa ren·cha·na an·da boo·at …
now	sekarang	se·ka·rang
tonight	malam ini	ma·lam i·ni
this weekend	akhir minggu ini	a·khir ming·goo i·ni

Would you like to go (for a) …?	Mau pergi …?	mow per·gi …
I feel like going (for a) …	Saya ingin pergi …	sa·ya ing·in per·gi …
coffee	minum kopi	mi·noom ko·pi
dancing	menari	me·na·ri
drink	minum	mi·noom
meal	makan	ma·kan
out somewhere	cari hiburan	cha·ri hi·boo·ran
walk	jalan-jalan	ja·lan ja·lan

Do you know a good restaurant?
Anda tahu restoran yang bagus?
an·da ta·hoo re·sto·ran yang ba·goos

Do you want to come to the concert with me?
Mau ikut saya ke konser?
mow i·koot sa·ya ke kon·ser

We're having a party.
Kami bikin pesta.
ka·mi bi·kin pe·sta

responding to invitations

Sure!
Pasti!
pa·sti

Yes, I'd love to.
Ya, saya senang.
ya sa·ya se·nang

That's very kind of you.
Aduh, Anda baik hati.
a·dooh an·da ba·ik ha·ti

beliefs & cultural differences
kepercayaan dan perbedaan budaya

Religion is an official pillar of Indonesian society, and all citizens must profess a state-approved *agama* (religion). They can be *Islam* (Muslim), *Katolik* (Catholic), *Protestan* (Protestant), *Hindu* (Hindu) or *Buda* (Buddhist). Even animist tribes or those who follow *kepercayaan tradisional* ke·per·cha·ya·an tra·di·si·o·nal (traditional beliefs) are officially considered 'Hindu', and religion is marked on the *KTP* ka·te·pe (identification cards) of all Indonesians. All approved religions are equal, and Indonesians will proudly declare theirs even if they don't practise it.

If you say *saya tidak beragama* sa·ya ti·dak be·ra·ga·ma (I'm not religious), an Indonesian will think that you're hiding your religion and, for Westerners, assume that you're a Christian.

Religion can be quite a touchy subject, so don't openly criticise the beliefs of anyone around you.

religion

What's your religion?
   Anda beragama apa?   an·da be·ra·ga·ma a·pa

I don't/rarely practise my religion.
   Saya tidak/kurang   sa·ya ti·dak/koo·rang
   taat beribadah.   ta·at be·ri·ba·dah

I'm (a) ...	*Agama saya ...*	a·ga·ma sa·ya ...
Buddhist	*Buda*	boo·da
Catholic	*Katolik*	ka·to·lik
Christian	*Kristen*	kri·sten
Hindu	*Hindu*	hin·doo
Jewish	*Yahudi*	ya·hoo·di
Muslim	*Islam*	is·lam
Protestant	*Protestan*	pro·te·stan

I (don't)	Saya (tidak)	sa·ya (ti·dak)
believe in ...	percaya kepada ...	per·cha·ya ke·pa·da ...
astrology	ramalan bintang	ra·ma·lan bin·tang
fate	nasib	na·sib
God	Tuhan	too·han
Can I ... here?	Bisa saya ... di sini?	bi·sa sa·ya ... di si·ni
Where can I ...?	Di mana saya bisa ...?	di ma·na sa·ya bi·sa ...
attend	ikut kebaktian	i·koot ke·bak·ti·an
a service		
attend mass	ikut misa	i·koot mi·sa
pray	sembahyang	sem·bah·yang
worship	memuja	me·moo·ja

cultural differences

I didn't mean to do/say anything wrong.
Saya tidak bermaksud — sa·ya ti·dak ber·mak·sood
lakukan/bilang yang salah. — la·koo·kan/bi·lang yang sa·lah

I don't want to offend you.
Saya tidak mau meng- — sa·ya ti·dak mow meng·
ganggu perasaan Anda. — gang·goo pe·ra·sa·an an·da

Is this a local or national custom?
Ini adat daerah atau — i·ni a·dat da·e·rah a·tow
nasional? — na·si·o·nal

What am I supposed to be doing?
Seharusnya saya — se·ha·roos·nya sa·ya
lakukan apa? — la·koo·kan a·pa

I'm sorry, it's against my beliefs/religion.
Maaf, ini dilarang — ma·af i·ni di·la·rang
kepercayaan/agama saya. — ke·per·cha·ya·an/a·ga·ma sa·ya

I'd rather not join in.
Saya tidak mau ikut. — sa·ya ti·dak mow i·koot

I'm not used to this.
Saya tidak terbiasa — sa·ya ti·dak ter·bi·a·sa
dengan ini. — deng·an i·ni

When's the museum open?
Jam berapa musium buka?   jam be·ra·pa moo·si·oom boo·ka

When's the gallery open?
Jam berapa galeri buka?   jam be·ra·pa ga·le·ri boo·ka

What kind of art are you interested in?
Anda tertarik pada seni apa?   an·da ter·ta·rik pa·da se·ni a·pa

What's in the collection?
Koleksinya apa saja?   ko·lek·si·nya a·pa sa·ja

What do you think of ...?
Apa pendapat Anda soal ...?   a·pa pen·da·pat an·da so·al ...

It's an exhibition of ...
Ini pameran ...   i·ni pa·me·ran ...

I'm interested in ...
Saya tertarik pada ...   sa·ya ter·ta·rik pa·da ...

I like the works of ...
Saya suka hasil kerjanya ...   sa·ya soo·ka ha·sil ker·ja·nya ...

It reminds me of ...
Itu ingatkan saya kepada ...   i·too ing·at·kan sa·ya ke·pa·da ...

religious art

kala	ka·la	demonic face seen over temple gateways
meru	me·roo	type of layered roof in Balinese temples
pura	poo·ra	Balinese temple or shrine
pura dalem	poo·ra da·lem	Balinese temple of the dead
pura puseh	poo·ra poo·seh	Balinese temple of origin
tau tau	ta·oo ta·oo	life-sized carved wooden effigies of the dead, placed outside cave graves in Sulawesi
temadu	te·ma·doo	carved ancestor totems

... art	seni ...	se·ni ...
impressionist	impressionisme	im·pre·si·o·nis·me
modern	modern	mo·dern
performance	pertunjukan	per·toon·joo·kan
traditional	tradisional	tra·di·si·o·nal
Western	barat	ba·rat
architecture	arsitektur	ar·si·tek·toor
artist	artis	ar·tis
artwork	seni	se·ni
carving (artwork)	ukiran	oo·ki·ran
carving (technique)	seni ukir	se·ni oo·kir
carver	pengukir	peng·oo·kir
craftsman	pengrajin	peng·ra·jin
curator	kurator	koo·ra·tor
design n	desain	de·sain
etching	etsa	et·sa
exhibit n	pameran	pa·me·ran
exhibition hall	ruang pameran	roo·ang pa·me·ran
handicraft	kerajinan tangan	ke·ra·ji·nan tang·an
handmade a	buatan tangan	boo·a·tan tang·an
installation	instalasi	in·sta·la·si
mass production	massa-produksi	ma·sa pro·dook·si
opening	pembukaan	pem·boo·ka·an
painter	pelukis	pe·loo·kis
painting (artwork)	lukisan	loo·ki·san
painting (technique)	seni lukis	se·ni loo·kis
period	zaman	za·man
permanent collection	koleksi permanen	ko·lek·si per·ma·nen
relief	relief	re·lif
sculptor	pematung	pe·ma·toong
sculpture/statue	patung	pa·toong
studio	studio	stoo·di·o
style n	aliran	a·li·ran
technique	teknik	tek·nik
typically (Balinese)	khas (Bali)	khas (ba·li)
weaving	tenunan	te·noo·nan
wood carving (artwork)	ukiran kayu	oo·ki·ran ka·yoo

sporting interests

What sport do you ...?	Olahraga mana yang Anda ...?	o·lah·ra·ga ma·na yang an·da ...
play	main	ma·in
follow	ikuti beritanya	i·koo·ti be·ri·ta·nya

I play/do ...	Saya main ...	sa·ya ma·in ...
I follow ...	Saya mengikuti ...	sa·ya meng·i·koo·ti ...
athletics	atletik	at·le·tik
badminton	bulu tangkis	boo·loo tang·kis
basketball	bola basket	bo·la bas·ket
karate	karate	ka·ra·te
scuba diving	menyelam	me·nye·lam
tennis	tenis	te·nis
volleyball	voli	vo·li

I ...	Saya ...	sa·ya ...
cycle	bersepeda	ber·se·pe·da
run	lari	la·ri
walk	jalan	ja·lan

Do you like (football)?
Anda suka (sepakbola)? an·da soo·ka (se·pak·bo·la)

Yes, very much.
Ya, sangat. ya sang·at

Not really.
Tidak terlalu. ti·dak ter·la·loo

I like watching it.
Saya suka nonton. sa·ya soo·ka non·ton

Who's your favourite sportsperson/team?
Atlet/Tim favorit Anda siapa? at·let/tim fa·vo·rit an·da si·a·pa

going to a game

Would you like to go to a game?
Anda ingin pergi — an·da ing·in per·gi
nonton pertandingan? — non·ton per·tan·ding·an

Who are you supporting?
Yang Anda jagokan siapa? — yang an·da ja·go·kan si·a·pa

Who's playing/winning?
Siapa yang main/menang — si·a·pa yang ma·in/me·nang

That was a … game!	*Pertandingan ini …!*	per·tan·ding·an i·ni …
bad	*buruk*	boo·rook
boring	*membosankan*	mem·bo·san·kan
great	*bagus sekali*	ba·goos se·ka·li

scoring

What's the score?	*Berapa skornya?*	be·ra·pa skor·nya
draw/even	*draw*	dro
love/nil (zero)	*nol*	nol
match-point	*match-point*	mech po·int

playing sport

Do you want to play?
Anda mau main? — an·da mow ma·in

Can I join in?
Boleh saya ikut? — bo·leh sa·ya i·koot

That would be great.
Bagus sekali. — ba·goos se·ka·li

I can't.
Saya tidak bisa. — sa·ya ti·dak bi·sa

I have an injury.
Saya ada cedera.   sa·ya a·da che·de·ra

Your/My point.
Dari Anda/saya.   da·ri an·da/sa·ya

Kick/Pass it to me!
Tendang/passing ke saya!   ten·dang/pa·sing ke sa·ya

You're a good player.
Anda pemain yang bagus.   an·da pe·ma·in yang ba·goos

Thanks for the game.
Terima kasih buat   te·ri·ma ka·sih boo·at
permainannya.   per·ma·i·nan·nya

Where's a good place to …?	*Di mana ada tempat yang bagus buat …?*	di ma·na a·da tem·pat yang ba·goos boo·at …
fish	*memancing*	me·man·ching
go horse riding	*berkuda*	ber·koo·da
run	*lari*	la·ri
snorkel	*snorkel*	snor·kel

Where's the nearest …?	*Di mana … yang terdekat?*	di ma·na … yang ter·de·kat
golf course	*lapangan golf*	la·pang·an golf
gym	*gym*	jim
swimming pool	*kolam renang*	ko·lam re·nang
tennis court	*lapangan tenis*	la·pang·an te·nis

What's the charge per …?	*Berapa sewanya per …?*	be·ra·pa se·wa·nya per …
day	*hari*	ha·ri
game	*game*	gem
hour	*jam*	jam
visit	*kunjungan*	koon·joong·an

Can I hire a …?	*Bisa saya sewa …?*	bi·sa sa·ya se·wa …
ball	*bola*	bo·la
bicycle	*sepeda*	se·pe·da
court	*lapangan*	la·pang·an
racquet	*raket*	ra·ket

sports talk

What a ...!	... bagus!	...ba·goos
goal	Golnya	gol·nya
hit	Pukulannya	poo·koo·lan·nya
kick	Tendangannya	ten·dang·an·nya
pass	Passingnya	pa·sing·nya
performance	Performannya	per·for·man·nya

Do I have to be a member to attend?
*Mesti jadi anggota buat
ikuti?*
me·sti ja·di ang·go·ta boo·at
i·koo·ti

Is there a women-only session?
*Ada saatnya buat
pemain wanita saja?*
a·da sa·at·nya boo·at
pe·ma·in wa·ni·ta sa·ja

Where are the changing rooms?
Di mana ruang ganti baju? di ma·na roo·ang gan·ti ba·joo

diving

menyelam

Where's a good diving site?
*Di mana lokasi menyelam
yang bagus?*
di ma·na lo·ka·si me·nye·lam
yang ba·goos

Is it a shore dive?
Ini penyelaman dari pantai? i·ni pe·nye·la·man da·ri pan·tai

Is it a boat dive?
*Ini penyelaman dari
perahu boat?*
i·ni pe·nye· la·man da·ri
pe·ra·hoo bot

How deep is the dive?
*Berapa dalam
menyelamnya?*
be·ra·pa da·lam
me·nye·lam·nya

Is the visibility good?
Visibilitasnya bagus? vi·si·bi·li·tas·nya ba·goos

I need an air fill.
Saya perlu mengisi udara. sa·ya per·loo meng·i·si oo·da·ra

Are there ...?	Ada ...?	a·da ...
currents	arus	a·roos
sharks	ikan hiu	i·kan hi·oo
whales	paus	pa·oos

I'd like to ...	Saya ingin ...	sa·ya ing·in ...
explore caves/	eksplorasi gua/	eks·plo·ra·si goo·a/
wrecks	rongsokan	rong·so·kan
go night diving	menyelam malam	me·nye·lam ma·lam
go scuba diving	menyelam	me·nye·lam
	dengan alat	deng·an a·lat
	pernapasan	per·na·pa·san
go snorkelling	snorkeling	snor·ke·ling
join a tour	ikut tour selam	i·koot toor se·lam
learn to dive	belajar	be·la·jar
	menyelam	me·nye·lam

I want to hire (a) ...	Saya mau sewa ...	sa·ya mow se·wa ...
buoyancy vest	vest pelampung	vest pe·lam·poong
diving equipment	alat menyelam	a·lat me·nye·lam
flippers	kaki katak	ka·ki ka·tak
mask	masker	ma·sker
regulator	regulator	re·goo·la·tor
snorkel	snorkel	snor·kel
tank	tangki	tang·ki
weight belt	sabuk beban	sa·book be·ban
wetsuit (diving)	pakaian selam	pa·kai·an se·lam

buddy n	teman	te·man
cave n	gua	goo·a
dive n	selam	se·lam
dive v	menyelam	me·nye·lam
diving boat	kapal penyelam	ka·pal pe·nye·lam
diving course	kursus menyelam	koor·soos me·nye·lam
night dive	menyelam malam	me·nye·lam ma·lam
wreck n	rongsokan	rong·so·kan

fishing

Where are the good spots?
Di mana titik pemancingan   di ma·na ti·tik pe·man·ching·an
yang bagus?   yang ba·goos

Do I need a fishing permit?
Saya perlu ijin memancing?   sa·ya per·loo i·jin me·man·ching

Do you do fishing tours?
Anda menjalankan   an·da men·ja·lan·kan
tour memancing?   toor me·man·ching

What's the best bait?
Umpan paling bagus apa?   oom·pan pa·ling ba·goos a·pa

Are they biting?
Mereka gigit umpannya?   me·re·ka gi·git oom·pan·nya

What kind of fish are you landing?
Ikan apa yang Anda   i·kan a·pa yang an·da
tangkap?   tang·kap

How much does it weigh?
Berapa bobotnya?   be·ra·pa bo·bot·nya

surfing

How do I get to the surf beaches?
Bagaimana saya sampai   ba·gai·ma·na sa·ya sam·pai
ke pantai surfing?   ke pan·tai soor·fing

Which beach has the best conditions today?
Pantai mana yang   pan·tai ma·na yang
kondisinya paling bagus   kon·di·si·nya pa·ling ba·goos
hari ini?   ha·ri i·ni

What are the best times to surf there?
Jam berapa paling pas   jam be·ra·pa pa·ling pas
buat surfing di sini?   boo·at soor·fing di si·ni

Where's the nearest/best ... break? | *Di mana break ... yang paling bagus/dekat?* | di ma·na brek ... yang pa·ling ba·goos/de·kat?
- **beach** | *pantai* | pan·tai
- **point** | *titik* | ti·tik
- **reef** | *karang* | ka·rang

Is the surf big or small?
Gelombangnya besar atau kecil? | ge·lom·bang·nya be·sar a·tow ke·chil

Does it work at high/low tide?
Bisa dilakukan saat pasang/surut? | bi·sa di·la·koo·kan sa·at pa·sang/soo·root

Do you know any secret spots?
Anda tahu tempat yang masih rahasia? | an·da ta·hoo tem·pat yang ma·sih ra·ha·si·a

Where can I find a surf shop?
Di mana saya dapat toko surfing? | di ma·na sa·ya da·pat to·ko soor·fing

Where can I ...? | *Di mana saya bisa ...?* | di ma·na sa·ya bi·sa ...
- **buy ...** | *beli ...* | be·li ...
- **rent ...** | *sewa ...* | se·wa ...
- **repair ...** | *reparasi ...* | re·pa·ra·si ...

water sports

olahraga air

Can I book a lesson?
Bisa saya ikut kursus? | bi·sa sa·ya i·koot koor·soos

Are there any ...? | *Ada ...?* | a·da ...
- **reefs** | *karang* | ka·rang
- **rips** | *gelombang* | ge·lom·bang
- **water hazards** | *bahaya perairan* | ba·ha·ya pe·ra·ir·an

sport

151

Can I hire (a) ...?	Bisa saya sewa ...?	bi·sa sa·ya se·wa ...
boat	perahu motor	pe·ra·hoo mo·tor
canoe (modern)	kanu	ka·noo
canoe (traditional)	sampan	sam·pan
kayak	kayak	ka·yak
life jacket	baju	ba·joo
	pelampung	pe·lam·poong
snorkelling gear	alat snorkeling	a·lat snor·ke·ling
water-skis	papan ski air	pa·pan ski a·ir
wetsuit (water-skiing)	pakaian ski	pa·kai·an ski

fighting in harmony

Although lacking the notoriety of kung fu and tae kwan do, Indonesia has its own style of martial arts – *pencak silat* pen·chak si·lat (lit: the harmony of fighting). Originally from Sumatra, the popularity of *pencak silat* has spread across the archipelago, and individual regions have developed their own distinct styles. Common rules and techniques allow competitions to take place throughout Indonesia and even internationally.

The study of *pencak silat* can be divided into three broad areas: *olahraga* o·lah·ra·ga (sport), *kesenian* ke·se·ni·an (art) and *tenaga dalam* te·ne·ga da·lam (inner power). The 'inner power' facet focuses on mind control and strength. *Pencak silat* is a recognised part of the national school curriculum, and is also offered at many universities.

Pencak silat can also be performed to music – routines cover key steps and transitions, and can incorporate weaponry or ornamental fans. In some regions, competitions and performances are carried out at weddings, harvest festivals and circumcision ceremonies.

weather

What's the weather like?
   Cuacanya bagaimana?   choo·a·cha·nya ba·gai·ma·na

What will the weather be like (tomorrow)?
   Bagaimana cuaca (besok)?   ba·gai·ma·na choo·a·cha (be·sok)

It's …

cloudy	*Berawan.*	be·ra·wan
cold	*Dingin.*	ding·in
fine	*Bagus.*	ba·goos
hot	*Panas.*	pa·nas
raining	*Hujan.*	hoo·jan
sunny	*Terang.*	te·rang
windy	*Berangin.*	be·rang·in

Where can I buy (a/an) …?	*Di mana saya bisa beli …?*	di ma·na sa·ya bi·sa be·li …
bathers	*baju renang*	ba·joo re·nang
hat	*topi*	to·pi
rain jacket	*jas hujan*	jas hoo·jan
sarong	*sarung*	sa·roong
sunscreen	*krim tabirsurya*	krim ta·bir·soor·ya
umbrella	*payung*	pa·yoong

eat & run

Need a picnic or rations for a long haul? Nearly all restaurants and stalls can pack you food for the road, and even soup can be put in a bag. Just say:

Please put it in a container.
   Minta dibungkus.   min·ta di·boong·koos

beach

Where's the best/nearest beach?
  Di mana pantai yang   di ma·na pan·tai yang
  paling bagus/dekat?   pa·ling ba·goos/de·kat

Is it safe to dive/swim here?
  Di sini aman buat   di si·ni a·man boo·at
  menyelam/berenang?   me·nye·lam/be·re·nang

What time is high/low tide?
  Jam berapa air   jam be·ra·pa a·ir
  pasang/surut?   pa·sang/soo·root

Do we have to pay?
  Kita harus bayar?   ki·ta ha·roos ba·yar

How much for a/an …?	*Berapa satu …?*	be·ra·pa sa·too …
chair	*kursi*	koor·si
hut	*pondok*	pon·dok
umbrella	*payung*	pa·yoong

For more on-the-water entertainment, see **sport**, page 145.

listen for ...		
Awas arus bawah!	a·was a·roos ba·wah	Be careful of the undertow!
Itu berbahaya!	i·too ber·ba·ha·ya	It's dangerous!

hiking

mendaki gunung

Is it safe?
  Di sana aman?   di sa·na a·man

Do we need a guide?
  Kita perlu penunjuk jalan?   ki·ta per·loo pe·noon·jook ja·lan

Where can I ...?	*Di mana saya bisa ...?*	di ma·na sa·ya bi·sa ...?
buy supplies	*beli bekal*	be·li be·kal
find someone who knows this area	*temukan seseorang yang mengerti daerah ini*	te·moo·kan se·se·o·rang yang men·ger·ti da·e·rah i·ni
get a map	*dapat peta*	da·pat pe·ta
hire hiking gear	*sewa alat untuk mendaki*	se·wa a·lat oon·took men·da·ki
How ...?	*Berapa ...?*	be·ra·pa ...
high is the climb	*tinggi mendakinya*	ting·gi men·da·ki·nya
long is the trail	*lama perjalanannya*	la·ma per·ja·la·nan·nya
Is the track ...?	*Jalannya ...?*	ja·lan·nya ...
clear	*jelas*	je·las
difficult	*susah*	soo·sah
scenic	*indah*	in·dah
Which is the ... route?	*Lewat mana paling...?*	le·wat ma·na pa·ling ...
easiest	*gampang*	gam·pang
most interesting	*menarik*	me·na·rik
shortest	*dekat*	de·kat
Where is/are (the) ...?	*Di mana ...?*	di ma·na ...
camping ground	*tempat kemping*	tem·pat kem·ping
nearest village	*kampung yang terdekat*	kam·poong yang ter·de·kat
water	*air*	a·ir
toilets	*tempat buang air*	tem·pat boo·ang a·ir
Do we need to take food/water?	*Kita perlu bawa makanan/air?*	ki·ta per·loo ba·wa ma·ka·nan/a·ir

When does it get dark?
Jam berapa mulai gelap?   jam be·ra·pa moo·lai ge·lap

Is there a hut?
Ada pondok?   a·da pon·dok

Where have you come from?
Anda baru dari mana?   an·da ba·roo da·ri ma·na

How long did it take?
Berapa lama perjalanannya?   be·ra·pa la·ma per·ja·la·nan·nya

Does this path go to (Semeru)?
Ini jalan ke (Semeru)?   i·ni ja·lan ke (se·me·roo)

Can I go through here?
Bisa saya lewat sini?   bi·sa sa·ya le·wat si·ni

Is the water OK to drink?
Air ini bisa diminum?   a·ir i·ni bi·sa di·mi·noom

I'm lost.
Saya tersesat.   sa·ya ter·se·sat

ecotourism

Indonesia is one of the earth's richest regions in terms of biodiversity, and its great variety of flora and fauna offers exceptional opportunities for ecotourism. Unfortunately, facilities in most conservation areas are either limited or absent, so those keen on exploring areas off the beaten track should head for the nearest village to make guiding and accommodation arrangements with the locals. Be prepared for camping rough if you're going deep in the rainforest, but guides usually make basic shelters so you won't need a tent.

I want to see birds/wildlife in this area.
    Saya mau lihat burung/   sa·ya mow li·hat boo·roong/
    satwa di daerah ini.   sat·wa di da·e·rah i·ni

What time is best for seeing …?
    Sekitar jam berapa paling   se·ki·tar jam be·ra·pa pa·ling
    cocok untuk melihat …?   cho·chok oon·took me·li·hat …

Can I see … here?
    Bisa saya lihat … di sini?   bi·sa sa·ya li·hat … di si·ni

I want to hire a guide.
    Saya mau sewa pemandu.   sa·ya mow se·wa pe·man·doo

How much for one day?
    Berapa untuk satu hari?   be·ra·pa oon·took sa·too ha·ri

I want to stay overnight in the forest.
    Saya mau bermalam   sa·ya mow ber·ma·lam
    di hutan.   di hoo·tan

Can you make a shelter?
    Anda bisa bikin pondok?   an·da bi·sa bi·kin pon·dok

Is this a …?	*Ini …?*	i·ni …
forestry post (ranger station)	*pos kehutanan*	pos ke·hoo·ta·nan
national park	*taman nasional*	ta·man na·si·o·nal
nature reserve	*cagar alam*	cha·gar a·lam
protected area	*kawasan konservasi*	ka·wa·san kon·ser·va·si
protected forest	*hutan lindung*	hoo·tan lin·doong
protected species	*jenis dilindungi*	je·nis di·lin·doong·i

What … is that?	Apa itu …?	a·pa i·too …
animal	binatang	bi·na·tang
flower	bunga	boo·nga
plant	tumbuhan	toom·boo·han
tree	pohon	po·hon
Is it a … species here?	Ini jenis … di sini?	i·ni je·nis … di si·ni
common	umum	oo·moom
endangered	terancam	te·ran·cham
	punah	poo·nah
protected	dilindungi	di·lin·doong·i
rare	langka	lang·ka

wildlife & habitats

geography

cliff	tebing	te·bing
earth (soil)	tanah	ta·nah
forest	hutan	hoo·tan
grassland	padang rumput	pa·dang room·poot
habitat	habitat	ha·bi·tat
mangrove	bakau	ba·kow
mountain	gunung	goo·noong
ocean	samudera	sa·moo·de·ra
peak	puncak	poon·chak
plateau	dataran tinggi	da·ta·ran ting·gi
rainforest	hutan hujan	hoo·tan hoo·jan
ravine	jurang	joo·rang
river	sungai	soong·ai
sea	laut	la·oot
stream	kali	ka·li
swamp	rawa	ra·wa
valley	lembah	lem·bah
waterfall	air terjun	a·ir ter·joon

SOCIAL

mammals

barking deer	kijang	ki·jang
bat	kelelawar	ke·le·la·war
bear	beruang	be·roo·ang
civet	musang	moo·sang
cuscus	kuskus	koos·koos
deer	rusa	roo·sa
elephant	gajah	ga·jah
gibbon	owa	o·wa
(tree) kangaroo	kanguru (pohon)	kan·goo·roo (po·hon)
leaf monkey	lutung	loo·toong
leopard	macan	ma·chan
mammal	mamalia	ma·ma·li·a
monkey	monyet	mo·nyet
mouse deer	kancil	kan·chil
orang-utan	orang hutan	o·rang hoo·tan
otter	berang-berang	be·rang be·rang
pangolin	trenggiling	treng·gi·ling
porcupine	landak	lan·dak
proboscis monkey	bekantan	be·kan·tan
rat	tikus	ti·koos
rhinoceros	badak	ba·dak
squirrel	tupai	too·pai
tiger	harimau	ha·ri·mow
wild animal	satwa	sat·wa
wild boar	babi hutan	ba·bi hoo·tan
wild cat	kucing hutan	koo·ching hoo·tan
wild cattle	sapi banten	sa·pi ban·ten
wild dog	ajag	a·jag

when nature calls …

Chances of an actual *kamar kecil* ka·mar ke·chil or *WC* we·se (both mean 'toilet') are slim if you're in the wilds of Indonesia. The phrase we've given you in this chapter – *Di mana tempat buang air?* – literally asks 'Where's a place to pee?'. You may be lucky enough to find a patch of bush just for that purpose …

ecotourism

159

birds

bird	*burung*	boo·roong
bird of paradise	*cendrawasih*	chen·dra·wa·sih
cassowary	*kasuari*	ka·soo·a·ri
cockatoo	*kakatua*	ka·ka·too·a
duck	*bebek*	be·bek
eagle	*elang*	e·lang
hornbill	*burung tahun*	boo·roong ta·hoon
kingfisher	*raja udang*	ra·ja oo·dang
mynah	*jalak*	ja·lak
owl	*burung hantu*	boo·roong han·too
parrot	*nuri*	noo·ri
peafowl	*merak*	me·rak
pheasant	*sempidan*	sem·pi·dan
pigeon	*merpati*	mer·pa·ti
pitta	*paok*	pa·ok
stork	*bangau*	ban·gow
sunbird	*burung madu*	boo·roong ma·doo

reptiles

cobra	*ular sendok*	oo·lar sen·dok
crocodile	*buaya*	boo·a·ya
gecko	*cecak*	che·chak
Komodo dragon	*biawak Komodo*	bi·a·wak ko·mo·do
lizard	*kadal*	ka·dal
monitor lizard	*biawak*	bi·a·wak
python	*ular sawah*	oo·lar sa·wah
reptile	*reptil*	rep·til
skink	*kadal*	ka·dal
snake	*ular*	oo·lar

marine life

coral	*karang*	ka·rang
dolphin	*lumba-lumba*	loom·ba loom·ba
(ornamental) fish	*ikan (hias)*	i·kan (hi·as)
jellyfish	*ubur-ubur*	oo·boor oo·boor
marine life	*biota laut*	bi·o·ta la·oot
shark	*ikan hiu*	i·kan hi·oo
tuna	*ikan cakalang*	i·kan cha·ka·lang
turtle	*penyu*	pe·nyoo
whale	*paus*	pa·oos

basics

dasar

breakfast	*sarapan*	sa·ra·pan
lunch	*makan siang*	ma·kan si·ang
dinner	*makan malam*	ma·kan ma·lam
snack	*makanan kecil*	ma·ka·nan ke·chil
eat v	*makan*	ma·kan
drink v	*minum*	mi·noom
Please.	*Silakan.*	si·la·kan
Thank you.	*Terima kasih.*	te·ri·ma ka·sih
I'd like …	*Saya mau …*	sa·ya mow …
I'm starving!	*Saya kelaparan!*	sa·ya ke·la·pa·ran

finding a place to eat

mencari tempat makan

Can you recommend a …?	*Bisa Anda rekomendasikan …*	bi·sa an·da re·ko·men·da·si·kan …
bar	*bar*	bar
café	*kafe*	ka·fe
eatery/foodstall	*warung*	wa·roong
restaurant (local style)	*rumah makan*	roo·mah ma·kan
restaurant (upmarket)	*restoran*	re·sto·ran

the writing's on the wall

Many eateries don't have *daftar makanan* daf·tar ma·ka·nan (menus) – the food available is usually advertised on the wall, the stall tarpaulin or the side of the *kakilima* ka·ki·li·ma (footpath).

Where would you go for (a) …?	*Anda ke mana kalau mau …?*	an·da ke ma·na ka·low mow …
celebration	*bikin acara*	bi·kin a·cha·ra
cheap meal	*cari makanan murah*	cha·ri ma·ka·nan moo·rah
local specialities	*cari masakan khas daerah*	cha·ri ma·sa·kan khas da·e·rah

I'd like to reserve a table for …	*Saya mau pesan meja …*	sa·ya mow pe·san me·ja …
(two) people	*untuk (dua) orang*	oon·took (doo·a) o·rang
(eight) o'clock	*pada jam (delapan)*	pa·da jam (de·la·pan)

Are you still serving food?
Masih ada makanan? ma·sih a·da ma·ka·nan

How long is the wait?
Mesti menunggu berapa lama? me·sti me·noong·goo be·ra·pa la·ma

at the restaurant

di restoran

What would you recommend?
Apa yang Anda rekomendasikan? a·pa yang an·da re·ko·men·da·si·kan

What's in that dish?
Hidangan itu isinya apa? hi·dang·an i·too i·si·nya a·pa

What's that called?
Namanya apa? na·ma·nya a·pa

I'll have that.
Saya minta itu. sa·ya min·ta i·too

Does it take long to prepare?
Apakah lama memasaknya? a·pa·kah la·ma me·ma·sak·nya

Is there a cover charge?
Ada cover charge? a·da ko·ver charj

Is service included in the bill?
Ongkos pelayanan sudah ong·kos pe·la·ya·nan soo·dah
termasuk di kuitansi? ter·ma·sook di koo·i·tan·si

Are these complimentary?
Ini gratis? i·ni gra·tis

Kami tutup. ka·mi too·toop	We're closed.
Kami penuh. ka·mi pe·nooh	We're full.
Sebentar. se·ben·tar	One moment.
Mau duduk di mana? mow doo·dook di ma·na	Where would you like to sit?
Anda perlu apa? an·da per·loo a·pa	What can I get for you?
Anda suka ... an·da soo·ka ...	Do you like ...?
Saya rekomendasikan ... sa·ya re·ko·men·da·si·kan ...	I suggest the ...
Anda ingin makanan itu dimasak dengan cara apa? an·da ing·in ma·ka·nan i·too di·ma·sak deng·an cha·ra a·pa	How would you like that cooked?
Selamat makan! se·la·mat ma·kan	Enjoy your meal!

eating out

Hidangan Pembuka	hi·dang·an pem·boo·ka	**Appetisers/ Entrées**
Aneka Sup	a·ne·ka soop	**Soups**
Selada	se·la·da	**Salads**
Hidangan Utama	hi·dang·an oo·ta·ma	**Main Courses**
Hidangan Penutup	hi·dang·an pe·noo·toop	**Desserts**
Minuman	mi·noo·man	**Drinks**
Aneka Minuman Ringan	a·ne·ka mi·noo·man ring·an	**Soft Drinks**
Aneka Jus	a·ne·ka joos	**Juices**
Aneka Teh	a·ne·ka teh	**Teas**
Aneka Kopi	a·ne·ka ko·pi	**Coffees**
Minuman Beralkohol	mi·noo·man be·ral·ko·hol	**Alcoholic Drinks**
Aneka Anggur	a·ne·ka ang·goor	**Wines**
Aneka Bir	a·ne·ka bir	**Beers**

I'd like (a/the) ..., please.	*Saya minta ...*	sa·ya min·ta ...
drink list	*daftar minuman*	daf·tar mi·noo·man
half portion	*setengah porsi*	se·teng·ah por·si
meal fit for a king	*makanan yang cocok untuk tamu dari jauh*	ma·ka·nan yang cho·chok oon·took ta·moo da·ri ja·ooh
menu (in English)	*daftar makanan (dalam Bahasa Inggris)*	daf·tar ma·ka·nan (da·lam ba·ha·sa ing·gris)
local speciality	*masakan khas daerah*	ma·sa·kan khas da·e·rah
nonsmoking section	*yang bebas asap rokok*	yang be·bas a·sap ro·kok
smoking section	*yang boleh merokok*	yang bo·leh me·ro·kok
table for (five)	*meja untuk (lima) orang*	me·ja oon·took (li·ma) o·rang
that dish	*hidangan itu*	hi·dang·an i·too

I'd like it	*Saya mau*	sa·ya mow
with/without …	*dengan/tanpa …*	deng·an/tan·pa …
cheese	*keju*	ke·joo
chilli	*cabe*	cha·be
chilli sauce	*saus cabe*	sows cha·be
garlic	*bawang putih*	ba·wang poo·tih
ketchup	*saus tomat*	sows to·mat
MSG	*vetsin*	vet·sin
oil	*minyak*	mi·nyak
peanuts	*kacang*	ka·chang
pepper	*lada*	la·da
salt	*garam*	ga·ram
soy sauce	*kecap*	ke·chap
vinegar	*cuka*	choo·ka

For other specific meal requests, see **vegetarian & special meals**, page 177, and for other tasty delights, see the **culinary reader**, page 179.

at the table

di meja

Please bring (a/the) ...	*Tolong bawa ...*	to·long ba·wa ...
bill	*kuitansi*	koo·i·tan·si
cloth	*kain*	ka·in
(wine) glass	*gelas (wine)*	ge·las (wain)
serviette	*serbet*	ser·bet

I didn't order this.
Saya tidak pesan ini.   sa·ya ti·dak pe·san i·ni

There's a mistake in the bill.
Ada yang salah di bonnya.   a·da yang sa·lah di bon·nya

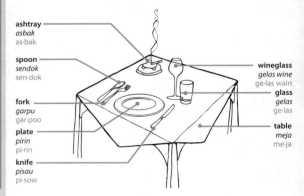

ashtray
asbak
as·bak

spoon
sendok
sen·dok

wineglass
gelas wine
ge·las wain

glass
gelas
ge·las

fork
garpu
gar·poo

table
meja
me·ja

plate
pirin
pi·rin

knife
pisau
pi·sow

FOOD

talking food

I love this dish.
  Saya sangat suka
  hidangan ini.

  sa·ya sang·at soo·ka
  hi·dang·an i·ni

I love the local cuisine.
  Saya sangat suka
  makanan daerah ini.

  sa·ya sang·at soo·ka
  ma·ka·nan da·e·rah i·ni

That was delicious!
  Ini enak sekali!

  i·ni e·nak se·ka·li

I'm full.
  Saya kenyang.

  sa·ya ke·nyang

My compliments to the chef.
  Sampaikan pujian
  buat kokinya.

  sam·pai·kan poo·ji·an
  boo·at ko·ki·nya

This is ...   *Ini ...*   i·ni ...
  (too) cold   *(terlalu) dingin*   (ter·la·loo) ding·in
  hot   *panas*   pa·nas
  salty   *asin*   a·sin
  spicy   *pedas*   pe·das
  spoiled   *busuk*   boo·sook
  superb   *luar biasa*   loo·ar bi·a·sa

food on five legs

Delicious food is available from roving food vendors known as *kaki lima* ka·ki li·ma (lit: 'five legs' – two wheels, a stand, plus the legs of the cook). Each *kaki lima* has a distinctive sound, depending on the snack that's being sold. Listen for the cry of *Bakso!* bak·so (advertising *bakso* noodles), or the wooden tock on the *sate* sa·te seller's bell.

methods of preparation

I'd like it …	Saya suka kalau itu …	sa·ya soo·ka ka·low i·too …
I don't want it …	Saya tidak mau itu …	sa·ya ti·dak mow i·too …
boiled	rebus	re·boos
broiled	panggang	pang·gang
fried	goreng	go·reng
grilled	bakar	ba·kar
mashed	tumbuk	toom·book
medium	setengah matang	se·teng·ah ma·tang
rare	masih mentah	ma·sih men·tah
reheated	dipanaskan ulang	di·pa·na·skan oo·lang
steamed	dikukus	di·koo·koos
well-done	sangat matang	sang·at ma·tang
without …	tanpa …	tan·pa …

street food

A huge variety of street food and drinks is available in Indonesia, often from a *warung* (eatery/foodstall) or a *kaki lima* (see the box on the previous page). Get your taste-buds ready – it's on the streets that you can sample the widest array of Indonesian food and drinks …

Does this drink contain tap water?
Minuman ini — mi·noo·man i·ni
mengandung air ledeng? — meng·an·doong a·ir le·deng

How long has this been in the sun?
Sudah berapa lama — soo·dah be·ra·pa la·ma
makanan ini terkena — ma·ka·nan i·ni ter·ke·na
sinar matahari? — si·nar ma·ta·ha·ri

I have a very weak stomach.
Perut saya sangat — pe·root sa·ya sang·at
gampang sakit. — gam·pang sa·kit

I'll have that one.
Saya mau yang itu. — sa·ya mow yang i·too

snack time

abon	a·bon	spiced & shredded meat
agar-agar	a·gar a·gar	jelly made with seaweed
bala bala	ba·la ba·la	vegetable fritter
dodol	do·dol	chewy, toffee-like sweet
emping	em·ping	rice or tapioca crackers
es krim	es krim	ice cream
gorengan	go·reng·an	fried snacks
kelepon	ke·le·pon	green rice balls with a palm-sugar centre
kerupuk	ke·roo·pook	prawn or rice crackers
ketan hitam	ke·tan hi·tam	black sticky rice served with coconut milk
kue (lapis)	koo·e (la·pis)	(layer) cake
kue sus	koo·e soos	custard-filled pastry
lemper	lem·per	sticky rice with *abon* filling wrapped in a banana leaf
lontong	lon·tong	cubes of pressed rice served with peanut sauce
lumpia	loom·pi·a	soft spring rolls
manisan	ma·ni·san	sweets
nasi liwet	na·si li·wet	rice cooked in coconut milk with egg or chicken
oncom	on·chom	soy-bean cake
onde-onde	on·de on·de	sesame balls with a green-bean centre
perkedel	per·ke·del	fried croquette with *abon* filling
pisang	pi·sang	fried banana
goreng	go·reng	
pukis	poo·kis	crescent-shaped cake
putu	poo·too	steamed cylindrical rice flour cakes with palm-sugar centres
rujak	roo·jak	fruit salad in a sour, spicy sauce
tahu isi	ta·hoo i·si	fried tofu with vegetable filling
tahu Sumedang	ta·hoo soo·me·dang	fried tofu from Sumedang
tempe goreng	tem·pe go·reng	fried tempeh
tiram	ti·ram	oysters

coffee cravings

Be ready to try some unique coffee combinations in Indonesia. In addition to Western-style brews, you can find *kopi telur* ko·pi te·loor (a glass of raw egg and sugar creamed together, then topped up with coffee), *kopi tubruk* ko·pi too·brook (freshly ground coffee tossed straight into the glass with sugar and boiling water) and *kopi jahe* ko·pi ja·he (coffee brewed with ginger). If you see *kopi pahit* ko·pi pa·hit (lit: bitter coffee) offered, it's simply a sugar-free coffee.

... coffee	*kopi ...*	ko·pi ...
black	*hitam*	hi·tam
decaffeinated	*tanpa kafein*	tan·pa ka·fe·in
iced	*es*	es
regular	*biasa*	bi·a·sa
white	*susu*	soo·soo

nonalcoholic drinks

minuman tanpa alkohol

boiled/hot water	*air matang/panas*	a·ir ma·tang/pa·nas
orange juice	*jus jeruk manis*	joos je·rook ma·nis
soft drink	*minuman ringan*	mi·noo·man ring·an
... mineral water	*air mineral ...*	a·ir mi·ne·ral ...
sparkling	*bersoda*	ber·so·da
still	*tanpa soda*	tan·pa so·da
(cup of) tea ...	*(secangkir) teh ...*	(se·chang·kir) teh ...
(glass of) coffee ...	*(segelas) kopi ...*	(se·ga·las) ko·pi ...
with (milk)	*dengan (susu)*	deng·an (soo·soo)
without (sugar)	*tanpa (gula)*	tan·pa (goo·la)

... tea	teh ...	teh ...
ginger	jahe	ja·he
green	hijau	hi·jow
lemon	jeruk	je·rook
sweet	manis	ma·nis

Or why not try *teh poci* teh po·chi – tea brewed with rock sugar in a clay pot?

alcoholic drinks

minuman beralkohol

a shot of (gin)	satu sloki (jenewer)	sa·too slo·ki (je·ne·wer)
a bottle/glass of ... wine	sebotol/segelas anggur ...	se·bo·tol/se·ge·las ang·goor ...
red	merah	me·rah
white	putih	poo·tih
a ... of beer	satu ... bir	sa·too ... bir
glass	gelas	ge·las
jug	pitcher	pi·cher
small bottle	botol kecil	bo·tol ke·chil
large bottle	botol besar	bo·tol be·sar

in the bar

di bar

If you're buying *sloki* slo·ki (shots) or *dobel* do·bel (double shots) of hard liquor, use the English names for your favourite spirits. The same goes for 'cocktails' and 'champagne'.

Excuse me.	Permisi.	per·mi·si
I'm next.	Saya yang berikut.	sa·ya yang be·ri·koot
I'll have ...	Saya mau ...	sa·ya mow ...

air jeruk	a·ir je·rook	citrus fruit juice or lemonade
air kelapa	a·ir ke·la·pa	coconut milk
air kelapa muda	a·ir ke·la·pa moo·da	coconut milk served in the coconut
es	es	ice • iced drink
es alpukat	es al·poo·kat	avocado mixed with ice, sugar & condensed milk or with chocolate syrup
es buah	es boo·ah	*es campur* with several fruits
es campur	es cham·poor	sweet drink of coconut milk, fruit, jelly & shaved ice
es cendol	es chen·dol	dessert-drink of green rice-flour jelly droplets, coconut milk & palm-sugar syrup
es dawet	es da·wet	see *es cendol*
es jeruk	es je·rook	citrus juice with ice & sugar syrup
es mangga	es mang·ga	mango shake
sari buah apel	sa·ri boo·ah a·pel	apple cider

Same again, please.
   Mau lagi, sama seperti tadi.   mow la·gi sa·ma se·per·ti ta·di
No ice, thanks.
   Tanpa es, terima kasih.   tan·pa es te·ri·ma ka·sih
I'll buy you a drink.
   Saya akan traktir   sa·ya a·kan trak·tir
   Anda segelas.   an·da se·ge·las

It's my round.
Saya yang traktir.   sa·ya yang trak·tir

What would you like?
Anda mau apa?   an·da mow a·pa

I don't drink alcohol.
Saya tidak minum   sa·ya ti·dak mow mi·noom
alkohol.   al·ko·hol

How much is that?
Harganya berapa?   har·ga·nya be·ra·pa

Do you serve meals here?
Ada layanan buat   a·da la·ya·nan boo·at
makan di sini?   ma·kan di si·ni

drinking up

waktu minum

Cheers!
Bersulang!   ber·soo·lang

I feel fantastic!
Top abis!   top a·bis

I think I've had one too many.
Aduh, rasanya   a·dooh ra·sa·nya
kebanyakan nenggak.   ke·ba·nya·kan neng·gak

I'm feeling drunk.
Saya mabuk.   sa·ya ma·book

eating out

I'm pissed.
Saya mabuk berat.
sa·ya ma·book be·rat

I feel ill.
Saya mual.
sa·ya moo·al

Where's the toilet?
Di mana kamar kecil?
di ma·na ka·mar ke·chil

I'm tired, I'd better go home.
*Saya capek, lebih
baik saya pulang.*
sa·ya cha·pek le·bih
ba·ik sa·ya poo·lang

Can you call a taxi for me?
*Bisa Anda panggilkan
taksi untuk saya?*
bi·sa an·da pang·gil·kan
tak·si oon·took sa·ya

I don't think you should drive.
*Saya pikir Anda sebaiknya
tidak menyopir sendiri.*
sa·ya pi·kir an·da se·ba·ik·nya
ti·dak me·nyo·pir sen·di·ri

local liquor

Indonesia has been a predominantly Muslim nation for centuries, so the locals don't have a strong tradition of making and drinking alcohol. There are, however, a few local drinks you might like to sample:

arak	a·rak	spirit distilled from palm sap or rice
arak attack	a·rak a·tak	*arak* mixed with lemonade or orange juice
brem	brem	type of *arak* distilled from white & black rice (Bali)
ciu	chi·oo	sugar-cane spirit
legen	le·gen	white alcohol from the fermented sap of the palm-tree flower (East Java)

What's the local speciality?
Apa yang khas daerah ini?   a·pa yang khas da·e·rah i·ni

What's that?
Itu apa?   i·too a·pa

Can I taste it?
Saya boleh mencicipi sedikit?   sa·ya bo·leh men·chi·chi·pi se·di·kit

Can I have a bag, please?
Boleh saya minta satu tas plastik?   bo·leh sa·ya min·ta sa·too tas pla·stik

I don't need a bag, thanks.
Saya tidak perlu tas, terima kasih.   sa·ya ti·dak per·loo tas te·ri·ma ka·sih

How much is (a kilo of rice)?
Berapa (sekilo beras)?   be·ra·pa (se·ki·lo be·ras)

How much does it cost?
Berapa harganya?   be·ra·pa har·ga·nya

I'd like …	*Saya mau …*	sa·ya mow …
(200) grams	*(dua ratus) gram*	(doo·a ra·toos) gram
a dozen	*satu lusin*	sa·too loo·sin
half a kilo	*setengah kilo*	se·teng·ah ki·lo
(two) kilos	*(dua) kilo*	(doo·a) ki·lo
a bottle	*satu botol*	sa·too bo·tol
a jar	*satu guci*	sa·too goo·chi
a packet	*satu bungkus*	sa·too boong·koos
(three) pieces	*(tiga) potong*	(ti·ga) po·tong
(six) slices	*(enam) iris*	(e·nam) i·ris
a tin	*satu kaleng*	sa·too ka·leng
(just) a little	*sedikit (saja)*	se·di·kit (sa·ja)
more	*lebih*	le·bih
some …	*beberapa …*	be·be·ra·pa …
that one	*yang itu*	yang i·too
this one	*yang ini*	yang i·ni

food stuff

cooked	*rebus*	re·boos
cured	*asin*	a·sin
dried	*kering*	ke·ring
fresh	*segar*	se·gar
frozen	*beku*	be·koo
raw	*menta*	men·ta
smoked	*asap*	a·sap

Less.	*Kurang.*	koo·rang
A bit more.	*Sedikit lagi.*	se·di·kit la·gi
Enough.	*Cukup.*	choo·koop

Do you have …?	*Ada …?*	a·da …
anything	*yang lebih*	yang le·bih
cheaper	*murah*	moo·rah
other kinds	*jenis lain*	je·nis la·in

Where can I find	*Di mana*	di ma·na
the … section?	*bagian …?*	ba·gi·an …
dairy	*susu*	soo·soo
fish	*ikan*	i·kan
frozen goods	*makanan beku*	ma·ka·nan be·koo
fruit and	*buah-buahan*	boo·ah boo·a·han
vegetable	*dan sayur-mayur*	dan sa·yoor ma·yoor
meat	*daging*	da·ging
poultry	*unggas*	oong·gas

Could I please	*Boleh saya*	bo·leh sa·ya
borrow a …?	*pinjam …?*	pin·jam …
chopping board	*talenan*	ta·le·nan
frying pan	*wajan*	wa·jan
knife	*pisau*	pi·sow
saucepan	*panci*	pan·chi
	bergangang	ber·gang·ang
steamer	*kukusan*	koo·koo·san

For more cooking implements, see the **dictionary**.

ordering food

Do you have ... food?	*Anda punya masakan ...?*	an·da poo·nya ma·sa·kan ...
Is there a ... restaurant nearby?	*Ada restoran ... dekat sini?*	a·da re·sto·ran ... de·kat si·ni
halal	*halal*	ha·lal
kosher	*khusus untuk orang Yahudi*	khoo·soos oon·took o·rang ya·hoo·di
vegetarian	*khusus untuk vegetarian*	khoo·soos oon·took ve·je·ta·ri·an

I don't eat ...
Saya tidak mau makan ...   sa·ya ti·dak mow ma·kan ...

Is it cooked in/with ...?
Ini dimasak dengan ...?   i·ni di·ma·sak deng·an ...

Could you prepare a meal without ...?
Bisa Anda siapkan   bi·sa an·da si·ap·kan
makanan tanpa ...?   ma·ka·nan tan·pa ...

butter	*mentega*	men·te·ga
eggs	*telur*	te·loor
fish	*ikan*	i·kan
fish sauce (Chinese)	*kecap ikan*	ke·chap i·kan
fish sauce (Indonesian)	*terasi*	te·ra·si
fish stock	*stok ikan*	stok i·kan
meat stock	*stok daging*	stok da·ging
oil	*minyak*	mi·nyak
pork	*daging babi*	da·ging ba·bi
poultry	*unggas*	oong·gas
red meat	*daging merah*	da·ging me·rah

Is this ...?	Ini ...?	i·ni ...
decaffeinated	bebas kafein	be·bas ka·fe·in
free of animal produce	bebas dari pemakaian hewan	be·bas da·ri pe·ma·kai·an he·wan
free-range	dari kampung	da·ri kam·poong
low-fat	rendah lemak	ren·dah le·mak
low in sugar	rendah gula	ren·dah goo·la
organic	bahan organik	ba·han or·ga·nik
salt-free	bebas garam	be·bas ga·ram

special diets & allergies

makanan khusus dan alergi

I'm on a special diet.
Saya punya
pantangan tertentu.
sa·ya poo·nya
pan·tang·an ter·ten·too

I'm vegan/vegetarian.
Saya pengikut aliran
vegan/vejetarian.
sa·ya peng·i·koot a·li·ran
ve·gan/ve·je·ta·ri·an

I'm (a) ...	Saya beragama ...	sa·ya be·ra·ga·ma ...
Buddhist	Buda	boo·da
Hindu	Hindu	hin·doo
Jewish	Yahudi	ya·hoo·di
Muslim	Islam	is·lam

I'm allergic to ...	Saya alergi terhadap ...	sa·ya a·ler·gi ter·ha·dap ...
dairy produce	hasil susu	ha·sil soo·soo
eggs	telur	te·loor
gelatine	gelatin	ge·la·tin
gluten	perekat	pe·re·kat
honey	madu	ma·doo
MSG	vetsin	vet·sin
nuts	biji-bijian	bi·ji bi·ji·an
peanuts	kacang tanah	ka·chang ta·nah
seafood	hasil laut	ha·sil la·oot
shellfish	kerang	ke·rang

culinary reader
daftar makanan dan minuman

This miniguide to Indonesian cuisine lists dishes and ingredients, and is designed to help you get the most out of your gastronomic experience by providing you with food terms that you may see on menus. For certain dishes we've marked the region or city where they're most popular.

A

abon a-bon *spiced & shredded meat*
acar a-char *pickled vegetables*
adas a-das *fennel*
aduk a-dook *scrambled*
agar-agar a-gar a-gar *gelatine-like substance found in seaweed*
alam a-lam *rice-flour* & **daun pandan** *pudding cooked in a banana-leaf cylinder (Bali)*
alpukat al-poo-kat *avocado*
ambu-ambu am-boo am-boo *tuna*
ampar tatak am-par ta-tak *'cut plate' – moist sweets in various shapes, colours & flavours (Kalimantan)*
ampiang dadiah am-pi-ang da-di-ah *buffalo-milk yogurt with palm syrup, coconut & rice (West Sumatra)*
anak domba a-nak dom-ba *lamb*
angsa ang-sa *goose*
apam/apem a-pam/a-pem *palm-sugar pancakes*
apokat a-po-kat *avocado*
ara a-ra *fig*
arem-arem a-rem a-rem *mixture of pressed rice, meat, sprouts, soy sauce, coconut & peanuts (East Java)*
asam a-sam *tamarind*
— **manis** ma-nis *'sour sweet' – term used for anything served in a sweet & sour sauce*
asinan a-si-nan *pickles*
aya kurik a-ya koo-rik *tuna (Pacific)*
ayam a-yam *chicken*
— **bakar** ba-kar *grilled chicken*
— **goreng** go-reng *fried chicken*
— **kampung** kam-poong *free-range chicken*
— **kebiri** ke-bi-ri *capon*
— **masak habang** ma-sak ha-bang *chicken cooked with chillies (Kalimantan)*
— **namargota** na-mar-go-ta *chicken cooked in spices & blood (Batak & North Sumatra)*
— **rica rica** ri-cha ri-cha *chicken with a paste of chilli, shallots, ginger & lime (North Sulawesi)*
— **taliwang** ta-li-wang *whole split chicken roasted over coconut husks, served with a peanut, tomato, chilli & lime dip (Lombok & Sumbawa)*

B

babat ba-bat *tripe*
babi ba-bi *pork*
— **guling** goo-ling *spit-roast pig stuffed with chilli, turmeric, garlic & ginger (Bali)*
— **hutan** hoo-tan *wild boar*
— **panggang** pang-gang *pork boiled in vinegar & pig blood with spices, then roasted (Batak)*
bacem ba-chem *tempeh, tofu or chicken cooked in stock & deep-fried in coconut oil*
bajigur ba-ji-goor *spiced coffee with coconut milk (West Java)*
bakasang ba-ka-sang *paste made by fermenting fish in a terracotta pot (North Sulawesi)*
bakmi bak-mi *rice-flour noodles*
— **goreng** go-reng *fried rice-flour noodles*
bakpao bak-pa-o *steamed bun with filling, often meat or bean paste*
bak pia patuk bak pi-a pa-took *mung-bean cake (Central Java)*
bakso bak-so *noodle & meatball soup*
— **ayam** a-yam *chicken soup with noodles & meatballs*

bakwan bak-wan *vegetable fritter (Central Java)*
— **malang** ma-lang *soup with noodles, meatballs & fried won tons (East Java)*

bami ba-mi *egg noodles*

bandrek ban-drek *ginger tea with coconut, palm sugar, cinnamon, peppercorns & shredded coconut (West Java)*

batagor ba-ta-gor *fried fish or meat dumplings with peanut sauce*

bawang ba-wang *generic term for onion or garlic*
— **bakung** ba-koong *leek*
— **bombay** bom-bey *onion*
— **cina** chi-na *spring onion*
— **goreng** go-reng *crispy fried shallots*
— **merah** me-rah *shallot*
— **perai** pe-rai *leek*
— **putih** poo-tih *garlic*

bayam ba-yam *spinach*

bebek be-bek *duck*
— **betutu** be-too-too *duck stuffed with spices, wrapped in banana leaves & coconut husks, then cooked in a pit of embers (Bali)*
— **panggang** pang-gang *roast duck or chicken with soy sauce*

belacan be-la-chan *see* **terasi**

belewa be-le-wa *cantaloupe • rockmelon*

belimbing be-lim-bing *starfruit*
— **wuluh** woo-looh *small fruit related to starfruit, used for its sour flavour*

belulut be-loo-loot *palm-tree fruit*

belut be-loot *eel*
— **asin** a-sin *dried baby eels*

bengkuang beng-koo-ang *yam bean*

beras be-ras *harvested raw rice*
— **belanda** be-lan-da *pearl barley*
— **coklat** chok-lat *brown rice*
— **merah** me-rah *red rice*

besaran be-sa-ran *mulberry*

bihun bi-hoon *small rice noodles*

bika ambon bi-ka am-bon *cake of egg, sugar, tapioca flour, coconut milk & palm wine (Aceh & North Sumatra)*

bingka kentang bing-ka ken-tang *sweet made with potato (Kalimantan)*

blumkol bloom-kol *cauliflower*

bongko bong-ko *kidney beans, coconut & spices cooked in a banana leaf*

brongkos brong-kos *beef & bean stew with kluwek (Central Java)*

buah boo-ah *fruit*
— **anggur** ang-goor *grapes*
— **buahan** boo-a-han *fruit*
— **buahan kering** boo-a-han ke-ring *dried fruit*

bubur boo-boor *congee • rice porridge*
— **ayam** a-yam *rice porridge with chicken*
— **jagung** ja-goong *hominy*
— **jeruk** je-rook *citrus fruit*
— **kacang hijau** ka-chang hi-jow *mung bean porridge with coconut milk*
— **kampiun** kam-pi-oon *mung bean porridge with banana, rice, yogurt & custard (West Sumatra)*
— **ketan hitam** ke-tan hi-tam *black rice porridge with coconut milk*
— **ketan hitam kacang hijau** ke-tan hi-tam ka-chang hi-jow *black rice & mung bean porridge*
— **lemu** le-moo *rice pudding*
— **tinotuan** ti-no-too-an *rice porridge with corn, cassava, pumpkin, fish paste & chilli (North Sulawesi)*

bumbu boom-boo *spice mix • spice paste • spice sauce*
— **kari** ka-ri *curry paste*

buncis boon-chis *beans • string beans*

bunga kol boon-ga kol *cauliflower*

burung boo-roong *bird*
— **dara** da-ra *pigeon*

C

cabai cha-bai *chilli*

cabe cha-be *bell pepper • chilli*
— **besar** be-sar *capsicum • pepper*
— **hijau** hi-jow *green chilli*
— **merah** me-rah *red chilli*
— **rawit** ra-wit *bird's eye chilli (small & hot)*

cakalang cha-ka-lang *tuna*

cakar ayam cha-kar a-yam *chicken claw*

cap jai chap chai *stir-fried vegetables*

cempedak chem-pe-dak *fruit similar to jackfruit but sweeter & more tender*

ceplok chep-lok *fried egg*

colenak cho-le-nak *fermented cassava with sweet coconut sauce (West Java)*

colo-colo cho-lo cho-lo *sauce made with citrus fruit & chilli (Maluku)*

coto makassar cho-to ma-ka-sar *soup of beef offal, pepper, cumin & lemongrass (South Sulawesi)*

cuka choo·ka *vinegar • sauce of chilli, palm sugar, garlic, vinegar & soy sauce, served with* **pempek** *(South Sumatra)*
— **jawa** ja·wa *palm blossom vinegar*
cumi-cumi choo·mi choo·mi *squid*

D

dabu-dabu da·boo da·boo *raw vegetables in a chilli & fish paste sauce (Maluku)*
dada da·da *breast • brisket*
dadar da·dar *omelette*
daging da·ging *meat*
— **anak domba** a·nak dom·ba *lamb*
— **anak sapi** a·nak sa·pi *veal*
— **babi** ba·bi *pork*
— **cincang** chin·chang *mince*
— **domba** dom·ba *mutton*
— **kambing** kam·bing *goat • mutton*
— **menjangan** men·jang·an *venison*
— **pinggang** ping·gang *sirloin*
— **sapi** sa·pi *beef*
daun da·oon *leaf*
— **bawang** ba·wang *spring onion*
— **jeruk purut** je·rook poo·root *kaffir lime leaf*
— **pandan** pan·dan *pandanus leaf • screwpine*
— **pisang** pi·sang *banana leaf*
delima de·li·ma *pomegranate*
direbus keras di·re·boos ke·ras *hard-boiled*
direbus setengah matang di·re·boos se·teng·ah ma·tang *soft-boiled*
domba dom·ba *mutton*
duku doo·koo *small, yellow-coloured fruit*
durian doo·ri·an *durian*

E

ebi e·bi *dried prawn*
empal genton em·pal gen·ton *beef & turmeric soup (West Java)*
emping em·ping *crackers made from dried* **melinjo** *nuts*
erom e·rom *sweet potato (Papua)*
es es *ice • iced drink*
— **alpukat** al·poo·kat *avocado mixed with ice, sugar & condensed milk or chocolate syrup*
— **durian** doo·ri·an *durian with ice & sugar syrup*

— **ketimun** ke·ti·moon *shredded cucumber with ice & sugar syrup*
— **nangka** nang·ka *jackfruit with ice & sugar syrup*
— **pallubutung** pa·loo·boo·toong *coconut custard & bananas in coconut milk & sugar syrup (South Sulawesi)*
— **teler** te·ler *'drunk ice' – coconut milk with fruit & ice*

G

gabus ga·boos *snakehead fish with a very meaty, salami-like flavour (Kalimantan)*
gado-gado ga·do ga·do *vegetables with peanut sauce (Jakarta)*
garang asem ga·rang a·sem *chicken innards, spices, starfruit & coconut milk cooked in a clay pot (Tegal & Central Java)*
gempol pleret gem·pol ple·ret *discs of spiced rice flour made with coconut milk (Central Java)*
geplak gep·lak *sticky rice sweet with palm sugar & coconut (Central Java)*
gepuk ge·pook *flattened & fried spiced beef (West Java)*
ginjal gin·jal *kidney*
goreng go·reng *fried • fry*
gowok go·wok *small purple-coloured fruit – eat the peel but not the seed*
gudeg goo·deg *jackfruit curry – young jackfruit & spices slowly cooked in coconut milk & served with chicken, egg or buffalo skin (Central Java)*
gula goo·la *sugar*
— **gula** goo·la *candy • lollies*
— **jawa** ja·wa *palm sugar*
— **kelapa** ke·la·pa *coconut palm sugar*
— **merah** me·rah *palm sugar*
gulai goo·lai *coconut curry*
— **ayam** a·yam *chicken coconut curry*
— **itik** i·tik *duck coconut curry*
— **kambing** kam·bing *goat coconut curry*
— **nangka** nang·ka *jackfruit coconut curry*
— **tahu** ta·hoo *tofu coconut curry*
gule goo·le *see* **gulai**
gurami goo·ra·mi *large freshwater fish*
gurita goo·ri·ta *octopus*

H

harawan ha·ra·wan *see* **gabus**
haring ha·ring *herring*
hati ha·ti *liver*
— **ayam** a·yam *chicken liver*

I

ikan i·kan *fish*
— **air tawar** a·ir ta·war *freshwater fish*
— **asam manis** a·sam ma·nis *sweet & sour fish*
— **asin** a·sin *salted fish*
— **bakar** ba·kar *grilled fish*
— **basah** ba·sah *fresh fish*
— **bawal** ba·wal *pomfret*
— **belado** be·la·do *fried fish covered in spring onions & chilli*
— **belida** be·li·da *large river fish*
— **bilis** bi·lis *anchovy*
— **bilis goreng kacang** bi·lis go·reng ka·chang *fried peanuts & anchovies*
— **brengkes** breng·kes *fish cooked in a spicy durian-based sauce (South Sumatra)*
— **cakalang** cha·ka·lang *tuna*
— **danau** da·now *freshwater fish*
— **garupa** ga·roo·pa *groper*
— **hiu** hi·oo *shark*
— **julung-julung** joo·loong joo·loong *garfish*
— **laut** la·oot *saltwater fish*
— **lele** le·le *catfish*
— **lemuru** le·moo·roo *sardine*
— **mas** mas *carp*
— **panada** pa·na·da *tuna pastry (North Sulawesi)*
— **pari** pa·ri *ray*
— **rica-rica** ri·cha ri·cha *fish with paste of shallots, chilli, ginger & lime (North Sulawesi)*
— **sarden** sar·den *sardine*
— **sebelah** se·be·lah *flatfish*
— **segar** se·gar *fresh fish*
— **teri** te·ri *anchovy • whitebait*
— **tongkol** tong·kol *mackerel • tuna*
intip in·tip *rice crackers*
itik i·tik *duck*

J

jagung ja·goong *corn • sweetcorn*
— **bakar** ba·kar *grilled corn*
jahe ja·he *ginger*
jaje ja·je *rice & tapioca cakes*
jamblang jam·blang *Java plum – small, purple fruit with sweet flesh similar to a ripe grape*
jambu jam·boo *guava*
— **air** a·ir *water apple – glossy white or pink bell-shaped fruit*
— **biji** bi·ji *guava*
— **klutuk** kloo·took *guava*
— **mete** me·te *cashew*
jamur ja·moor *mushrooms*
jengkol jeng·kol *starchy fruit used in savoury dishes*
jeroan je·ro·an *entrails • giblets • offal*
jeruk je·rook *citrus fruit • orange*
— **asam** a·sam *lemon*
— **bali** ba·li *pomelo*
— **baras** ba·ras *small tangerine-like orange*
— **garut** ga·root *tangerine*
— **keriput** ke·ri·poot *grapefruit*
— **limau** li·mow *green lime*
— **mandarin** man·da·rin *mandarin*
— **manis** ma·nis *orange*
— **muntis** moon·tis *pomelo*
— **nipis** ni·pis *lemon • lime*
— **purut** poo·root *kaffir lime*
jerunga je·roong·a *pomelo*
jicama ji·cha·ma *yam bean*

K

kacang ka·chang *bean • nut • pulse*
— **asin** a·sin *salted peanuts*
— **belimbing** be·lim·bing *pea*
— **buncis** boon·chis *green bean • pea*
— **hijau** hi·jow *mung bean*
— **jawa** ja·wa *lima bean*
— **mente** men·te *cashew*
— **merah** me·rah *red kidney bean*
— **panjang** pan·jang *chickpea • yard-long bean*
— **putih** poo·tih *peanut*
— **tanah** ta·nah *peanut*
kakap ka·kap *snapper*
kalio ka·li·o *rendang that hasn't been fully reduced*

kalkun kal-koon *turkey*
kambing kam-bing *goat*
kangkung kang-koong *cress • water spinach*
kantan kan-tan *ginger bud*
kapal selam ka-pal se-lam **pempek** *with a boiled egg inside (Sumatra)*
kapri ka-pri *snow pea*
kapur ka-poor *lime*
karak ka-rak *rice crackers*
kare ka-re *coconut curry (see also gulai)*
karedok ka-re-dok *Sundanese salad with yard-long beans, bean sprouts & cucumber with a spicy sauce (West Java)*
kawaok ka-wa-ok *fried forest rat (North Sulawesi)*
kayu manis ka-yoo ma-nis *'sweet wood' – cinnamon*
kecap ke-chap *sauce • soy sauce*
— **asin** a-sin *salty soy sauce*
— **manis** ma-nis *sweet soy sauce*
kedelai ke-de-lai *soybean*
keju ke-joo *cheese*
kelapa ke-la-pa *coconut*
— **kopyor** kop-yor *coconut with loose flesh that's made into ice cream*
— **muda** moo-da *young coconut*
kelembak ke-lem-bak *rhubarb*
kelepon ke-le-pon *rice-flour dumpling coloured green with daun pandan with palm-sugar centre & rolled in coconut (Central Java)*
kelinci ke-lin-chi *rabbit*
kelor ke-lor *hot soup with kangkung & other vegetables (Lombok)*
keluang ke-loo-ang *fruit bat (North Sulawesi)*
kembang kol kem-bang kol *cauliflower*
kemiri ke-mi-ri *candlenut*
kencur ken-choor *ginger-like rhizome often called 'lesser galangal'*
kentang ken-tang *potato*
— **goreng** go-reng *fried potatoes*
— **keripik** ke-ri-pik *crisps • potato chips*
— **panggang** pang-gang *roast potatoes*
kepala susu ke-pa-la soo-soo *cream*
kepiting ke-pi-ting *crab*
kerang ke-rang *clam • mussels*
— **laut** la-oot *abalone*
— **kerangan** ke-rang-an *shellfish*
kerapu ke-ra-poo *perch*
kerbau ker-bow *buffalo*
kering ke-ring *dried*

kerupuk ke-roo-pook *prawn crackers*
— **jagung** ja-goong *fried corn kernels*
— **kulit** koo-lit *cow or buffalo skin*
— **ubi** oo-bi *sweet potato crisps*
— **udang** oo-dang *prawn crackers*
kesemak ke-se-mak *persimmon*
ketan ke-tan *glutinous rice*
— **hitam** hi-tam *black rice*
ketimun ke-ti-moon *cucumber*
ketoprak ke-to-prak *tofu, noodles & bean sprouts with soy & peanut sauce (Jakarta)*
ketumbar ke-toom-bar *coriander used for the seeds*
ketupat ke-too-pat *rice steamed in boxes made from fancily woven coconut palms*
— **kandangan** kan-dang-an *broiled river fish & pressed rice swimming in lime-flavoured coconut sauce (Kalimantan)*
— **tahu** ta-hoo *pressed rice, bean sprouts & tofu with soy & peanut sauce (West Java)*
kijing ki-jing *clam*
kismis kis-mis *currant • raisin*
kluwek kloo-wek *seed that adds an earthy flavour to dishes & darkens their colour*
kobis ko-bis *broccoli*
kodok ko-dok *frog*
kohu-kohu ko-hoo ko-hoo *fish salad with citrus fruit & chilli (Maluku)*
kol kol *cabbage*
— **merah** me-rah *red cabbage*
— **mini** mi-ni *Brussel sprouts*
— **putih** poo-tih *white cabbage*
kolak ko-lak *fruit in coconut milk*
krecek kre-chek *beef or buffalo skin, often served with gudeg*
kroket kro-ket *mashed potato cake with minced meat filling*
krupuk kroo-pook *cracker*
kuah koo-ah *gravy • sauce*
kuaytau koo-ey-tow *flat rice noodles*
kubis koo-bis *broccoli*
kucai koo-chai *chives*
kue koo-e *cake • cookie*
— **kering** ke-ring *pastry*
— **pengantin** peng-an-tin *wedding cake*
kulit koo-lit *peel • skin*
kumut koo-moot *solids from cooking coconut milk*
kunyit koo-nyit *turmeric*
kurma koor-ma *dates*

L

labu la·boo *pumpkin · squash*
— **siam** si·am *kind of pumpkin*
lada la·da *pepper*
— **merah** me·rah *cayenne*
— **rimba** rim·ba *mouth-numbing pepper (Batak)*
lak lak lak lak *small pancake with palm sugar & coconut (Bali)*
laksa lak·sa *spicy noodle soup with coconut milk*
lalap la·lap *raw vegetable salad served with* **sambal**
lalapan la·la·pan *raw vegetable salad*
laor la·or *see* **nyale**
laos la·os *galangal*
lawar la·war *salad of chopped coconut, garlic & chilli with pork or chicken meat & blood (Bali)*
leci le·chi *lychee*
lele le·le *catfish*
lemper lem·per *sticky rice with a meat filling, steamed in a banana leaf*
leunca len·cha *small bittermelon, poisonous unless eaten when green*
lenggang leng·gang *chopped* **pempek** *mixed in an omelette (South Sumatra)*
lengkeng leng·keng *longan*
lobak lo·bak *radish*
— **cina** chi·na *turnip*
lombok lom·bok *chilli (see also* **cabe**)
lontong lon·tong *rice steamed in banana leaves & sliced into cubes*
lotek lo·tek *peanut sauce with vegetables & pressed rice (Central Java)*
lumpia loom·pi·a *fried spring rolls filled with prawns & bean sprouts (Semarang)*

M

madu ma·doo *honey*
makanan laut ma·ka·nan la·oot *seafood*
mangga mang·ga *mango*
manggis mang·gis *mangosteen, a fruit with purple skin & sweet white flesh*
manis ma·nis *sweet a*
manisan ma·ni·san *sweets*
— **pala** pa·la *preserve made with the fruit of the nutmeg*
markisa mar·ki·sa *passionfruit*

martabak mar·ta·bak *crispy-skin omelette with cucumber, garlic, shallots & meat · sweet, chunky pancake with toppings like banana, chocolate sauce, condensed milk & nuts*
— **habang** ha·bang *variety of dishes cooked with red chillies (Kalimantan)*
melinjo me·lin·jo *nut from the gnetum tree, used to make* **emping**
mentega men·te·ga *butter · margarine*
merica me·ri·cha *pepper*
mi/mie mee *noodles*
— **goreng** go·reng *fried noodles with vegetables & sometimes meat*
— **kocok** ko·chok *beef & egg noodle soup (West Java)*
— **kuah** koo·ah *noodle soup*
— **pangsit** pang·sit *won ton & noodle soup*
— **rebus** re·boos *noodle soup*
— **toprak** to·prak *beef noodle soup with tempeh, peanuts & spinach*
mihun mee·hoon *small rice noodles*
miju-miju mi·joo mi·joo *lentil*
mutiara moo·ti·a·ra *sago droplets used in sweets & drinks (Maluku)*

N

nangka nang·ka *jackfruit*
nasi na·si *cooked rice*
— **campur** cham·poor *rice with a selection of meat & vegetable dishes on one plate*
— **gabah** ga·bah *brown rice*
— **goreng** go·reng *fried rice cooked with chilli, eggs, vegetables &* **kecap manis**
— **goreng istimewa** go·reng i·sti·me·wa *nasi goreng crowned with a fried egg*
— **gudeg** goo·deg *unripe jackfruit cooked in coconut milk & served with rice, pieces of chicken & spices*
— **gurih** goo·rih *rice cooked in coconut milk*
— **jenggo** jeng·go *white rice with spicy sauce served in a banana leaf*
— **kuning** koo·ning *rice cooked in turmeric*
— **lengko** leng·ko *rice with tofu, tempeh, bean sprouts, cucumber & peanut sauce (West Java)*

— **liwet** li-wet *rice cooked with coconut milk, garlic, shallots & kumut, served with chicken or egg (Central Java)*
— **pecel** pe-chel *salad similar to gado-gado, with boiled papaya leaves, tapioca, bean sprouts, string beans, tempeh, cucumber, coconut shavings & peanut sauce*
— **putih** poo-tih *plain white rice*
— **rames** ra-mes *rice with several meat & vegetable dishes on one plate*
— **rawon** ra-won *rice with spicy hot beef soup, fried onions & spicy sauce*
— **goreng spesial** go-reng spe-si-al *see* **nasi goreng istimewa**
— **tambanan** tam-ba-nan *brown rice (Tambanan)*
— **timbel** tim-bel *rice cooked in banana leaves served with sambal, chicken, tofu, salted fish or tempeh (West Java)*
— **uduk** oo-dook *rice cooked in coconut milk served with meat, tofu or vegetables (Jakarta)*
nenas ne-nas *pineapple*
nyale nya-le *marine glow-worm, usually fried into a croquette*

O

onde-onde on-de on-de *sesame balls with a sweet mung-bean filling*
opor ayam o-por a-yam *chicken in pepper & coconut curry, with galangal, coriander seeds & lemongrass (Central Java)*
orak-arik o-rak a-rik *vegetables fried with pepper (Central Java)*
oret o-ret *sausage*
oseng-oseng o-seng o-seng *fried kangkung, yard-long beans & soy sauce (Central Java)*
— **ayam** a-yam **oseng-oseng** *with chicken (Central Java)*
— **jamur** ja-moor **oseng-oseng** *with dog (Central Java)*
otak o-tak *brains*

P

pais pa-is *see* **pepes**
pakis pa-kis *fernshoots, commonly used in* **sambals** *& fish dishes*
palai pa-lai *see* **pepes**

pamerasan pa-me-ra-san *buffalo meat in black sauce (Central Sulawesi)*
pange pang-e *fish stuffed with spiced egg (West Sumatra)*
panggang pang-gang *baked • roasted*
pangsit pang-sit *soup with meat dumplings • won ton*
pa'piong pa pi-ong *pork stuffed into bamboo tubes with vegetables & roasted over coals (Central Sulawesi)*
pare-pare pa-re pa-re *green rice-flour sweet with a palm-sugar filling (Kalimantan)*
pecel pe-chel *peanut sauce with spinach & bean sprouts (Java) • spicy sauce made from chilli, peanuts & tomato*
— **lele** le-le *deep-fried catfish served with rice &* **pecel**
pelecing pe-le-ching *sauce of chilli, prawn paste & tomato (Lombok)*
pempek pem-pek *deep-fried fish & sago dumpling (South Sumatra)*
pencuci mulut pen-choo-chi moo-loot *'mouth cleaner' – dessert*
pengsi peng-si *cockles*
— **maninjau** ma-nin-jow *cockles with chilli sauce (West Sumatra)*
pepes pe-pes *steamed or roasted in banana leaves*
— **ayam** a-yam *spiced chicken steamed in banana leaves*
— **ikan** i-kan *fish spiced & then cooked in banana leaves*
perkedel per-ke-del *croquette or fritter, often made with corn or potato*
— **jagung** ja-goong *corn fritters*
permen per-men *candy • lollies • sweets*
pete pe-te *large odorous bean that grows in a massive pod*
peterseli pe-ter-se-li *parsley*
petis ikan pe-tis i-kan *fish paste*
pindang pin-dang *spicy clear fish soup with soy & tamarind (South Sumatra)*
pisang pi-sang *banana*
— **bakar** ba-kar *bananas grilled over hot coals, flattened in a wooden press, then sprinkled with palm sugar & coconut*
— **goreng** go-reng *fried banana fritters*
— **kepok** ke-pok *banana used in cooking, similar to plantain*
— **molen** mo-len *banana wrapped in pastry & fried*
polong po-long *legumes*

potongan babi po·tong·an ba·bi pork chops

pukis poo·kis *crescent-shaped cake*

pulut poo·loot *glutinous rice*

putu poo·too *steamed coconut cylinder with a palm-sugar centre*

puyuh poo·yooh *quail*

R

rambutan ram·boo·tan *rambutan – red fruit covered in soft, hairy spines with lychee-like flesh*

rawon ra·won *hearty beef stew with kluwek (Java)*

rebung re·boong *bamboo shoot*

rembang rem·bang *sour fruit*

remis re·mis *mussel • scallop*

rempah-rempah gulai ikan rem·pah rem·pah goo·lai i·kan *whole, gutted saltwater fish flavoured with turmeric & tamarind seeds & cooked in a coconut curry (West Sumatra)*

rempeyek rem·pe·yek *peanut & rice-flour crackers fried in coconut oil*

rendang ren·dang *beef or buffalo coconut curry (West Sumatra)*

rica ri·cha *chilli*

   — rica ri·cha *dish prepared with a spicy paste of chillies, shallots, ginger & lime (North Sulawesi)*

roti ro·ti *bread • pastry*

   — bakar ba·kar *toast • bread with a filling of jam, chocolate or cheese fried on a hot plate*

   — jala ja·la *'bread net' – fried threads of batter eaten with curry (Aceh & North Sumatra)*

   — kadet ka·det *bread roll*

rujak roo·jak *fruit served with a sour, spicy sauce of peanuts, sugar & chilli*

   — cingur chin·goor *peanut sauce with cow skin & lips (Central Java)*

rumput laut room·poot la·oot *seaweed*

RW er·wey *dog – usually served shredded, fried & very spicy (North Sulawesi & other Christian areas)*

S

sago sa·go *starchy food extracted from a variety of palm tree*

saguer sa·goo·er *palm sap wine*

salak sa·lak *brown snake-skin fruit of the zalacca palm*

sambal sam·bal *chilli sauce or paste which contains chillies, garlic or shallots & salt*

   — badjak bad·jak *thick, dark chilli sauce with shallots, sugar, tamarind, galangal & prawn paste*

   — brandal bran·dal *chilli sauce with shallots & prawn paste*

   — buah boo·ah *chilli sauce with fruit (South Sumatra)*

   — jeruk je·rook *chilli sauce made with lime juice, lime peel, salt & vinegar*

   — leunca len·cha *chilli sauce made with leunca (West Java)*

   — terasi te·ra·si *chilli sauce with lime & roasted prawn paste*

   — ulek oo·lek *chilli sauce with vinegar & chilli*

sangsang sang·sang *rich, meaty dish made with pig or dog (Batak)*

santan san·tan *coconut milk*

sares sa·res *dish made with chilli, coconut juice & banana palm pith (Lombok)*

sate sa·te *grilled on skewers*

   — ayam a·yam *chicken satay*

   — daging da·ging *beef satay*

   — kambing kam·bing *goat satay*

   — kelinci ke·lin·chi *rabbit satay*

   — lilit li·lit *satay of minced, spiced meat pressed onto skewers (Bali)*

   — madura ma·doo·ra *satay served with rice & a sweet & spicy soy sauce (Madura)*

   — padang pa·dang *satay served with pressed rice & a smooth peanut sauce (West Sumatra)*

   — pusut poo·soot *skewered sausage-shaped mixture of grated coconut, meat & brown sugar (Lombok & Bali)*

saus sows *sauce*

   — cabe cha·be *chilli sauce*

   — ikan i·kan *fish sauce*

   — kacang ka·chang *peanut sauce*

   — tiram ti·ram *oyster sauce*

   — tomat to·mat *ketchup • tomato sauce*

sawi sa·wi *Chinese cabbage*

sawo kecik sa·wo ke·chik *small, plum-shaped fruit with white grainy flesh*

sayur sa·yoor *vegetable (often used to describe vegetable dishes)*

   — asam a·sam *sour vegetables in clear broth*

— asam rembang a·sam rem·bang
rembang soup (Kalimantan)
— hutan hoo·tan wild greens
— kapau ka·pow cabbage, jackfruit &
shallot shoots in coconut milk (West
Sumatra)
— sayuran sa·yoo·ran vegetables
se'i se i smoked beef (Timor)
selai se·lai jam
— jeruk je·rook marmalade
selasih se·la·sih type of basil with an
aniseed-like flavour
seledri se·le·dri celery
semangka se·mang·ka melon • watermelon
sepat se·pat tart-tasting dish of shredded
fish in a sour sauce of coconut & young
mango (Sumbawa)
sepek se·pek bacon
serabi se·ra·bi pancakes made with rice
flour, coconut milk & **daun pandan**,
topped with chocolate, banana or
jackfruit (Solo)
serai se·rai lemongrass
serebuk se·re·book vegetables mixed with
grated coconut (Lombok)
sereh se·reh lemongrass
serombotan se·rom·bo·tan salad of chilli,
watercress, bean sprouts, yard-long
beans & coconut (Bali)
serundeng se·roon·deng garnish of roast
coconut, soybeans, shallots, tamarind &
chilli (Central Java)
setengah masak se·teng·ah ma·sak
rare steak
singkong sing·kong cassava • manioc
siobak si·o·bak minced pig's head, stomach,
tongue & skin cooked with spices (Bali)
sirih si·rih betel nut
sirsak sir·sak soursop
soba so·ba buckwheat
sohun so·hoon bean-flour vermicelli
sop sop soup • clear, light broth
— buntut boon·toot ox-tail soup
— kental ken·tal chowder
— konro kon·ro beef-rib soup with
kluwek (South Sulawesi)
soto so·to soup, usually a well-seasoned
broth (see also **sop**)
— ayam a·yam chicken soup
— bandung ban·doong
beef & vegetable soup with lemongrass
(Bandung & West Java)

— banjar ban·jar chicken broth made
creamy by mashing & mixing boiled
eggs into the stock
(Banjarmasin & Kalimantan)
— betawi be·ta·wi soup with every
part of the cow, including the marrow,
and made creamy with coconut milk
(Jakarta)
— buntut boon·toot ox-tail soup
— kudus koo·doos chicken & egg soup
(Kudus & Central Java)
— lamongan la·mong·an chicken soup
with noodles, rice & spices (Lamongan,
East Java)
— madura ma·doo·ra soup of beef, lime,
pepper, peanuts, chilli & ginger (Madura)
— pekalongan pe·ka·long·an tripe &
soy soup (Pekalongan & Central Java)
— tegal te·gal beef & noodle soup
(Tegal & Central Java)
srikaya sri·ka·ya custard apples • green
custard of sticky rice, sugar, coconut
milk & egg (South Sumatra)
— nangka nang·ka sweet made with
jackfruit (Kalimantan)
sukun soo·koon breadfruit
sumsum soom·soom marrow
suntek soon·tek water chestnut
susu soo·soo milk
— bubuk boo·book powdered milk
— kacang ka·chang soy milk
— kedelai ke·de·lai soy milk
— kental ken·tal condensed milk
— masam kental ma·sam ken·tal yogurt
— panas pa·nas hot milk

T

tahu ta·hoo beancurd • tofu
— gejrot gej·rot fried, chopped tofu in
spiced soy sauce (West Java)
— goreng go·reng fried tofu
— isi i·si tofu stuffed with bean sprouts &
other vegetables, covered in batter &
deep-fried
— Sumedang soo·me·dang plain,
deep-fried tofu (Sumedang & West Java)
tape ta·pe strange-tasting speciality made
by peeling, boiling & fermenting cassava
or rice in yeast
tauge tow·ge bean sprouts

tekwan tek·wan *small* **pempek** *dumplings & seaweed in a mildly sweet stock (South Sumatra)*

telur te·loor *egg*
— **ceplok** chep·lok *poached egg*
— **dadar** da·dar *omelette*
— **goreng** go·reng *fried egg • omelette*
— **ikan** i·kan *fish roe*
— **rebus** re·boos *boiled egg*
— **setengah matang** se·teng·ah ma·tang *half-cooked egg*

tempeh tem·pe *fermented soybean cake*
— **goreng** go·reng *fried tempeh*
— **kering** ke·ring *sweet & crispy fried tempeh*
— **mendoang** men·do·ang *thin, fried tempeh (Mendoang & Central Java)*
— **penyet** pe·nyet *deep-fried tempeh*

tempoyak tem·po·yak *accompaniment of prawn paste, lime juice, chilli & fermented durian (South Sumatra)*

temusu te·moo·soo *cow-skin sausage with spiced egg filling (West Sumatra)*

tenggiri teng·gi·ri *mackerel*

tengkleng teng·kleng *goat curry with coconut milk & all parts of the goat (Central Java)*

tepung te·poong *flour*

terasi te·ra·si *dark & very pungent prawn paste*

terung te·roong *aubergine • eggplant*
— **belado** be·la·do *eggplant with chilli sauce*
— **hijau** hi·jow *zucchini*

terwelu ter·we·loo *hare*

timbul tim·bool *breadnut*

timbungan bi siap tim·boong·an bi si·ap *sharp-tasting chicken soup with minced chicken, tamarind, sugar & starfruit leaves (Bali)*

timun ti·moon *cucumber*
— **urap** oo·rap *sliced cucumber with grated coconut, onion & garlic (Lombok)*

tiram ti·ram *oyster*

tom tom *duck or chicken cooked with spices in a banana leaf (Bali)*

tongkol tong·kol *tuna • tunny*

tongseng tong·seng *meat or chicken in coconut milk & spices*

tuak too·ak *palm sap wine*

tulang too·lang *bone*
— **iga** i·ga *spare rib*
— **kering** ke·ring *shank*
— **rusuk** roo·sook *ribs*

tumpang toom·pang *boiled tempeh crushed & mixed with coconut milk (Central Java)*

U

ubi oo·bi *sweet potato*
— **goreng** go·reng *deep-fried sweet potato*
— **kayu** ka·yoo *cassava root*
— **rendang** ren·dang *diced sweet potato cooked in coconut milk & spices, then deep-fried (West Sumatra)*

udang oo·dang *prawns • shrimp*
— **galah** ga·lah *giant prawns*
— **karang** ka·rang *crayfish • lobster*

ulat sagu oo·lat sa·goo *sago grubs, mostly eaten fried (Papua)*

ulen oo·len *roasted brick of sticky rice with peanut sauce (West Java)*

urab oo·rab *salad of boiled & diced yard-long beans, coconut, chilli, prawn paste, shallots, salt & garlic (Bali)*

W

walua wa·loo·a *pumpkin*
— **dongo** dong·o *coconut drink with black rice-flour drops (Central Java)*
— **kacang** ka·chang *coconut drink with nuts (Central Java)*

wortel wor·tel *carrot*

emergencies

keadaan darurat

Help!	Tolong!	to·long
Stop!	Berhenti!	ber·hen·ti
Thief!	Pencuri!	pen·choo·ri
Fire!	Api!	a·pi
Go away!	Pergi!	per·gi
Watch out!	Hati-hati!	ha·ti ha·ti

Call the police!
Panggil polisi! pang·gil po·li·si

Call a doctor!
Panggil dokter! pang·gil dok·ter

Call an ambulance!
Panggil ambulansi! pang·gil am·boo·lan·si

There's been an accident!
Baru saja terjadi ba·roo sa·ja ter·ja·di
kecelekaan! ke·che·le·ka·an

Could you please help?
Bisa Anda menolong? bi·sa an·da me·no·long

Can I use your phone?
Boleh saya pakai telpon bo·leh sa·ya pa·kai tel·pon
genggamnya? geng·gam·nya

signs

Polisi	po·li·si	**Police**
Pos Polisi	pos po·li·si	**Police Station**
Rumah Sakit	roo·mah sa·kit	**Hospital**
Unit Gawat	oo·nit ga·wat	**Emergency**
Darurat	da·roo·rat	**Department**

I'm lost.
Saya tersesat.   sa·ya ter·se·sat

Where are the toilets?
Di mana kamar kecil?   di ma·na ka·mar ke·chil

Do you think it is safe to travel to (Aceh) now?
Anda pikir saat ini   an·da pi·kir sa·at i·ni
aman ke (Aceh)?   a·man ke (a·cheh)

Is it safe …?	*Ini aman …?*	i·ni a·man …
at night	*pada malam hari*	pa·da ma·lam ha·ri
for gay people	*untuk orang gay*	oon·took o·rang gey
for travellers	*untuk*	oon·took
	pelancong	pe·lan·chong
for women	*untuk*	oon·took
	perempuan	pe·rem·poo·an
on your own	*sendiri*	sen·di·ri

Is there danger	*Ada bahaya …*	a·da ba·ha·ya …
of … here/there?	*di sini/sana?*	di si·ni/sa·na
demonstrations	*demonstrasi*	de·mon·stra·si
earthquakes	*gempa bumi*	gem·pa boo·mi
flooding	*banjir*	ban·jir
landslides	*tanah lonsor*	ta·nah lon·sor
terrorism	*terrorisme*	te·ro·ris·me
volcanic	*letusan*	le·too·san
eruptions	*gunung api*	goo·noong a·pi

police

Where's the police station?
Di mana ada pos polisi?   di ma·na a·da pos po·li·si

I want to report an offence.
Saya mau lapor kejahatan.   sa·ya mow la·por ke·ja·ha·tan

I have insurance.
Saya punya asuransi.   sa·ya poo·nya a·soo·ran·si

It was him/her.
Itu dia.   i·too di·a

I've been …	Saya …	sa·ya …
He/She has been …	Dia …	di·a …
assaulted	diserang	di·se·rang
raped	diperkosa	di·per·ko·sa
robbed	dirampok	di·ram·pok

He/She tried	Dia mencoba	di·a men·cho·ba
to … me.	… saya.	… sa·ya
assault	menyerang	me·nye·rang
rape	memperkosa	mem·per·ko·sa
rob	merampok	me·ram·pok

I've lost my …	… saya hilang.	… sa·ya hi·lang
My … was/	… saya dicuri.	… sa·ya di·choo·ri
were stolen.		
bag	Tas	tas
jewellery	Barang	ba·rang
	perhiasan	per·hi·a·san
money	Uang	oo·ang
papers	Dokumen	do·koo·men

What am I accused of?
Saya dituduh apa?　　　saya di·too·dooh a·pa

I'm sorry.
Saya menyesal.　　　　sa·ya me·nye·sal

I didn't do it.
Saya tidak melakukannya.　sa·a ti·dak me·la·koo·kan·nya

I didn't realise I was doing anything wrong.
Saya tidak menyadari　　sa·ya ti·dak me·nya·da·ri
saya melakukan sesuatu　sa·ya me·la·koo·kan se·soo·a·too
yang salah.　　　　　　yang sa·lah

Can I pay an on-the-spot fine?
Boleh saya bayar denda　bo·leh sa·ya ba·yar den·da
langsung di sini?　　　　lang·soong di si·ni

I want to contact my embassy/consulate.
Saya mau hubungi　　　sa·ya mow hoo·boong·i
kedutaan/konsulat saya.　ke·doo·ta·an/kon·soo·lat sa·ya

Can I make a phone call?
Bolehkah saya menelpon?　bo·leh·kah sa·ya me·nel·pon

Can I have a lawyer (who speaks English)?

Bolehkah saya   bo·leh·kah sa·ya
mendapatkan pengacara   men·da·pat·kan peng·a·cha·ra
(berbahasa Inggris)?   (ber·ba·ha·sa ing·gris)

This drug is for personal use.

Obat ini untuk keperluan   o·bat i·ni oon·took ke·per·loo·an
pribadi saya.   pri·ba·di sa·ya

I have a prescription for this drug.

Saya punya catatan   sa·ya poo·nya cha·ta·tan
soal obat ini.   so·al o·bat i·ni

---

the police may say ...

Anda dituduh melakukan ...	an·da di·too·dooh me·la·koo·kan ...	You're charged with ...
Dia dituduh melakukan ...	di·a di·too·dooh me·la·koo·kan ...	He/She is charged with ...
gangguan keamanan	gang·goo·an ke·a·ma·nan	disturbing the peace
memiliki (barang illegal)	me·mi·li·ki (ba·rang i·le·gal)	possession (of illegal substances)
pencurian	pen·choo·ri·an	theft
penyerangan	pe·nye·rang·an	assault
Anda dituduh ...	an·da di·too·dooh ...	You're charged with ...
Dia dituduh ...	di·a di·too·dooh ...	He/She is charged with ...
punya visa lewat batas waktu	poo·nya vi·sa le·wat ba·tas wak·too	overstaying a visa
tidak punya visa	ti·dak poo·nya vi·sa	not having a visa
Ini denda ...	i·ni den·da ...	It's a ... fine.
melampui batas kecepatan	me·lam·poo·i ba·tas ke·che·pa·tan	speeding
parkir	par·kir	parking

doctor

dokter

Where's the nearest …?	Di mana … yang terdekat?	di ma·na … yang ter·de·kat
dentist	dokter gigi	dok·ter gi·gi
doctor	dokter	dok·ter
emergency department	unit gawat darurat	oo·nit ga·wat da·roo·rat
hospital	rumah sakit	roo·mah sa·kit
medical centre	puskesmas	poos·kes·mas
optometrist	ahli kacamata	ah·li ka·cha·ma·ta
(night) pharmacy	apotek (malam)	a·po·tek (ma·lam)

I need a doctor (who speaks English).
Saya perlu dokter   sa·ya per·loo dok·ter
(berbahasa Inggris).   (ber·ba·ha·sa ing·gris)

Could I see a female doctor?
Boleh saya perlu   bo·leh sa·ya per·loo
dokter yang perempuan?   dok·ter yang pe·rem·poo·an

Could the doctor come here?
Bisa dokternya   bi·sa dok·ter·nya
datang ke sini?   da·tang ke si·ni

Is there an after-hours emergency number?
Ada nomor unit   a·da no·mor oo·nit
gawat darurat?   ga·wat da·roo·rat

I've run out of my medication.
Obat saya habis.   o·bat sa·ya ha·bis

This is my usual medicine.
Biasanya obat saya ini.   bi·a·sa·nya o·bat sa·ya i·ni

My child weighs (20) kilos.
Bobot anak saya   bo·bot a·nak sa·ya
(duapuluh) kilo.   (doo·a·poo·looh) ki·lo

What's the correct dosage?
Dosis yang tepat berapa?   do̅·sis yang te·pat be·ra·pa

I don't want a blood transfusion.
Saya tidak mau   sa·ya ti̅·dak mow
transfusi darah.   trans·foo·si da·rah

Please use a new syringe.
Tolong, pakai jarum   to·long pa·kai ja·room
suntik yang baru.   soon·tik yang ba·roo

I have my own syringe.
Saya punya jarum   sa·ya poo·nya ja·room
suntik sendiri.   soon·tik sen·di·ri

I've been vaccinated against …	*Saya diimmunisasi terhadap …*	sa·ya di·i·moo·ni·sa·si ter·ha·dap …
He/She has been vaccinated against …	*Dia diimmunisasi terhadap …*	di·a di·i·moo·ni·sa·si ter·ha·dap …
hepatitis A/B/C	*hepatitis A/B/C*	he·pa·ti·tis a/be/che
tetanus	*tetanus*	te·ta·noos
typhoid	*tifus*	ti·foos
I need new …	*Saya perlu … yang baru.*	sa·ya per·loo … yang ba·roo
contact lenses	*lensa kontak*	len·sa kon·tak
glasses	*kacamata*	ka·cha·ma·ta

My prescription is …
Resep saya …   re·sep sa·ya …

How much will it cost?
Berapa harganya?   be·ra·pa har·ga·nya

Can I have a receipt for my insurance?
Boleh saya minta kuitansi   bo·leh sa·ya min·ta koo·i·tan·si
untuk asuransi saya?   oon·took a·soo·ran·si sa·ya

symptoms & conditions

I'm sick.
Saya sakit. — sa·ya sa·kit

My friend/child is (very) sick.
Teman/Anak saya — te·man/a·nak sa·ya
sakit (sekali). — sa·kit (se·ka·li)

It hurts here.
Sakit di sini. — sa·kit di si·ni

He/She is having a/an …	*Dia punya …*	di·a poo·nya …
allergic reaction	*alergi*	a·ler·gi
asthma attack	*asma kambuh*	as·ma kam·booh
baby (right now)	*(sedang)*	(se·dang)
	melahirkan	me·la·hir·kan
epileptic fit	*menderita*	men·de·ri·ta
	serangan	se·rang·an
	epilepsi	e·pi·lep·si
heart attack	*kena serangan*	ke·na se·rang·an
	jantung	jan·toong

I've been …	*Saya …*	sa·ya …
He/She has been …	*Dia …*	di·a …
injured	*kena luka*	ke·na loo·ka
vomiting	*muntah*	moon·tah

I feel …	*Saya merasa …*	sa·ya me·ra·sa …
anxious	*gelisah*	ge·li·sah
better	*lebih sehat*	le·bih se·hat
depressed	*tertekan*	ter·te·kan
dizzy	*pusing*	poo·sing
hot and cold	*meriang*	me·ri·ang
nauseous	*mual*	moo·al
shivery	*menggigil*	meng·gi·gil
strange	*aneh*	a·neh
weak	*lemah*	le·mah
worse	*lebih buruk*	le·bih boo·rook

the doctor may say ...

Apa masalahnya?
a·pa ma·sa·lah·nya — **What's the problem?**

Sakit di mana?
sa·kit di ma·na — **Where does it hurt?**

Anda demam?
an·da de·mam — **Do you have a temperature?**

Sudah berapa lama seperti ini?
soo·dah be·ra·pa
la·ma se·per·ti i·ni — **How long have you been like this?**

Sudah pernah dapat gejala seperti ini sebelumnya?
soo·dah per·nah da·pat
ge·ja·la se·per·ti i·ni
se·be·loom·nya — **Have you had this before?**

Masih berapa lama perjalanannya?
ma·sih be·ra·pa la·ma
per·ja·la·nan·nya — **How long are you travelling for?**

Anda aktif berhubungan seksual?
an·da ak·tif
ber·hoo·boong·an sek·soo·al — **Are you sexually active?**

Pernah berhubungan seks tanpa kondom?
per·nah ber·hoo·boong·an
seks tan·pa kon·dom — **Have you had unprotected sex?**

Anda ...?	an·da ...	**Do you ...?**
minum	mi·noom	**drink**
merokok	me·ro·kok	**smoke**
pakai narkoba	pa·kai nar·ko·ba	**take drugs**

Anda ...?	an·da ...	**Are you ...?**
alergi terhadap sesuatu	a·ler·gi ter·ha·dap se·soo·a·too	**allergic to anything**
sedang dalam pengobatan	se·dang da·lam peng·o·ba·tan	**on medication**

Anda harus masuk ke rumah sakit.
an·da ha·roos ma·sook
ke roo·mah sa·kit
You need to be admitted to hospital.

Kalau kembali ke negara Anda, mesti periksa lagi.
ka·low kem·ba·li ke ne·ga·ra
an·da me·sti pe·rik·sa la·gi
You should have it checked when you go home.

Anda harus pulang ke negaranya untuk diobati.
an·da ha·roos poo·lang ke
ne·ga·ra·nya oon·took di·o·ba·ti
You should return home for treatment.

Anda cemas tanpa alasan.
an·da che·mas tan·pa a·la·san
You're a hypochondriac.

I'm dehydrated.
   Saya mengalami dehidrasi.   sa·ya meng·a·la·mi de·hi·dra·si

I can't sleep.
   Saya tidak bisa tidur.   sa·ya ti·dak bi·sa ti·door

I think it's the medication I'm on.
   Saya pikir obat ini   sa·ya pi·kir o·bat i·ni
   yang saya minum.   yang sa·ya mi·noom

I'm on medication for ...
   Saya biasa minum   sa·ya bi·a·sa mi·noom
   obat untuk ...   o·bat oon·took ...

He/She is on medication for ...
   Dia biasa minum   di·a bi·a·sa mi·noom
   obat untuk ...   o·bat oon·took ...

I have (a) ...
   Saya punya ...   sa·ya poo·nya ...

He/She has (a) ...
   Dia punya ...   di·a poo·nya ...

I've recently had (a) ...
   Saya baru-baru punya ...   sa·ya ba·roo ba·roo poo·nya ...

He/She has recently had (a) ...
   Dia baru-baru punya ...   di·a ba·roo ba·roo poo·nya ...

asthma	*asma*	as·ma
cold n	*pilek*	pi·lek
constipation	*sembelit*	sem·be·lit
cough n	*batuk*	ba·took
diabetes	*penyakit kencing manis*	pe·nya·kit ken·ching ma·nis
diarrhoea	*mencret*	mench·ret
dysentery	*disentri*	di·sen·tri
fever	*demam*	de·mam
headache	*sakit kepala*	sa·kit ke·pa·la
nausea	*mual*	moo·al
malaria	*malaria*	ma·la·ri·a
pain n	*perasaan sakit*	pe·ra·sa·an sa·kit
rabies	*penyakit anjing gila*	pe·nya·kit an·jing gi·la
sore throat	*sakit tenggorokan*	sa·kit teng·go·ro·kan

women's health

(I think) I'm pregnant.
(Saya pikir) Saya hamil.   (sa·ya pi·kir) sa·ya ha·mil

I'm on the pill.
Saya minum pil   sa·ya mi·noom pil
pencegah kehamilan.   pen·che·gah ke·ha·mi·lan

I haven't had my period for (six) weeks.
Saya tidak menstruasi   sa·ya ti·dak men·stroo·a·si
sudah (enam) minggu.   soo·dah (e·nam) ming·goo

I've noticed a lump here.
Saya mendapati ada   sa·ya men·da·pa·ti a·da
pembengkakan di sini.   pem·beng·ka·kan di si·ni

Anda pakai alat kontrasepsi?
an·da pa·kai a·lat
kon·tra·sep·si | **Are you using contraception?**

Kapan terakhir kali datang bulan?
ka·pan te·ra·khir ka·li
da·tang boo·lan | **When did you last have your period?**

Anda sedang menstruasi?
an·da se·dang men·stroo·a·si | **Are you menstruating?**

Anda hamil?
an·da ha·mil | **Are you pregnant?**

Anda hamil.
an·da ha·mil | **You're pregnant.**

Do you have something for (period pain)?

Ada obat untuk (menstruasi)? — a·da o·bat oon·took (men·stroo·a·si)

I have a ...	*Saya punya infeksi ...*	sa·ya poo·nya in·fek·si ...
urinary tract infection	*di kandung kemih*	di kan·doong ke·mih
yeast infection	*ragi*	ra·gi

I need a/the ...	*Saya perlu ...*	sa·ya per·loo ...
contraception	*kontrasepsi*	kon·tra·sep·si
morning-after pill	*pil telat bulan*	pil te·lat boo·lan
pregnancy test	*tes kehamilan*	tes ke·ha·mi·lan

parts of the body

My ... hurts.
   ... saya sakit.   ... sa·ya sa·kit

I can't move my ...
   Saya tidak bisa   sa·ya ti·dak bi·sa
   mengerakkan ... saya.   men·ge·ra·kan ... sa·ya

I have a cramp in my ...
   ... saya kram.   ... sa·ya kram

My ... is swollen.
   ... saya bengkak.   ... sa·ya beng·kak

For other parts of the body, see the **dictionary**.

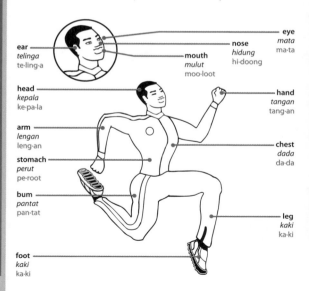

eye
mata
ma·ta

nose
hidung
hi·doong

mouth
mulut
moo·loot

ear
telinga
te·ling·a

head
kepala
ke·pa·la

hand
tangan
tang·an

arm
lengan
leng·an

chest
dada
da·da

stomach
perut
pe·root

bum
pantat
pan·tat

leg
kaki
ka·ki

foot
kaki
ka·ki

allergies

I have a skin allergy.
Kulit saya alergi.   koo·lit sa·ya a·ler·gi

I'm allergic	*Saya alergi*	sa·ya a·ler·gi
to ...	*terhadap ...*	ter·ha·dap ...
He/She is	*Dia alergi*	di·a a·ler·gi
allergic to ...	*terhadap ...*	ter·ha·dap ...
antibiotics	*antibiotik*	an·ti·bi·o·tik
anti-inflammatories	*antiradang*	an·ti·ra·dang
aspirin	*aspirin*	as·pi·rin
bees	*tawon*	ta·won
codeine	*kodein*	ko·de·in
penicillin	*penicillin*	pe·ni·chi·lin
pollen	*tepung sari*	te·poong sa·ri
sulphur-based drugs	*obat pakai bahan dasar belerang*	o·bat pa·kai ba·han da·sar be·le·rang
inhaler	*inhaler*	in·ha·ler
injection	*suntikan*	soon·ti·kan
antihistamines	*antihistamin*	an·ti·hi·sta·min

For food-related allergies, see **special diets & allergies**, page 178.

alternative treatments

I don't use (Western medicine).
Saya tidak pakai (obat barat).   sa·ya ti·dak pa·kai (o·bat ba·rat)

I would like to see a local medicine man.
Saya mau dipanggilkan   sa·ya mow di·pang·gil·kan
dukun tradisional.   doo·koon tra·di·si·o·nal

I prefer ...	*Saya lebih suka ...*	sa·ya le·bih soo·ka ...
Can I see	*Boleh saya*	bo·leh sa·ya
someone who	*bertemu ahli ...?*	ber·te·moo ah·li ...
practises ...?		
acupuncture	*pengobatan*	peng·o·ba·tan
	dengan tusukan	deng·an too·soo·kan
	jarum	ja·room
traditional	*pengobatan*	peng·o·ba·tan
medicine	*tradisional*	tra·di·si·o·nal

For other kinds of alternative medicine, see the **dictionary**.

pharmacist

ahli farmasi

I need something for (a headache).
Saya perlu sesuatu sa·ya per·loo se·soo·a·too
untuk (sakit kepala). oon·took (sa·kit ke·pa·la)

Do I need a prescription for (antihistamines)?
Perlu resep untuk per·loo re·sep oon·took
(antihistamin)? (an·ti·hi·sta·min)

I have a prescription.
Saya punya resep. sa·ya poo·nya re·sep

How many times a day?
Berapa kali sehari? be·ra·pa ka·li se·ha·ri

Will it make me drowsy?
Itu akan bikin i·too a·kan bi·kin
saya mengantuk? sa·ya meng·an·took

antimalarials	*obat malaria*	o·bat ma·la·ri·a
antiseptic n	*antiseptik*	an·ti·sep·tik
contraceptives	*kontrasepsi*	kon·tra·sep·si
painkillers	*penawar sakit*	pe·na·war sa·kit
rehydration salts	*garam anti*	ga·ram an·ti
	dehidrasi	de·hi·dra·si
thermometer	*termometer*	ter·mo·me·ter

For more pharmaceutical items, see the **dictionary**.

Dua/tiga kali sehari (dengan makanan).
doo·a/ti·ga ka·li se·ha·ri (deng·an ma·ka·nan) **Twice/three times a day (with food).**

Sebelum makanan.
se·be·loom ma·ka·nan **Before food.**

Sesudah makanan.
se·soo·dah ma·ka·nan **After food.**

Sudah pernah minum ini sebelumnya?
soo·dah per·nah mi·noom i·ni se·be·loom·nya **Have you taken this before?**

Anda harus minum sampai habis.
an·da ha·roos mi·noom sam·pai ha·bis **You must complete the course.**

dentist

I have a …	*Gigi saya …*	gi·gi sa·ya …
broken tooth	*patah*	pa·tah
cavity	*berlobang*	ber·lo·bang
toothache	*sakit*	sa·kit

I've lost a filling.
Tambalan gigi saya copot. tam·ba·lan gi·gi sa·ya cho·pot

My dentures are broken.
Gigi palsu saya pecah. gi·gi pal·soo sa·ya pe·chah

My gums hurt.
Gusi saya sakit. goo·si sa·ya sa·kit

I don't want it extracted.
Saya tidak mau itu   sa·ya ti·dak mow i·too
dicabut.   di·cha·boot

Ouch!
Aduh!   a·dooh

I need a/an ...   *Saya perlu ...*   sa·ya per·loo ...
anaesthetic   *penawar sakit*   pe·na·war sa·kit
filling   *tambalan*   tam·ba·lan

the dentist may say ...

Buka lebar.
  boo·ka le·bar   **Open wide.**

Tidak sakit sama sekali.
  ti·dak sa·kit sa·ma se·ka·li   **This won't hurt a bit.**

Gigit ini.
  gi·git i·ni   **Bite down on this.**

Jangan bergerak.
  jang·an ber·ge·rak   **Don't move.**

Berkumur.
  ber·koo·moor   **Rinse!**

Nanti kembali lagi, saya belum selesai.
  nan·ti kem·ba·li la·gi   **Come back, I haven't**
  ˆsa·ya be·loom se·le·sai   **finished!**

You'll find the English words marked as adjective a, noun n, verb v, singular sg, plural pl, informal inf, polite pol, adverb adv, exclusive excl and inclusive incl where necessary. All Indonesian verbs are provided in the active form, and some also have the root word in square brackets – for more information, see the **phrasebuilder**. For language related to flora, fauna and the environment, see **ecotourism**, page 157.

A

aboard *di atas* di a·tas
abortion *aborsi* a·bor·si
about *tentang* ten·tang
above *di atas* di a·tas
abroad *luar negeri* loo·ar ne·ge·ri
accident *kecelakaan* ke·che·le·ka·an
accommodation *tempat menginap* tem·pat meng·i·nap
account (bank) n *rekening* re·ke·ning
across *seberang* se·be·rang
activist n *aktivis* ak·ti·vis
actor *pemain film* pe·ma·in film
acupuncture *pengobatan dengan tusukan jarum* peng·o·ba·tan deng·an too·soo·kan ja·room
adaptor *adaptor* a·dap·tor
addiction *kecanduan* ke·chan·doo·an
address n *alamat* a·la·mat
administration *administrasi* ad·mi·ni·stra·si
administrator *pengatur* peng·a·toor
admission (entry) *masuk* ma·sook
admit (let in) v *menerima [terima]* me·ne·ri·ma [te·ri·ma]
adult n&a *dewasa* de·wa·sa
advertisement *iklan* ik·lan
advice *saran* sa·ran
afraid *takut* ta·koot
after *sesudah* se·soo·dah
afternoon *sore* so·re
aftershave *aftershave* af·ter·shev
again *lagi* la·gi
age n *umur* oo·moor
agnostic n *agnostis* ag·no·stis
agree *setuju* se·too·joo
agriculture *pertanian* per·ta·ni·an
ahead *di depan* di de·pan
aid n *bantuan* ban·too·an

AIDS *AIDS* eds
air *udara* oo·da·ra
air-conditioned *dengan AC* deng·an a·se
air conditioning *AC* a·se
airline *maskapai penerbangan* ma·ska·pai pe·ner·bang·an
airmail *pos udara* pos oo·da·ra
airplane *pesawat* pe·sa·wat
airport *bandara* ban·da·ra
airport tax *pajak bandara* pa·jak ban·da·ra
aisle (on plane) *gang* gang
alarm clock *weker* we·ker
alcohol *alkohol* al·ko·hol
alive *hidup* hi·doop
all *semua* se·moo·a
allergic *alergi* a·ler·gi
alley *gang* gang
almond *amandel* a·man·del
almost *hampir* ham·pir
alone *sen dirian* sen·di·ri·an
already *sudah* soo·dah
also *juga* joo·ga
altar *altar* al·tar
altitude *ketinggian* ke·ting·gi·an
always *selalu* se·la·loo
ambassador *duta besar* doo·ta be·sar
ambulance *ambulans* am·boo·lans
America *Amerika* a·me·ri·ka
anaemia *anemi* a·ne·mi
ancient *kuno* koo·no
and *dan* dan
angry *marah* ma·rah
animal *binatang* bi·na·tang
ankle *pergelangan kaki* per·ge·lang·an ka·ki
another *yang lain* yang la·in
answer n *jawaban* ja·wa·ban
answer v *menjawab [jawab]* men·ja·wab [ja·wab]
ant *semut* se·moot
antibiotics *antibiotik* an·ti·bi·o·tik

antinuclear *antinuklir* an·ti·nook·lir
antiques *barang antik* ba·rang an·tik
antiseptic *penangkal infeksi* n
pe·nang·kal in·fek·si
any(thing) *apa saja* a·pa sa·ja
anytime *kapan saja* ka·pan sa·ja
anywhere *di mana saja* di ma·na sa·ja
apartment *apartemen* a·par·te·men
appendix *usus buntu* oo·soos boon·too
apple *apel* a·pel
appointment *janji* jan·ji
April *April* a·pril
archaeological *kepurbakalaan*
ke·poor·ba·ka·la·an
architect *arsitek* ar·si·tek
architecture *arsitektur* ar·si·tek·toor
argue *membantah [bantah]*
mem·ban·tah [ban·tah]
arm (body) *lengan* leng·an
arrest v *menangkap [tangkap]*
me·nang·kap [tang·kap]
arrival *kedatangan* ke·da·tang·an
arrive *datang* da·tang
art *seni* se·ni
art gallery *galeri seni* ga·le·ri se·ni
artist *seniman* se·ni·man
artwork *karya seni* kar·ya se·ni
ashtray *asbak* as·bak
Asia *Asia* a·si·a
ask (a question) *bertanya [tanya]*
ber·ta·nya [ta·nya]
ask (for something) *minta* min·ta
asleep *tidur* ti·door
aspirin *aspirin* as·pi·rin
assault n *serangan* se·rang·an
assist *membantu [bantu]*
mem·ban·too [ban·too]
assistance *bantuan* ban·too·an
asthma *asma* as·ma
at (location) *di* di
at (time) *pada* pa·da
athletics *atletik* at·le·tik
atmosphere (of place) *suasana* soo·a·sa·na
atmosphere (of planet) *atmosfir* at·mos·fir
aubergine *terung* te·roong
August *Agustus* a·goo·stoos
aunt *bibi* bi·bi
Australia *Australia* a·oo·stra·li·a
automated teller machine *ATM* a·te·em
autumn *musim gugur* moo·sim goo·goor
avenue *jalan raya* ja·lan ra·ya
avocado *alpukat* al·poo·kat
awful *mengerikan* meng·e·ri·kan

B

B&W *hitam-putih* hi·tam poo·tih
baby *bayi* ba·yi
baby food *makanan bayi* ma·ka·nan ba·yi
baby powder *bedak bayi* be·dak ba·yi
babysitter *pengasuh anak*
peng·a·sooh a·nak
back (body) *punggung* poong·goong
back (position) *kembali* kem·ba·li
backpack *ransel* ran·sel
bacon *sepek* se·pek
bad (general) *jelek* je·lek
bad (weather) *buruk* boo·rook
bag *tas* tas
baggage *bagasi* ba·ga·si
baggage allowance *bagasi yang
diijinkan* ba·ga·si yang di·i·jin·kan
baggage claim *pengambilan barang*
peng·am·bi·lan ba·rang
bait (fishing) *umpan* oom·pan
bakery *toko roti* to·ko ro·ti
balance (account) *saldo* sal·do
balcony *balkon* bal·kon
ball (sport) *bola* bo·la
banana *pisang* pi·sang
band (music) *band* band
bandage n *pembalut* pem·ba·loot
bank *bank* bank
bank account *rekening bank*
re·ke·ning bank
banknote *uang kertas* oo·ang ker·tas
baptism *pembaptisan* pem·bap·ti·san
bar *bar* bar
barber *tukang cukur* too·kang choo·koor
bargain v *menawar [tawar]*
me·na·war [ta·war]
baseball *baseball* bes·bol
basket *keranjang* ke·ran·jang
basketball *bola basket* bo·la bas·ket
bath n&v *mandi* man·di
bathing suit *baju renang* ba·joo re·nang
bathroom *kamar mandi* ka·mar man·di
battery (car) *aki* a·ki
battery (small) *baterai* ba·te·rai
be *adalah* a·da·lah
beach *pantai* pan·tai
beach volleyball *voli pantai* vo·li pan·tai
bean *buncis* boon·chis
beautiful (scenery/thing) *indah* in·dah
beautiful (woman) *cantik* chan·tik
beauty salon *salon kecantikan*
sa·lon ke·chan·ti·kan

because *karena* ka·re·na
bed *tempat tidur* tem·pat ti·door
bedding *kain tempat tidur*
 ka·in tem·pat ti·door
bed linen *sepre* sep·re
bedroom *kamar tidur* ka·mar ti·door
bee *tawon* ta·won
beef *daging sapi* da·ging sa·pi
beer *bir* bir
before *sebelum* se·be·loom
beggar *pengemis* peng·e·mis
begin *mulai* moo·lai
behind *di belakang* di be·la·kang
Belgium *Belgia* bel·gi·a
below *di bawah* di ba·wah
beside *di samping* di sam·ping
best *terbaik* ter·ba·ik
bet n *taruhan* ta·roo·han
better *lebih baik* le·bih ba·ik
between *antara* an·ta·ra
Bible *alkitab* al·ki·tab
bicycle *sepeda* se·pe·da
big *besar* be·sar
bigger *lebih besar* le·bih be·sar
biggest *terbesar* ter·be·sar
bike *sepeda* se·pe·da
bike chain *rantai gembok sepeda*
 ran·tai gem·bok se·pe·da
bike lock *kunci sepeda* koon·chi se·pe·da
bike shop *toko sepeda* to·ko se·pe·da
bill (account) *kuitansi* koo·i·tan·si
bill (note) *uang kertas* oo·ang ker·tas
binoculars *teropong* te·ro·pong
bird *burung* boo·roong
birth certificate *surat lahir* soo·rat la·hir
birthday *hari ulang tahun*
 ha·ri oo·lang ta·hoon
biscuit *biskuit* bis·koo·it
bite (dog/insect) n *gigitan* gi·gi·tan
bite v *menggigit [gigit]* meng·gi·git [gi·git]
bitter *pahit* pa·hit
black *hitam* hi·tam
black market *pasar gelap* pa·sar ge·lap
bladder *kandung kemih* kan·doong ke·mih
blanket *selimut* se·li·moot
bleed *mengeluarkan darah*
 meng·e·loo·ar·kan da·rah
blind a *buta* boo·ta
blister n *lepuh* le·pooh
blocked *diblokir* di·blo·kir
blood *darah* da·rah
blood group *golongan darah*
 go·long·an da·rah

blood pressure *tekanan darah*
 te·ka·nan da·rah
blood test *pemeriksaan darah*
 pe·me·rik·sa·an da·rah
blue *biru* bi·roo
board (plane/ship) v *naik* na·ik
board bag *tas papan selancar*
 tas pa·pan se·lan·char
boarding house *rumah kos* roo·mah kos
boarding pass *pas naik* pas na·ik
boat (general) *kapal* ka·pal
boat (local) *perahu* pe·ra·hoo
body *badan* ba·dan
body board *papan selancar*
 pa·pan se·lan·char
boil v *merebus [rebus]* me·re·boos [re·boos]
boiled *rebus* re·boos
boiled egg *telur rebus* te·loor re·boos
boiled water *air matang* a·ir ma·tang
bone *tulang* too·lang
book n *buku* boo·koo
book v *memesan [pesan]*
 me·me·san [pe·san]
booked out *dipesan penuh*
 di·pe·san pe·nooh
bookshop *toko buku* to·ko boo·koo
boot (shoe) *sepatu tinggi* se·pa·too ting·gi
border *perbatasan* per·ba·ta·san
bored *bosan* bo·san
boring *membosankan* mem·bo·san·kan
borrow *meminjam [pinjam]*
 me·min·jam [pin·jam]
botanic garden *kebun raya* ke·boon ra·ya
both *keduanya* ke·doo·a·nya
bottle *botol* bo·tol
bottle opener *alat pembuka botol*
 a·lat pem·boo·ka bo·tol
bottom (body) *pantat* pan·tat
bottom (position) *di bawah* di ba·wah
bowl n *mangkuk* mang·kook
box n *kotak* o·tak
boxing (sport) *tinju* tin·joo
boy *anak laki-laki* a·nak la·ki la·ki
boyfriend *pacar laki-laki* pa·char la·ki la·ki
bra *beha* be·ha
brain *otak* o·tak
brakes *rem* rem
brandy *brendi* bren·di
brave a *berani* be·ra·ni
bread *roti* ro·ti
break (bone) n&v *patah* pa·tah
break down v *rusak* roo·sak
breakfast *sarapan* sa·ra·pan

breast (body) *dada* da·da
breathe *bernapas [napas]*
ber·na·pas [na·pas]
bribe n *sogok* so·gok
bribe v *menyogok [sogok]*
me·nyo·gok [so·gok]
bridge (structure) n *jembatan* jem·ba·tan
briefcase *tas kantor* tas kan·tor
bright (colour) a *terang* te·rang
bring *membawa [bawa]*
mem·ba·wa [ba·wa]
brochure *brosur* bro·soor
broken *patah* pa·tah
broken down *rusak* roo·sak
bronchitis *bronkhitis* bron·khi·tis
brother (older) *kakak laki-laki*
ka·kak la·ki la·ki
brother (younger) *adik laki-laki*
a·dik la·ki la·ki
brown n *coklat* chok·lat
bruise n *luka memar* loo·ka me·mar
Brunei *Brunei* broo·ney
brush n *sikat* si·kat
bucket *ember* em·ber
Buddhist n *penganut Buda*
peng·a·noot boo·da
budget n *anggaran* ang·ga·ran
buffet *bupet* boo·pet
bug n *hama* ha·ma
build *membangun [bangun]*
mem·bang·oon [bang·oon]
builder *tukang bangunan*
too·kang bang·oo·nan
building *gedung* ge·doong
burn n *bakar* ba·kar
burnt *terbakar* ter·ba·kar
bus (city) *bis kota* bis ko·ta
bus (intercity) *bis antar kota* bis an·tar ko·ta
business *bisnis* bis·nis
business class *kelas bisnis* ke·las bis·nis
businessperson *pedagang* pe·da·gang
business trip *perjalanan bisnis*
per·ja·la·nan bis·nis
bus station *terminal bis* ter·mi·nal bis
bus stop *halte bis* hal·te bis
busy (place) *ramai* ra·mai
busy (time) *sibuk* si·book
but *tetapi* te·ta·pi
butcher *tukang daging* too·kang da·ging
butter *mentega* men·te·ga
butterfly *kupu-kupu* koo·poo koo·poo
buttons *kancing* kan·ching
buy *membeli [beli]* mem·be·li [be·li]

C

cabin *kabin* ka·bin
café *kafe* ka·fe
cake *kue* koo·e
cake shop *toko kue* to·ko koo·e
calculator *mesin hitung* me·sin hi·toong
calendar *kalender* ka·len·der
call (phone) v *menelpon [telpon]*
me·nel·pon [tel·pon]
calm *tenang* te·nang
camera *tustel* too·stel
camera shop *toko tustel* to·ko too·stel
camp v *berkemah [kemah]*
ber·ke·mah [ke·mah]
camping ground *kemping* kem·ping
can (tin) *kaleng* ka·leng
can (be able) *bisa* bi·sa
can (have permission) *boleh* bo·leh
can opener *alat pembuka kaleng*
a·lat pem·boo·ka ka·leng
Canada *Kanada* ka·na·da
cancel *membatalkan [batal]*
mem·ba·tal·kan [ba·tal]
cancer *kanker* kan·ker
candle *lilin* li·lin
candy *gula-gula* goo·la goo·la
cantaloupe *belewa* be·le·wa
car *mobil* mo·bil
caravan *karavan* ka·ra·van
cardiac arrest *perhentian jantung*
per·hen·ti·an jan·toong
cards (playing) *kartu (main)* kar·too (ma·in)
care (for someone) v *memelihara [pelihara]*
me·me·li·ha·ra [pe·li·ha·ra]
car hire *penyewaan mobil*
pe·nye·wa·an mo·bil
car owner *pemilik mobil* pe·mi·lik mo·bil
car park *tempat parkir* tem·pat par·kir
carpenter *tukang kayu* too·kang ka·yoo
car registration *pendaftaran mobil*
pen·daf·ta·ran mo·bil
carrot *wortel* wor·tel
carry *memikul [pikul]* me·mi·kool [pi·kool]
cash n *kontan* kon·tan
cash (a cheque) v *menukar [tukar] (cek)*
me·noo·kar [too·kar] (chek)
cashew *jambu monyet* jam·boo mo·nyet
cashier *kasir* ka·sir
cash register *mesin kas* me·sin kas
casino *kasino* ka·si·no
cassette *kaset* ka·set
castle *benteng* ben·teng

cat *kucing* koo·ching
cathedral *katedral* ka·te·dral
Catholic *Katolik* ka·to·lik
cave n *gua* goo·a
CD *CD* see·dee
celebrate *merayakan* me·ra·ya·kan
celebration *perayaan* pe·ra·ya·an
cemetery *kuburan* koo·boo·ran
cent *sen* sen
centimetre *sentimeter* sen·ti·me·ter
centre n *pusat* poo·sat
ceramic *keramik* ke·ra·mik
certificate *surat keterangan* soo·rat ke·te·rang·an
chain n *rantai* ran·tai
chair n *kursi* koor·si
champagne *sampanye* sam·pa·nye
championships *kejuaraan* ke·joo·a·ra·an
chance n *kesempatan* ke·sem·pa·tan
change n *perubahan* pe·roo·ba·han
change (coins) n *uang kecil* oo·ang ke·chil
change (money) v *menukar [tukar]* me·noo·kar [too·kar]
changing rooms *kamar ganti pakaian* ka·mar gan·ti pa·kai·an
charming *luwes* loo·wes
chat up v *merayu* me·ra·yoo
cheap *murah* moo·rah
cheat n *menipu* me·ni·poo
cheat v *menipu [tipu]* me·ni·poo [ti·poo]
check (banking) n *cek* chek
check (bill) n *kuitansi* koo·i·tan·si
check v *memeriksa [periksa]* me·me·rik·sa [pe·rik·sa]
check-in (desk) *(tempat) mendaftarkan diri* (tem·pat) men·daf·tar·kan di·ri
checkpoint *pos pemeriksaan* pos pe·me·rik·sa·an
cheese *keju* ke·joo
chef *koki* ko·ki
chemist (pharmacist) *ahli kimia* ah·li ki·mi·a
chemist (pharmacy) *apotek* a·po·tek
cheque (banking) *cek* chek
chess *catur* cha·toor
chess board *papan catur* pa·pan cha·toor
chest (body) *dada* da·da
chewing gum *permen karet* per·men ka·ret
chicken *ayam* a·yam
chicken pox *cacar air* cha·char a·ir
chickpea *kacang panjang* ka·chang pan·jang
child *anak* a·nak

childminding *penjagaan anak* pen·ja·ga·an a·nak
children *anak-anak* a·nak a·nak
child seat *kursi anak* koor·si a·nak
chilli *cabe* cha·be
chilli sauce *saus cabe* sows cha·be
China *Cina* chi·na
chocolate *coklat* chok·lat
cholera *kolera* ko·le·ra
choose *memilih [pilih]* me·mi·lih [pi·lih]
chopping board *talenan* ta·le·nan
Christian n *Kristen* kri·sten
Christian name *pranama* pra·na·ma
Christmas *Natal* na·tal
Christmas Day *Hari Natal* ha·ri na·tal
Christmas Eve *Malam Natal* ma·lam na·tal
church *gereja* ge·re·ja
cigar *serutu* se·roo·too
cigarette *rokok* ro·kok
cigarette lighter *geretan* ge·re·tan
cinema *bioskop* bi·os·kop
circus *sirkus* sir·koos
citizenship *kewarganegaraan* ke·war·ga·ne·ga·ra·an
city *kota* ko·ta
city centre *pusat kota* poo·sat ko·ta
civil rights *hak penduduk* hak pen·doo·dook
class n *kelas* ke·las
classical *klasik* kla·sik
classical art *seni klasik* se·ni kla·sik
classical theatre *sandiwara klasik* san·di·wa·ra kla·sik
class system *sistem pengkelasan* si·stem peng·ke·la·san
clean a *bersih* ber·sih
clean v *membersihkan* mem·ber·sih·kan
cleaning *pembersihan* pem·ber·si·han
client *langganan* lang·ga·nan
cliff *tebing* te·bing
climb v *naik* na·ik
cloakroom *tempat penggantungan jas* tem·pat peng·gan·toong·gan jas
clock n *jam* jam
close a *berdekatan* ber·de·ka·tan
close v *menutup [tutup]* me·noo·toop [too·toop]
closed *tutup* too·toop
clothesline *tali jemuran* ta·li je·moo·ran
clothing *pakaian* pa·kai·an
clothing store *toko pakaian* to·ko pa·kai·an
cloud n *awan* a·wan
cloudy *berawan* be·ra·wan
clove cigarettes *kretek* kre·tek

club *klub* kloob
clutch (car) *kopeling* ko·pe·ling
coach (bus) *bis* bis
coach (trainer) *pelatih* pe·la·tih
coast n *pantai* pan·tai
coat n *jas* jas
cocaine *kokain* ko·ka·in
cockroach *kacoa* ka·cho·a
cocoa *coklat* chok·lat
coconut *kelapa* ke·la·pa
coffee *kopi* ko·pi
coins *uang logam* oo·ang lo·gam
cold (temperature) n&a *dingin* ding·in
cold (flu) n *pilek* pi·lek
colleague *teman sekerja* te·man se·ker·ja
collect call
  menelpon dibayar oleh si penerima
  me·nel·pon di·ba·yar o·leh si pe·ne·ri·ma
college *sekolah tinggi* se·ko·lah ting·gi
colour *warna* war·na
comb n *sisir* si·sir
come (arrive) *datang* da·tang
come from (origin) *berasal [asal]*
  be·ra·sal [a·sal]
comedy *komedi* ko·me·di
comfortable *menyenangkan*
  me·nye·nang·kan
commission *komisi* ko·mi·si
communications (profession)
  komunikasi ko·moo·ni·ka·si
communion *komuni* ko·moo·ni
communist n *komunis* ko·moo·nis
companion *rekan* re·kan
company (business) *perusahaan*
  pe·roo·sa·ha·an
compass *kompas* kom·pas
complain *mengeluh [keluh]*
  meng·e·looh [ke·looh]
complaint *keluhan* ke·loo·han
complimentary (free) *gratis* gra·tis
computer *komputer* kom·poo·ter
concert *konser* kon·ser
concussion *gegar* ge·gar
conditioner *pelembab* pe·lem·bab
condom *kondom* kon·dom
conference *konperensi* kon·pe·ren·si
confession (religious) *pengakuan*
  peng·a·koo·an
confirm (booking) *konfirmasi* kon·fir·ma·si
congratulations *ucapan selamat*
  oo·cha·pan se·la·mat
connection (objects/ideas) n *hubungan*
  hoo·boong·an

connection (transport) n *sambungan*
  sam·boong·an
conservative n *konservatif* kon·ser·va·tif
constipation *sembelit* sem·be·lit
construction *pembangunan*
  pem·bang·oo·nan
consulate *konsulat* kon·soo·lat
contact lenses *lensa kontak* len·sa kon·tak
contact lens solution *larutan untuk lensa
  kontak* la·roo·tan oon·took len·sa kon·tak
contraceptive n *kontrasepsi* kon·tra·sep·si
contract n *kontrak* kon·trak
convent *biara* bi·a·ra
cook n *tukang masak* too·kang ma·sak
cook v *masak* ma·sak
cooking *masakan* ma·sa·kan
cool (temperature) *sejuk* se·jook
corkscrew *kotrek* ko·trek
corn *jagung* ja·goong
corner *sudut* soo·doot
corrupt a *korup* ko·roop
corruption *korupsi* ko·roop·si
cosmetics *bahan kecantikan*
  ba·han ke·chan·ti·kan
cost (object) *harga* har·ga
cost (service) *biaya* bi·a·ya
cotton *katun* ka·toon
cotton balls *kapas kesehatan*
  ka·pas ke·se·ha·tan
cotton buds *kapas pembersih telinga*
  ka·pas pem·ber·sih te·ling·a
cough n&v *batuk* ba·took
cough medicine *obat batuk* o·bat ba·took
count v *menghitung [hitung]*
  meng·hi·toong [hi·toong]
country *negara* ne·ga·ra
countryside *daerah luar kota*
  da·e·rah loo·ar ko·ta
coupon *kupon* koo·pon
court (legal) *pengadilan* peng·a·di·lan
cover charge *cover charge* ka·ver charj
cow *sapi* sa·pi
crab *kepiting* ke·pi·ting
cracker *krupuk* kroo·pook
crafts *kerajinan* ke·ra·ji·nan
crash n *tabrakan* ta·bra·kan
crazy *gila* gi·la
cream (food) *kepala susu* ke·pa·la soo·soo
cream (lotion) *krim* krim
crèche *taman pra-sekolah*
  ta·man pra se·ko·lah
credit n *kredit* kre·dit
credit card *kartu kredit* kar·too kre·dit

cremation *pembakaran mayat* pem·ba·ka·ran ma·yat
cricket (insect) *jengkerik* jeng·ke·rik
cricket (sport) *kriket* kri·ket
crop n *panen* pa·nen
cross (religious) *salib* sa·lib
crowded *ramai* ra·mai
cucumber *ketimun* ke·ti·moon
cup *cangkir* chang·kir
cupboard *lemari* le·ma·ri
currency exchange *penukaran uang* pe·noo·ka·ran oo·ang
current (electricity) *arus listrik* a·roos li·strik
current affairs *berita hangat* be·ri·ta hang·at
curry *kari* ka·ri
custom (tradition) *adat* a·dat
customs (immigration) *bea dan cukai* be·a dan choo·kai
cut n *luka* loo·ka
cut v *memotong [potong]* me·mo·tong [po·tong]
cute (baby) *mungil* moong·il
cutlery *alat-alat makan* a·lat a·lat ma·kan
cycle v *naik sepeda* na·ik se·pe·da
cycling *bersepeda* ber·se·pe·da
cyclist *penyuka olahraga sepeda* pe·nyoo·ka o·lah·ra·ga se·pe·da

D

dad *bapak* ba·pak
daily *harian* ha·ri·an
damaged *rusak* roo·sak
dance n *tarian* ta·ri·an
dance v *menari [tari]* me·na·ri [ta·ri]
dancing *tarian* ta·ri·an
dangerous *berbahaya* ber·ba·ha·ya
dark (colour) a *tua* too·a
dark (night) a *gelap* ge·lap
date (appointment) *janji* jan·ji
date (day) *tanggal* tang·gal
date of birth *tanggal kelahiran* tang·gal ke·la·hi·ran
date (person) v *berpacaran* ber·pa·cha·ran
daughter *anak perempuan* a·nak pe·rem·poo·an
dawn *subuh* soo·booh
day *hari* ha·ri
day after tomorrow *lusa* loo·sa
day before yesterday *kemarin dulu* ke·ma·rin doo·loo
dead a *mati* ma·ti

deaf *tuli* too·li
death *kematian* ke·ma·ti·an
December *Desember* de·sem·ber
decide *memutus* me·moo·toos
deep *dalam* da·lam
deforestation *penebangan hutan* pe·ne·bang·an hoo·tan
degrees (temperature) *derajat* de·ra·jat
delayed *tertunda* ter·toon·da
delicious *enak* e·nak
delirious *gila* gi·la
deliver *mengantarkan [antar]* meng·an·tar·kan [an·tar]
democracy *demokrasi* de·mo·kra·si
demonstration (protest) *demonstrasi* de·mon·stra·si
Denmark *Denmark* den·mark
dental floss *benang gigi* be·nang gi·gi
dentist *dokter gigi* dok·ter gi·gi
deodorant *deodoran* de·o·do·ran
depart *berangkat* be·rang·kat
department store *toko serbaada* to·ko ser·ba·a·da
departure *keberangkatan* ke·be·rang·ka·tan
departure gate *pintu keberangkatan* pin·too ke·be·rang·ka·tan
deposit (bank) n *deposito* de·po·si·to
deposit (luggage) v *menitip [titip]* me·ni·tip [ti·tip]
descendent *keturunan* ke·too·roo·nan
desert *padang pasir* pa·dang pa·sir
design n *desain* de·sain
dessert *pencuci mulut* pen·choo·chi moo·loot
destination *tujuan* too·joo·an
detail *perincian* pe·rin·chi·an
develop (film) *mencuci [cuci]* men·choo·chi [choo·chi]
diabetes *kencing manis* ken·ching ma·nis
dial tone *nada pilih* na·da pi·lih
diaper *popok* po·pok
diaphragm (contraceptive) *diafrakma* di·a·frak·ma
diarrhoea *mencret* mench·ret
diary *buku harian* boo·koo ha·ri·an
dice *dadu* da·doo
dictionary *kamus* ka·moos
die *meninggal* me·ning·gal
diet n *diet* di·et
different *berbeda* ber·be·da
difficult *susah* soo·sah
digital a *digital* di·gi·tal
dining car *kereta makan* ke·re·ta ma·kan

dinner *makan malam* ma·kan ma·lam
direct a *langsung* lang·soong
direct-dial *dial langsung* di·al lang·soong
direction *jurusan* joo·roo·san
director *direktur* di·rek·toor
dirty *kotor* ko·tor
disabled *cacat* cha·chat
disco *disko* dis·ko
discount n *diskon* dis·kon
discrimination *diskriminasi* dis·kri·mi·na·si
disease *penyakit* pe·nya·kit
dish n *piring* pi·ring
disk (CD-ROM) *disk CD* disk see·dee
disk (floppy) *disket kecil* dis·ket ke·chil
distance n *jarak* ja·rak
dive v *menyelam [selam]* me·nye·lam [se·lam]
diving *selam* se·lam
diving boat *kapal penyelam* ka·pal pe·nye·lam
diving course *kursus menyelam* koor·soos me·nye·lam
diving equipment *alat selam* a·lat se·lam
divorce n *cerai* che·rai
divorced *bercerai* ber·che·rai
dizzy *pusing* poo·sing
do *melakukan [lakukan]* me·la·koo·kan [la·koo·kan]
doctor *dokter* dok·ter
documentary *film dokumenter* film do·koo·men·ter
dog *anjing* an·jing
dole *uang sokongan* oo·ang so·kong·an
doll *boneka* bo·ne·ka
dollar *dolar* do·lar
door *pintu* pin·too
double a *dobol* do·bol
double bed *tempat tidur untuk dua orang* tem·pat ti·door oon·took doo·a o·rang
double room *kamar untuk dua orang* ka·mar oon·took doo·a o·rang
down adv *turun* too·roon
downhill *turun gunung* too·roon goo·noong
dozen *lusin* loo·sin
dream n&v *mimpi* mim·pi
dress n *baju rok* ba·joo rok
dried *kering* ke·ring
dried fruit *buahan kering* boo·a·han ke·ring
drink (alcoholic) n *minuman (keras)* mi·noo·man (ke·ras)
drink v *minum* mi·noom
drive v *menyopir* me·nyo·pir

drivers licence *SIM (Surat Ijin Mengemudi)* sim (soo·rat i·jin meng·e·moo·di)
drug (illegal) *narkoba* nar·ko·ba
drug (prescription) *obat* o·bat
drug addiction *pecandu* pe·chan·doo
drug dealer *pedagang narkoba* pe·da·gang nar·ko·ba
drug store *toko obat* to·ko o·bat
drug trafficking *perdagangan narkoba* per·da·gang·an nar·ko·ba
drug user *pemakai narkoba* pe·ma·kai nar·ko·ba
drum n *tambur* tam·boor
(be) drunk *mabuk* ma·book
dry a *kering* ke·ring
dry (clothes) v *jemur* je·moor
dry (oneself) v *berjemur* ber·je·moor
dry season *musim kemarau* moo·sim ke·ma·row
duck *bebek* be·bek
dummy (pacifier) *dot* dot
DVD *DVD* dee·vee·dee
dysentery *disentri* di·sen·tri

E

each *setiap* se·ti·ap
ear *telinga* te·ling·a
early *lekas* le·kas
earn *mendapat* men·da·pat
earplugs *penyumbat telinga* pe·nyoom·bat te·ling·a
earrings *anting-anting* an·ting an·ting
Earth *bumi* boo·mi
earthquake *gempa bumi* gem·pa boo·mi
east *timur* ti·moor
Easter *Paskah* pas·kah
East Timor *Timor Leste* ti·mor le·ste
easy *gampang* gam·pang
eat v *makan* ma·kan
economy *ekonomi* e·ko·no·mi
economy class *kelas ekonomi* ke·las e·ko·no·mi
ecstasy (drug) *ekstasi* ek·sta·si
eczema *eksema* ek·se·ma
education *pendidikan* pen·di·di·kan
egg *telur* te·loor
eggplant *terung* te·roong
elections *pemilihan* pe·mi·li·han
electrical store *toko barang-barang elektronik* to·ko ba·rang ba·rang e·lek·tro·nik
electrician *montir listrik* mon·tir li·strik

electricity *listrik* li·strik
elevator *lift* lift
email *email* i·mel
embarassed *malu* ma·loo
embassy *kedutaan* ke·doo·ta·an
emergency *darurat* da·roo·rat
emotional *emosionil* e·mo·si·o·nil
employee *karyawan* kar·ya·wan
employer *atasan* a·ta·san
empty *a kosong* ko·song
end *n akhir* a·khir
endangered species *jenis terancam punah* je·nis te·ran·cham poo·nah
engaged (to marry) *bertunangan* ber·too·nang·an
engaged (phone) *sibuk* si·book
engagement (appointment) *janji* jan·ji
engagement (to marry) *pertunangan* per·too·nang·an
engine *mesin* me·sin
engineer *insinyur* in·si·nyoor
engineering *keahlian teknik* ke·ah·li·an tek·nik
England *Inggris* ing·gris
English (language/nationality) *Inggris* ing·gris
enjoy (oneself) *menikmati* me·nik·ma·ti
enough *cukup* choo·koop
enter *masuk* ma·sook
entrance *pintu masuk* pin·too ma·sook
envelope *amplop* am·plop
environment *lingkungan* ling·koong·an
epilepsy *epilepsi* e·pi·lep·si
equality *persamaan* per·sa·ma·an
equal opportunity *kesempatan yang sama* ke·sem·pa·tan yang sa·ma
escalator *lift* lift
essential *yang terpenting* yang ter·pen·ting
estate agency *agen perumahan* a·gen pe·roo·ma·han
euro *euro* yoo·ro
Europe *Eropa* e·ro·pa
evening *malam* ma·lam
every *setiap* se·ti·ap
everybody *semua orang* se·moo·a o·rang
every day *setiap hari* se·ti·ap ha·ri
everything *segala sesuatu* se·ga·la se·soo·a·too
exactly *persis* per·sis
example *contoh* chon·toh
excellent *ulung* oo·loong
excess (baggage) *kelebihan* ke·le·bi·han
exchange *n penukaran* pe·noo·ka·ran

exchange *v menukarkan [tukar]* me·noo·kar·kan [too·kar]
exchange rate *kurs* koors
excluded *tidak termasuk* ti·dak ter·ma·sook
excuse *n alasan* a·la·san
exhibition *pameran* pa·me·ran
exit *n pintu keluar* pin·too ke·loo·ar
expensive *mahal* ma·hal
experience *pengalaman* peng·a·la·man
exploitation *eksploitasi* eks·plo·i·ta·si
express *a ekspres* eks·pres
express mail *pos kilat* pos ki·lat
extension (visa) *perpanjangan* per·pan·jang·an
eye(s) *mata* ma·ta
eye drops *obat mata* o·bat ma·ta

F

fabric *kain* ka·in
face *muka* moo·ka
factory *pabrik* pab·rik
factory worker *karyawan pabrik* kar·ya·wan pab·rik
faint *v pingsan* ping·san
fall (autumn) *n musim gugur* moo·sim goo·goor
fall *v jatuh* ja·tooh
family *keluarga* ke·loo·ar·ga
family name *fam* fam
famous *terkenal* ter·ke·nal
fan (handheld) *kipas tangan* ki·pas tang·an
fan (machine) *kipas angin* ki·pas ang·in
fan (supporter) *penggemar* peng·ge·mar
fanbelt *tali kipas* ta·li ki·pas
far *jauh* ja·ooh
fare *n ongkos* ong·kos
farm *kebun* ke·boon
farmer *petani* pe·ta·ni
fashion *mode* mo·de
fast *adv cepat* che·pat
fat *a gemuk* ge·mook
father *bapak* ba·pak
father-in-law *bapak mertua* ba·pak mer·too·a
faucet *keran* ke·ran
(someone's) fault *salah* sa·lah
faulty *cacad* cha·chad
fax *faks* faks
February *Februari* feb·roo·a·ri
feed *v memberi makanan* mem·be·ri ma·ka·nan
feel (touch) *v merasa [rasa]* me·ra·sa [ra·sa]

feeling(s) *perasaan* pe·ra·sa·an
female (animal) n&a *betina* be·ti·na
female (human) n&a *perempuan* pe·rem·poo·an
fence n *pagar* pa·gar
ferry n *kapal feri* ka·pal fe·ri
festival *pesta* pe·sta
fever *demam* de·mam
few *sedikit* se·di·kit
fiancé(e) *tunangan* too·nang·an
fiction *fiksi* fik·si
field n *ladang* la·dang
fight n *pertengkaran* per·teng·ka·ran
fill v *mengisi [isi]* meng·i·si [i·si]
film (camera/cinema) *film* film
film speed *kecepatan film* ke·che·pa·tan film
filtered *saring* sa·ring
fin (swimming) *kaki katak* ka·ki ka·tak
fine n *denda* den·da
fine a *baik* ba·ik
find v *dapat* da·pat
finger *jari* ja·ri
finish n *akhir* a·khir
finish v *menyelesaikan [selesai]* me·nye·le·sai·kan [se·le·sai]
finished *lengkap* leng·kap
Finland *Finlandia* fin·lan·di·a
fire *api* a·pi
firewood *kayu bakar* ka·yoo ba·kar
first a *pertama* per·ta·ma
first-aid kit *kotak pertolongan pertama* ko·tak per·to·long·an per·ta·ma
first class *kelas satu* ke·las sa·too
first name *pranama* pra·na·ma
fish n *ikan* i·kan
fishing *pemancingan* pe·man·ching·an
fishing line *garis pemancingan* ga·ris pe·man·ching·an
fishing rod *tangkai pancing* tang·kai pan·ching
fish monger *penjual ikan* pen·joo·al i·kan
fish shop *toko ikan* to·ko i·kan
flag *bendera* ben·de·ra
flannel *pelanel* pe·la·nel
flare (boating) n *flare fler*
flash (camera) *blitz* blits
flashlight (torch) *senter* sen·ter
flat (apartment) n *apartemen* a·par·te·men
flat a *datar* da·tar
flea *kutu* koo·too
fleamarket *pasar loak* pa·sar lo·ak
flight (air) *penerbangan* pe·ner·bang·an

flippers *kaki katak* ka·ki ka·tak
float (fishing) n *pengapung* peng·a·poong
flood n *banjir* ban·jir
floor (room) *lantai* lan·tai
floor (storey) *tingkat* ting·kat
florist *toko bunga* to·ko boong·a
flour *tepung* te·poong
flower n *bunga* boong·a
flu *flu* floo
fluent *lancar* lan·char
flute *suling* soo·ling
fly n *lalat* la·lat
fly v *terbang* ter·bang
foggy *berkabut* ber·ka·boot
follow *ikut* i·koot
food *makanan* ma·ka·nan
food stall *warung* wa·roong
foot (body) *kaki* ka·ki
football (soccer) *sepakbola* se·pak·bo·la
footpath *jalan setapak* ja·lan se·ta·pak
for (duration) *selama* se·la·ma
for (purpose) *untuk* oon·took
foreign *asing* a·sing
foreigner *orang asing* o·rang a·sing
forest *hutan* hoo·tan
forever *selalu* se·la·loo
forget *lupa* loo·pa
forgive *memaafkan* me·ma·af·kan
fork *garpu* gar·poo
fortnight *dua minggu* doo·a ming·goo
fortune teller *ahli nujum* ah·li noo·joom
foyer *serambi* se·ram·bi
fracture (bone) n *retak* re·tak
fragile *gampang pecah* gam·pang pe·chah
France *Perancis* pe·ran·chis
free (available/unbound) *bebas* be·bas
free (gratis) *gratis* gra·tis
freeze v *membeku [beku]* mem·be·koo [be·koo]
fresh *segar* se·gar
Friday *Jumat* joo·mat
fridge *kulkas* kool·kas
fried *goreng* go·reng
friend *teman* te·man
frog *kodok* ko·dok
from *dari* da·ri
front *depan* de·pan
frozen *dibekukan* di·be·koo·kan
frozen foods *makanan beku* ma·ka·nan be·koo
fruit *buah* boo·ah
fry v *goreng* go·reng
frying pan *wajan* wa·jan

full (location) *penuh* pe·nooh
full (of food) *kenyang* ke·nyang
full-time *penuh* pe·nooh
funeral *pemakaman* pe·ma·ka·man
funny *lucu* loo·choo
furniture *mebel* me·bel
future n *masa depan* ma·sa de·pan

G

game (sport) *pertandingan* per·tan·ding·an
garage *garasi* ga·ra·si
garbage *sampah* sam·pah
garden n *kebun* ke·boon
gardener *tukang kebun* too·kang ke·boon
gardening *perkebunan* per·ke·boo·nan
garlic *bawang putih* ba·wang poo·tih
gas (cooking) *gas LPG* gas el·pi·ji
gas (petrol) *bensin* ben·sin
gas cartridge *pelor gas* pe·lor gas
gate (airport, etc) *pintu* pin·too
gauze *kabut tipis* ka·boot ti·pis
gay (homosexual) *gay* gey
gearbox *girboks* gir·boks
Germany *Jerman* jer·man
get *dapat* da·pat
get off (bus/train) *turun* too·roon
gift *hadiah* ha·di·ah
gin *jenewer* je·ne·wer
girl (preteen) *anak perempuan*
   a·nak pe·rem·poo·an
girl (teenage & above) *cewek* che·wek
girlfriend *pacar perempuan*
   pa·char pe·rem·poo·an
give v *kasih* ka·sih
glad *senang* se·nang
glandular fever *demam kelenjar*
   de·mam ke·len·jar
glass (drinking) *gelas* ge·las
glasses (optical) *kaca mata* ka·cha ma·ta
gloves *sarung tangan* sa·roong tang·an
glue n *lem* lem
go *pergi* per·gi
go out *mencari [cari] hiburan*
   men·cha·ri [cha·ri] hi·boo·ran
go out with (date) *berpacaran dengan*
   ber·pa·cha·ran deng·an
go shopping *belanja* be·lan·ja
goal (score/structure) *gol* gol
goalkeeper *kiper* ki·per
goat *kambing* kam·bing
god (general) *dewa* de·wa
God (mostly Christian) *Tuhan* too·han

God (mostly Muslim) *Allah* al·lah
goggles (swimming) *kaca mata (renang)*
   ka·cha ma·ta (re·nang)
gold n *emas* e·mas
golf ball *bola golf* bo·la golf
golf course *lapangan golf* la·pang·an golf
good (general) *bagus* ba·goos
good (person) *baik* ba·ik
goods (possessions) *barang* ba·rang
government *pemerintah* pe·me·rin·tah
gram *gram* gram
grammar *tatabahasa* ta·ta·ba·ha·sa
grandchild *cucu* choo·choo
grandfather *kakek* ka·kek
grandmother *nenek* ne·nek
grape *anggur* ang·goor
grateful *berterima kasih* ber·te·ri·ma ka·sih
grave n *kuburan* koo·boo·ran
great (fantastic) *jago* ja·go
green *hijau* hi·jow
greengrocer *penjual sayuran*
   pen·joo·al sa·yoo·ran
grey *abu-abu* a·boo a·boo
grocery *toko pangan* to·ko pang·an
group n *kelompok* ke·lom·pok
grow *tumbuh* toom·booh
guaranteed *dijamin* di·ja·min
guess v *menerka [terka]* me·ner·ka [ter·ka]
guest *tamu* ta·moo
guesthouse *losmen* los·men
guide (audio/person) *pemandu*
   pe·man·doo
guidebook *buku panduan perjalanan*
   boo·koo pan·doo·an per·ja·la·nan
guide dog *anjing penuntun*
   an·jing pe·noon·toon
guided tour *tour* toor
guilty *bersalah* ber·sa·lah
gum (mouth) *gusi* goo·si
gun *senjata* sen·ja·ta
gym (place) *gym* jim
gynaecologist *ahli kandungan*
   ah·li kan·doong·an

H

habit *kebiasaan* ke·bi·a·sa·an
hair *rambut* ram·boot
hairbrush *sikat rambut* si·kat ram·boot
haircut *potong rambut* po·tong ram·boot
hairdresser *ahli rias rambut*
   ah·li ri·as ram·boot
halal *halal* ha·lal

half n *setengah* se·teng·ah
hallucination *khayalan* kha·ya·lan
hammer n *palu* pa·loo
hammock *tempat tidur gantong*
   tem·pat ti·door gan·tong
hand *tangan* tang·an
handbag *tas tangan* tas tang·an
handicrafts *kerajinan tangan*
   ke·ra·ji·nan tang·an
handkerchief *saputangan* sa·poo·tang·an
handlebars *gagang sepeda*
   ga·gang se·pe·da
handmade *buatan tangan*
   boo·a·tan tang·an
handsome (man) *ganteng* gan·teng
happy *senang* se·nang
harassment *gangguan* gang·goo·an
harbour *pelabuhan* pe·la·boo·han
hard (difficult) *susah* soo·sah
hard (not soft) *keras* ke·ras
hard-boiled *direbus keras* di·re·boos ke·ras
hardware store *toko perkakas*
   to·ko per·ka·kas
hat *topi* to·pi
have *punya* poo·nya
have a cold *punya pilek* poo·nya pi·lek
have fun *bersenang-senang*
   ber·se·nang se·nang
hay fever *berdemam* ber·de·mam
he *dia* di·a
head *kepala* ke·pa·la
headache *sakit kepala* sa·kit ke·pa·la
headcloth (Muslim women) *jilbab* jil·bab
headlights *lampu besar* lam·poo be·sar
health *kesehatan* ke·se·ha·tan
healthy *sehat* se·hat
hear *mendengar [dengar]*
   men·deng·ar [deng·ar]
hearing aid *alat bantu dengar*
   a·lat ban·too deng·ar
heart *jantung* jan·toong
heart attack *serangan jantung*
   se·rang·an jan·toong
heart condition *penyakit jantung*
   pe·nya·kit jan·toong
heat *kepanasan* ke·pa·na·san
heavy (weight) *berat* be·rat
helmet *helm* helm
help n *bantuan* ban·too·an
help v *menolong [tolong]*
   me·no·long [to·long]
hepatitis *radang hati* ra·dang ha·ti
her (object/possessive) *dia* di·a

herbalist *ahli jamu* ah·li ja·moo
herbs *jamu* ja·moo
here *di sini* di si·ni
heroin *heroin* he·ro·in
high (height) *tinggi* ting·gi
high blood pressure *tekanan darah tinggi*
   te·ka·nan da·rah ting·gi
highchair *kursi tinggi* koor·si ting·gi
high school *SMA (sekolah menengah atas)*
   e·se·ma (se·ko·lah me·nen·gah a·tas)
highway *jalan raya* ja·lan ra·ya
hike n *mendakian* men·da·ki·an
hike v *mendaki* men·da·ki
hiking *mendakian* men·da·ki·an
hiking boots *sepatu pendaki*
   se·pa·too pen·da·ki
hiking route *rute pendaki* roo·te pen·da·ki
hill *bukit* boo·kit
him *dia* di·a
Hindu n *Hindu* hin·doo
hire n *sewa* se·wa
hire v *menyewa [sewa]* me·nye·wa [se·wa]
his *dia* di·a
historical *bersejarah* ber·se·ja·rah
history *sejarah* se·ja·rah
hitchhike v *menggonceng [gonceng]*
   meng·gon·cheng [gon·cheng]
HIV *HIV* ha·ee·ve
hobby *hobi* ho·bi
holiday *hari raya* ha·ri ra·ya
holidays *liburan* li·boo·ran
Holy Week *minggu suci* ming·goo soo·chi
home *rumah* roo·mah
homeless *orang jalanan* o·rang ja·la·nan
homemaker *ibu rumah tangga*
   i·boo roo·mah tang·ga
homeopathy *homeopathy* ho·me·o·pa·ti
homesick *rindu kampung*
   rin·doo kam·poong
homosexual n *homo* ho·mo
honest *jujur* joo·joor
honey *madu* ma·doo
honeymoon *bulan madu* boo·lan ma·doo
hooks (fishing) *kail* ka·il
horny *terangsang* te·rang·sang
horoscope *primbon* prim·bon
horse (riding) *(tunggang) kuda*
   (toong·gang) koo·da
hospital *rumah sakit* roo·mah sa·kit
hospitality *keramahtamahan*
   ke·ra·mah·ta·ma·han
hot (spicy) *pedas* pe·das
hot (temperature) *panas* pa·nas

hotel *hotel* ho·tel
hot water *air panas* a·ir pa·nas
hour *jam* jam
house *rumah* roo·mah
housework *pekerjaan rumah tangga* pe·ker·ja·an roo·mah tang·ga
how *bagaimana* ba·gai·ma·na
how many/much *berapa* be·ra·pa
hug v *memeluk [peluk]* me·me·look [pe·look]
huge *sangat besar* sang·at be·sar
humanities *ilmu sastera* il·moo sa·ste·ra
human resources *sumberdaya manusia* soom·ber·da·ya ma·noo·si·a
human rights *hak asasi manusia (HAM)* hak a·sa·si ma·noo·si·a (ham)
humid *lembab* lem·bab
hundred *ratus* ra·toos
hungry *lapar* la·par
hunt *berburu [buru]* ber·boo·roo [boo·roo]
hunting *pemburuan* pem·boo·roo·an
hurt v *sakit* sa·kit
husband *suami* soo·a·mi

I

I *saya* sa·ya
ice *es* es
ice cream *es krim* es krim
identification *pengenalan* peng·e·na·lan
identification card *KTP (Kartu Tanda Penduduk)* ka·te·pe (kar·too tan·da pen·doo·dook)
idiot *bodoh* bo·doh
if *kalau* ka·low
ill *sakit* sa·kit
immigration *imigrasi* i·mi·gra·si
important *penting* pen·ting
impossible *tidak mungkin* ti·dak moong·kin
in *dalam* da·lam
in (six) days *dalam (enam) hari lagi* da·lam (e·nam) ha·ri la·gi
in a hurry *tergesa-gesa* ter·ge·sa ge·sa
in front of *di depan* di de·pan
included *termasuk* ter·ma·sook
income tax *pajak penghasilan* pa·jak peng·ha·si·lan
India *India* in·di·a
indicator *penunjuk* pe·noon·jook
indigenous *asli* as·li
indigestion *salah cerna* sa·lah cher·na
Indonesia *Indonesia* in·do·ne·si·a

Indonesian (language) *Bahasa Indonesia* ba·ha·sa in·do·ne·si·a
Indonesian (person) *orang Indonesia* o·rang in·do·ne·si·a
indoor *di dalam* di da·lam
industry *industri* in·doo·stri
inequality *ketidaksamaan* ke·ti·dak·sa·ma·an
infection *infeksi* in·fek·si
inflammation *radang* ra·dang
influenza *flu* floo
information *keterangan* ke·te·rang·an
ingredient *bahan* ba·han
inject *menyuntikkan [suntik]* me·yoon·ti·kan [soon·tik]
injection *jarum suntik* ja·room soon·tik
injured *berluka* ber·loo·ka
injury *luka* loo·ka
inner tube *ban dalam* ban da·lam
innocent a *tidak bersalah* ti·dak ber·sa·lah
insect *serangga* se·rang·ga
insect repellent *obat nyamuk* o·bat nya·mook
inside *di dalam* di da·lam
instructor *pelatih* pe·la·tih
insurance *asuransi* a·soo·ran·si
interesting *menarik* me·na·rik
international *internasional* in·ter·na·si·o·nal
Internet *internet* in·ter·net
Internet café *warnet* war·net
interpreter *juru bahasa* joo·roo ba·ha·sa
intersection *simpang* sim·pang
interview n *wawancara* wa·wan·cha·ra
invite v *mengundang [undang]* meng·oon·dang [oon·dang]
Ireland *Irlandia* ir·lan·di·a
iron (clothes) *setrika listrik* se·tri·ka li·strik
island *pulau* poo·low
Israel *Israel* is·ra·el
it *ini* i·ni
IT *TI (Teknologi Informatika)* te·i (tek·no·lo·gi in·for·ma·ti·ka)
Italy *Italia* i·ta·li·a
itch n *gatal* ga·tal
itinerary *rencana perjalanan* ren·cha·na per·ja·la·nan
IUD *spiral* spi·ral
ivory n *gading* ga·ding

J

jacket *jaket* ja·ket
jackfruit *nangka* nang·ka
jail n *penjara* pen·ja·ra

January *Januari* ja·noo·a·ri
Japan *Jepang* je·pang
jar *kendi* ken·di
jaw *rahang* ra·hang
jealous *iri hati* i·ri ha·ti
jeans *celana jeans* che·la·na jins
jeep *jip* jip
jet lag *jet lag* jet leg
jewellery *perhiasan* per·hi·a·san
Jewish *Yahudi* ya·hoo·di
job *pekerjaan* pe·ker·ja·an
jogging *jogging* jo·ging
joke n *lelucon* le·loo·chon
journalist *wartawan* war·ta·wan
journey *perjalanan* per·ja·la·nan
judge (court) n *hakim* ha·kim
juice *jus* joos
July *Juli* joo·li
jumper (sweater) *sweater* swe·ter
June *Juni* joo·ni
just (only) *saja* sa·ja
just (recently) *baru* ba·roo
justice *keadilan* ke·a·di·lan

K

kerosene *minyak tana* mi·nyak ta·na
ketchup *saus tomat* sows to·mat
key *kunci* koon·chi
kick v *menyepak* me·nye·pak
kidney *ginjal* gin·jal
kill *membunuh [bunuh]*
  mem·boo·nooh [boo·nooh]
kilogram *kilogram* ki·lo·gram
kilometre *kilometer* ki·lo·me·ter
kind a *baik hati* ba·ik ha·ti
kindergarten *taman kanak-kanak*
  ta·man ka·nak ka·nak
king *raja* ra·ja
kiosk *kios* ki·os
kiss n *ciuman* chi·oo·man
kitchen *dapur* da·poor
knapsack *ransel* ran·sel
knee *lutut* loo·toot
knife *pisau* pi·sow
know (someone) *kenal* ke·nal
know (something) *tahu* ta·hoo

L

labourer *karyawan* kar·ya·wan
lake *danau* da·now
lamb (meat) *daging anak domba*
  da·ging a·nak dom·ba

land n *tanah* ta·nah
landlady *pemilik rumah* pe·mi·lik roo·mah
landlord *tuan rumah* too·an roo·mah
language *bahasa* ba·ha·sa
laptop *laptop* lap·top
large *besar* be·sar
last (final) *terakhir* te·ra·khir
last (previous) *sebelumnya* se·be·loom·nya
late (not on time) *terlambat* ter·lam·bat
later *nanti* nan·ti
laugh v *tertawa* ter·ta·wa
launderette *tempat cuci otomat*
  tem·pat choo·chi o·to·mat
laundry (clothes) *cucian* choo·chi·an
laundry (room) *ruang cuci* roo·ang choo·chi
law (rule/profession) *hukum* hoo·koom
lawyer *pengacara* peng·a·cha·ra
laxatives *obat pencahar* o·bat pen·cha·har
lazy *malas* ma·las
leader *pemimpin* pe·mim·pin
leaf n *daun* da·oon
learn v *belajar* be·la·jar
leather n *kulit* koo·lit
lecture n *kuliah* koo·li·ah
lecturer *dosen* do·sen
left (direction) *kiri* ki·ri
left luggage *barang simpanan*
  ba·rang sim·pa·nan
left-luggage office *kantor penitipan*
  barang kan·tor pe·ni·ti·pan ba·rang
left-wing *sayap kiri* sa·yap ki·ri
leg (body) *kaki* ka·ki
legal *sah* sah
legislation *perundang-undangan*
  pe·roon·dang oon·dang·an
lemon *jeruk asam* je·rook a·sam
lemonade *air jeruk* a·ir je·rook
length *panjang* pan·jang
lens (camera) *lensa* len·sa
Lent *bulan puasa Masehi*
  boo·lan poo·a·sa ma·se·hi
lentil *miju-miju* mi·joo mi·joo
lesbian v *lesbi* les·bi
less *kurang* koo·rang
letter (mail) *surat* soo·rat
liar *pembohong* pem·bo·hong
library *perpustakaan* per·poo·sta·ka·an
lice *kutu* koo·too
license n *ijin* i·jin
license plate number *nomor pelat*
  no·mor pe·lat
lie (not stand) v *baring* ba·ring
lie (not tell the truth) v *bohong* bo·hong

life *hidup* hi·doop
life jacket *baju pelampung*
  ba·joo pe·lam·poong
lift (elevator) *lift* lift
light (electric) n *lampu* lam·poo
light (natural) n *cahaya* cha·ha·ya
light (weight) a *ringan* ring·an
light bulb *bola lampu* bo·la lam·poo
lighter (cigarette) *geretan* ge·re·tan
light meter *meteran lampu*
  me·te·ran lam·poo
like v *suka* soo·ka
lime (fruit) *kapur* ka·poor
linen (material) *linan* li·nan
linen (sheets) *sepre* se·pre
linguist *ahli bahasa* ah·li ba·ha·sa
lip balm *balsem bibir* bal·sem bi·bir
lips *bibir* bi·bir
lipstick *gincu* gin·choo
listen v *mendengar [dengar]*
  men·deng·ar [deng·ar]
little (quantity) *sedikit* se·di·kit
little (size) *kecil* ke·chil
live (be alive) v *hidup* hi·doop
live (reside) v *tinggal* ting·gal
liver *hati* ha·ti
local a *lokal* lo·kal
location *lokasi* lo·ka·si
lock n *kunci* koon·chi
lock v *mengunci* meng·oon·chi
locked *dikunci* di·koon·chi
lollies *gula-gula* goo·la goo·la
long (measurement) *panjang* pan·jang
long (time) *lama* la·ma
look v *melihat [lihat]* me·li·hat [li·hat]
look after *memelihara [pelihara]*
  me·me·li·ha·ra [pe·li·ha·ra]
look for *mencari [cari]* men·cha·ri [cha·ri]
lookout *pengintai* peng·in·tai
loom n *alat tenun* a·lat te·noon
loose *longgar* long·gar
loose change *recehan* re·che·han
lose *menghilangkan* meng·hi·lang·kan
lost (object) *kehilangan* ke·hi·lang·an
lost (person) *tersesat* ter·se·sat
lost property office *kantor kehilangan*
  barang kan·tor ke·hi·lang·an ba·rang
(a) lot *banyak* ba·nyak
lotion *cairan* cha·i·ran
loud *keras* ke·ras
love n&v *cinta* chin·ta
lover *kekasih* ke·ka·sih
low *rendah* ren·dah

low blood pressure *tekanan darah*
  rendah te·ka·nan da·rah ren·dah
lubricant *pelicin* pe·li·chin
luck *untung* oon·toong
lucky *beruntung* be·roon·toong
luggage *bagasi* ba·ga·si
luggage lockers *loker untuk bawaan*
  lo·ker oon·took ba·wa·an
luggage tag *penanda bagasi*
  pe·nan·da ba·ga·si
lump *pembengkakan* pem·beng·ka·kan
lunch *makan siang* ma·kan si·ang
lung *paru-paru* pa·roo pa·roo
lures (fishing) *umpan* oom·pan
luxury a *mewah* me·wah

M

machine *mesin* me·sin
made (of) *dibuat (dari)* di·boo·at (da·ri)
magazine *majalah* ma·ja·lah
magician *tukang sihir* too·kang si·hir
mail (letters) n *kiriman* ki·ri·man
mail (system) n *pos* pos
mail v *kirim* ki·rim
mailbox *kotak pos* ko·tak pos
main a *utama* oo·ta·ma
main road *jalan raya* ja·lan ra·ya
main square *lapangan* la·pang·an
make v *membuat [buat]*
  mem·boo·at [boo·at]
make-up n *dandanan* dan·da·nan
malaria *malaria* ma·la·ri·a
Malaysia *Malaysia* ma·lai·si·a
male (animal) n&a *jantan* jan·tan
male (person) n&a *laki-laki* la·ki la·ki
man (male) n *pria* pri·a
manager (business) *pemimpin* pe·mim·pin
manager (team) *manajer* ma·na·jer
mango *mangga* mang·ga
manual worker *pekerja kasar*
  pe·ker·ja ka·sar
many *banyak* ba·nyak
map *peta* pe·ta
March *Maret* ma·ret
margarine *margarina* mar·ga·ri·na
marijuana *ganja* gan·ja
marital status *kedudukan perkawinan*
  ke·doo·doo·kan per·ka·wi·nan
market *pasar* pa·sar
marriage *perkawinan* per·ka·wi·nan
married *kawin* ka·win
marry *menikah* me·ni·kah

martial arts *seni bela diri rakyat* se·ni be·la di·ri rak·yat
mask n *topeng* to·peng
mass (Catholic) *misa* mi·sa
massage n&v *pijat* pi·jat
masseur/masseuse *tukang pijat* too·kang pi·jat
mat n *tikar* ti·kar
match (game) n *pertandingan* per·tan·ding·an
matches (lighting) *korek api* ko·rek a·pi
material (clothing) *bahan baju* ba·han ba·joo
mattress *kasur* ka·soor
May *Mei* mey
maybe *mungkin* moong·kin
mayor *walikota* wa·li·ko·ta
me *saya* sa·ya
meal *makanan* ma·ka·nan
measles *campak* cham·pak
meat *daging* da·ging
mechanic *montir* mon·tir
media *media* me·di·a
medicine (drug) *obat* o·bat
medicine (profession) *kedokteran* ke·dok·te·ran
meditation *meditasi* me·di·ta·si
meet (first time) v *bertemu* ber·te·moo
meet (get together) v *berjumpa [jumpa]* ber·joom·pa [joom·pa]
melon *semangka* se·mang·ka
member *anggota* ang·go·ta
memory card *memory card* me·mo·ri kard
menstruation *menstruasi* men·stroo·a·si
menu *daftar makanan* daf·tar ma·ka·nan
message *pesan* pe·san
metal n *logam* lo·gam
metre *meter* me·ter
microwave oven *oven gelombang mikro* o·ven ge·lom·bang mik·ro
midday *siang* si·ang
midnight *tengah malam* teng·ah ma·lam
migraine *migren* mi·gren
military a *tentara* ten·ta·ra
military service *tugas tentara* too·gas ten·ta·ra
milk *susu* soo·soo
millimetre *milimeter* mi·li·me·ter
million *juta* joo·ta
mince *daging cincang* da·ging chin·chang
mineral water *air mineral* a·ir mi·ne·ral
minibus *bemo* be·mo
minister (politics) *menteri* men·te·ri

minute *menit* me·nit
mirror *cermin* cher·min
miscarriage *keguguran* ke·goo·goo·ran
Miss *Nona* no·na
miss (person) *rindu* rin·doo
miss (transport) *terlambat* ter·lam·bat
mistake n *salah* sa·lah
mix v *campur* cham·poor
mobile phone *HP* ha·pe
modem *modem* mo·dem
modern *modern* mo·dern
moisturiser *pelembab* pe·lem·bab
monastery *biara* bi·a·ra
Monday *Senin* se·nin
money *uang* oo·ang
monk *biarawan* bi·a·ra·wan
monkey *monyet* mo·nyet
month *bulan* boo·lan
monument *monumen* mo·noo·men
moon *bulan* boo·lan
more *lebih* le·bih
morning *pagi* pa·gi
morning sickness *muak di waktu pagi* moo·ak di wak·too pa·gi
mosque *mesjid* mes·jid
mosquito *nyamuk* nya·mook
mosquito coil *obat nyamuk* o·bat nya·mook
mosquito net *kelambu* ke·lam·boo
mother *ibu* i·boo
mother-in-law *ibu mertua* i·boo mer·too·a
motorbike *sepeda motor* se·pe·da mo·tor
motorboat *perahu motor* pe·ra·hoo mo·tor
motorway *jalan tol* ja·lan tol
mountain *gunung* goo·noong
mountain bike *sepeda gunung* se·pe·da goo·noong
mountaineering *mendaki gunung* men·da·ki goo·noong
mountain hut *pondok pendaki* pon·dok pen·da·ki
mountain path *jalan gunung* ja·lan goo·noong
mountain range *pegunungan* pe·goo·noong·an
mouse *tikus* ti·koos
mouth *mulut* moo·loot
movie *film* film
Mr *Bapak* ba·pak
Mrs *Ibu* i·boo
Ms *Ibu* i·boo
mud *lumpur* loom·poor
mum *ibu* i·boo
mumps *beguk* be·gook

murder n *pembunuhan* pem·boo·noo·han
murder v *membunuh [bunuh]*
mem·boo·nooh [boo·nooh]
muscle *otot* o·tot
museum *musium* moo·si·oom
mushroom *jamur* ja·moor
music *musik* moo·sik
music shop *toko musik* to·ko moo·sik
musician *pemain musik* pe·ma·in moo·sik
Muslim n&a *Islam* is·lam
mussel *remis* re·mis
mute *a bisu* bi·soo
mutton *daging domba* da·ging dom·ba
my *saya* sa·ya

N

nail clippers *gunting kuku*
goon·ting koo·koo
name n *nama* na·ma
napkin *serbet* ser·bet
nappy *popok* po·pok
nappy rash *ruam* roo·am
nationality *kebangsaan* ke·bang·sa·an
national park *taman nasional*
ta·man na·si·o·nal
nature *alam* a·lam
nausea *mual* moo·al
near adv *dekat* de·kat
nearby *berdekatan* ber·de·ka·tan
nearest *terdekat* ter·de·kat
necessary *perlu* per·loo
neck n *leher* le·her
necklace *kalung* ka·loong
need v *perlu* per·loo
needle (sewing/syringe) *jarum* ja·room
negatives (photos) *gambar negatip*
gam·bar ne·ga·tip
net *jala* ja·la
Netherlands *Belanda* be·lan·da
network *jaringan* ja·ring·an
never *tidak pernah* ti·dak per·nah
new *baru* ba·roo
news *berita* be·ri·ta
newsagency *agen berita* a·gen be·ri·ta
newspaper *koran* ko·ran
newsstand *kios koran* ki·os ko·ran
New Year's Day *Hari Tahun Baru*
ha·ri ta·hoon ba·roo
New Year's Eve *Malam Tahun Baru*
ma·lam ta·hoon ba·roo
New Zealand *Selandia Baru*
se·lan·di·a ba·roo

next *yang berikutnya* yang be·ri·koot·nya
next (time) *depan* de·pan
next to *di samping* di sam·ping
nice *baik* ba·ik
nickname *nama panggilan*
na·ma pang·gi·lan
night *malam* ma·lam
night market *pasar malam* pa·sar ma·lam
night out *rekreasi malam*
rek·re·a·si ma·lam
no *tidak* ti·dak
noisy *ribut* ri·boot
none *tidak satu pun* ti·dak sa·too poon
nonsmoking *dilarang merokok*
di·la·rang me·ro·kok
noodles *mie* mee
noon *siang* si·ang
north *utara* oo·ta·ra
Norway *Norwegia* nor·we·gi·a
nose *hidung* hi·doong
not (with nouns) *bukan* boo·kan
not (with verbs) *tidak* ti·dak
nothing *tidak ada* ti·dak a·da
not yet *belum* be·loom
November *November* no·vem·ber
now *sekarang* se·ka·rang
nuclear energy *tenaga nuklir*
te·na·ga nook·lir
nuclear testing *percobaan nuklir*
per·cho·ba·an nook·lir
number n *nomor* no·mor
numberplate *pelat nomor polisi*
pe·lat no·mor po·li·si
nun *biarawati* bi·a·ra·wa·ti
nurse n *jururawat* joo·roo·ra·wat
nut (food) *kacang* ka·chang

O

oar(s) *dayung* da·yoong
occupation *pekerjaan* pe·ker·ja·an
ocean *samudera* sa·moo·de·ra
October *Oktober* ok·to·ber
off (power) *mati* ma·ti
off (spoiled) *busuk* boo·sook
offense (legal) *pelanggaran* pe·lang·ga·ran
office *kantor* kan·tor
office worker *pegawai* pe·ga·wai
often *sering* se·ring
oil (cooking) *minyak* mi·nyak
oil (crude) *oli* o·li
old (object) *lama* la·ma
old (person) *tua* too·a*

Olympic Games *Pertandingan Olympiade* per·tan·ding·an o·lim·pi·a·de
omelette *telur goreng* te·loor go·reng
on (location) *di* di
on (power) *hidup* hi·doop
on time *tepat waktu* te·pat wak·too
on top of *di atas* di a·tas
once *sekali* se·ka·li
one *satu* sa·too
one-way (ticket) *satu kali jalan* sa·too ka·li ja·lan
onion *bawang bombay* ba·wang bom·bey
only *hanya* ha·nya
open (business) a *buka* boo·ka
open v *membuka [buka]* mem·boo·ka [boo·ka]
opening hours *jam buka* jam boo·ka
opera *opera* o·pe·ra
operation (medical) *pembedahan* pem·be·da·han
operator (telephone) *penghubung* peng·hoo·boong
opinion *pendapat* pen·da·pat
opposite *lawan* la·wan
optometrist *ahli kacamata* ah·li ka·cha·ma·ta
or *atau* a·tow
orange (colour) *jingga* jing·ga
orange (fruit) *jeruk manis* je·rook ma·nis
orchestra *orkes* or·kes
order n *pesanan* pe·sa·nan
order v *memesan [pesan]* me·me·san [pe·san]
ordinary *biasa* bi·a·sa
organise *mengatur [atur]* meng·a·toor [a·toor]
orgasm *syahwat* shah·wat
original a *asli* as·li
other *lain* la·in
our excl *kami* ka·mi
our incl *kita* ki·ta
out of order *rusak* roo·sak
outside *luar* loo·ar
ovarian cyst *kista induk telur* ki·sta in·dook te·loor
ovary *induk telur* in·dook te·loor
oven *kompor* kom·por
overdose n *terlalu banyak takaran* ter·la·loo ba·nyak ta·ka·ran
overnight *sepanjang malam* se·pan·jang ma·lam
overseas *luar negeri* loo·ar ne·ge·ri
owe v *berhutang* ber·hoo·tang

owner *pemilik* pe·mi·lik
oxygen *oksigen* ok·si·gen
oyster *tiram* ti·ram
ozone layer *lapisan ozon* la·pi·san o·zon

P

pacemaker *alat pacu jantung* a·lat pa·choo jan·toong
pacifier (dummy) *dot* dot
package *paket* pa·ket
packet (general) *bungkus* boong·koos
padlock *gembok gantung* gem·bok gan·toong
page n *halaman* ha·la·man
pain n *perasaan sakit* pe·ra·sa·an sa·kit
painful *menyakitkan* me·nya·kit·kan
painkillers *penawar sakit* pe·na·war sa·kit
painter (artist) *pelukis* pe·loo·kis
painter (trade) *tukang cat* too·kang chat
painting (picture) *lukisan* loo·ki·san
painting (the art) *seni lukis* se·ni loo·kis
pair n *sepasang* se·pa·sang
palace *istana* i·sta·na
pan *panci* pan·chi
pants (trousers) *celana* che·la·na
panty liners *pembalut tipis* pem·ba·loot ti·pis
pap smear *papsmir* pap·smir
paper *kertas* ker·tas
paperwork *pekerjaan kertas* pe·ker·ja·an ker·tas
paraplegic *cacat kaki* cha·chat ka·ki
parcel *paket* pa·ket
parents *orang tua* o·rang too·a
park n *taman* ta·man
park (a car) v *memarkir [parkir]* me·mar·kir [par·kir]
parliament *parlemen* par·la·men
part n *bagian* ba·gi·an
party (fiesta) *pesta* pe·sta
party (political) *partai* par·tai
pass (go by) v *melewatkan [lewat]* me·le·wat·kan [le·wat]
pass (kick/throw) v *memberikan [beri]* mem·be·ri·kan [be·ri]
passenger *penumpang* pe·noom·pang
passport (number) (nomor) *paspor* (no·mor) pas·por
past n *masa lalu* ma·sa la·loo
pastry *kue kering* koo·e ke·ring
path *jalan kecil* ja·lan ke·chil
pattern *pola* po·la

pay v *membayar [bayar]* mem·ba·yar [ba·yar]
payment *bayaran* ba·ya·ran
pea *kacang buncis* ka·chang boon·chis
peace *damai* da·mai
peanut *kacang tanah* ka·chang ta·nah
pedal n *pedal* pe·dal
pedestrian *pejalan kaki* pe·ja·lan ka·ki
pen *pena* pe·na
pencil *pensil* pen·sil
penis *zakar* za·kar
penknife *pisau lipat* pi·sow li·pat
pensioner *pensiunan* pen·si·oo·nan
people *rakyat* rak·yat
pepper (bell) *cabe* cha·be
pepper (black) *lada* la·da
per (day) *per (hari)* per (ha·ri)
per cent *persen* per·sen
perfect *sempurna* sem·poor·na
performance *pertunjukan* per·toon·joo·kan
performance art *seni pertunjukan* se·ni per·toon·joo·kan
perfume n *minyak harum* mi·nyak ha·room
period pain *sakit menstruasi* sa·kit men·stroo·a·si
permission *ijin* i·jin
permit n *ijin* i·jin
person *orang* o·rang
petition *petisi* pe·ti·si
petrol *bensin* ben·sin
petrol station *pompa bensin* pom·pa ben·sin
pharmacy *apotek* a·po·tek
the Philippines *Filipina* fi·li·pi·na
phone n *telpon* tel·pon
phone book *buku telpon* boo·koo tel·pon
phone box *boks telpon* boks tel·pon
phone card *kartu telpon* kar·too tel·pon
photo *foto* fo·to
photograph v *memotret [potret]* me·mo·tret [po·tret]
photographer *tukang potret* too·kang po·tret
photography *fotografi* fo·to·gra·fi
piano *piano* pi·a·no
pick (axe) *beliung* be·li·oong
pick up v *memungut [pungut]* me·moong·oot [poong·oot]
pickles *asinan* a·si·nan
pickpocket *copet* cho·pet
picnic n *piknik* pik·nik
picture *gambar* gam·bar
pie *pastei* pa·stey

piece *potongan* po·tong·an
pig *babi* ba·bi
pill *pil* pil
the pill *pil kontrasepsi* pil kon·tra·sep·si
pillow *bantal* ban·tal
pillowcase *sarung bantal* sa·roong ban·tal
pineapple *nenas* ne·nas
pink *merah muda* me·rah moo·da
place n *tempat* tem·pat
place of birth *tempat kelahiran* tem·pat ke·la·hi·ran
plane *pesawat* pe·sa·wat
planet *planit* pla·nit
plant n *tumbuhan* toom·boo·han
plastic *plastik* pla·stik
plate *piring* pi·ring
plateau *dataran tinggi* da·ta·ran ting·gi
platform *peron* pe·ron
play (theatre) n *drama* dra·ma
play (game) v *bermain [main]* ber·ma·in [ma·in]
play (music) v *main* ma·in
plug (bath) n *penutup bak mandi* pe·noo·toop bak man·di
plug (electricity) *steker* ste·ker
plumber *tukang patri* too·kang pa·tri
PO box *kotak pos* ko·tak pos
pocket *kantung* kan·toong
pocket knife *pisau pilat* pi·sow pi·lat
poetry *puisi* poo·i·si
point v *menunjuk [tunjuk]* me·noon·jook [toon·jook]
poisonous *beracun* be·ra·choon
police (officer) *polisi* po·li·si
police station *kantor polisi* kan·tor po·li·si
policy *polis* po·lis
politician *politikus* po·li·ti·koos
politics *politik* po·li·tik
pollen *serbuk sari* ser·book sa·ri
pollution *polusi* po·loo·si
pool (game) *bilyar* bil·yar
pool (swimming) *kolam renang* ko·lam re·nang
poor (money) *miskin* mis·kin
popular *populer* po·poo·ler
pork *daging babi* da·ging ba·bi
port (harbour) *pelabuhan* pe·la·boo·han
portrait sketcher *pelukis potret* pe·loo·kis po·tret
positive a *positip* po·si·tip
possible *mungkin* moong·kin
post v *mengirim [kirim]* meng·i·rim [ki·rim]
postage *perangko* pe·rang·ko

postcard *kartu pos* kar·too pos
post code *kode pos* ko·de pos
post office *kantor pos* kan·tor pos
poster *plakat* pla·kat
pot (ceramics) *guci* goo·chi
pot (cooking) *panci* pan·chi
potato *kentang* ken·tang
pottery *tembikar* tem·bi·kar
pound (money) *pound* pa·oond
poverty *kemiskinan* ke·mis·ki·nan
powder n *pupur* poo·poor
power *kuasa* koo·a·sa
prawn *udang* oo·dang
prayer *doa* do·a
prayer book *buku doa* boo·koo do·a
prefer *lebih suka* le·bih soo·ka
pregnancy test kit *tes kehamilan*
 tes ke·ha·mi·lan
pregnant *hamil* ha·mil
prehistoric art *seni prasejarah*
 se·ni pra·se·ja·rah
premenstrual tension
 ketegangan sebelum menstruasi
 ke·te·gang·an se·be·loom men·stroo·a·si
prepare *menyiapkan [siapkan]*
 me·nyi·ap·kan [si·ap·kan]
prescription *resep* re·sep
present (gift) *hadiah* ha·di·ah
present (time) n *sekarang* se·ka·rang
president *presiden* pre·si·den
pressure (tyre) n *tekanan* te·ka·nan
pretty *cantik* chan·tik
price (goods) n *harga* har·ga
price (service) n *ongkos* ong·kos
priest (Catholic) *pastor* pa·stor
priest (Buddhist/Hindu/Protestant)
 pendeta pen·de·ta
prime minister *perdana menteri*
 per·da·na men·te·ri
print n *cetakan* che·ta·kan
printer (computer) *printer* prin·ter
prison *penjara* pen·ja·ra
prisoner *orang hukuman*
 o·rang hoo·koo·man
private *pribadi* pri·ba·di
private hospital *rumah sakit swasta*
 roo·mah sa·kit swa·sta
problem *masalah* ma·sa·lah
produce v *memproduksi [produksi]*
 mem·pro·dook·si [pro·dook·si]
profession *pekerjaan* pe·ker·ja·an
profit *keuntungan* ke·oon·toong·an
program n *program* pro·gram

projector *proyektor* pro·yek·tor
promise n v *berjanji [janji]* ber·jan·ji [jan·ji]
prostitute n *pelacur* pe·la·choor
protect v *melindungi [lindung]*
 me·lin·doong·i [lin·doong]
protest n *protes* pro·tes
protest v *memprotes [protes]*
 mem·pro·tes [pro·tes]
Protestant n *Protestan* pro·te·stan
provisions *ketentuan* ke·ten·too·an
pub *tempat minum* tem·pat mi·noom
public gardens *taman umum*
 ta·man oo·moom
public phone *telpon umum*
 tel·pon oo·moom
public toilet *WC umum* we·se oo·moom
pull v *menarik [tarik]* me·na·rik [ta·rik]
pump n *pompa* pom·pa
pumpkin *labu* la·boo
puncture n *lubang* loo·bang
pure *bersih* ber·sih
purified water *air penyulingan*
 a·ir pe·nyoo·ling·an
purple *ungu* oong·oo
purse *dompet* dom·pet
push v *mendorong [dorong]*
 men·do·rong [do·rong]
put *menyimpan [simpan]*
 me·nyim·pan [sim·pan]

Q

qualifications *kwalifikasi* kwa·li·fi·ka·si
quality *kwalitas* kwa·li·tas
quarantine *karantina* ka·ran·ti·na
quarter (fraction) n *perempat* pe·rem·pat
queen *ratu* ra·too
question n *pertanyaan* per·ta·nya·an
question v *bertanya [tanya]*
 ber·ta·nya [ta·nya]
queue n *antri* an·tri
quick *cepat* che·pat
quiet *sepi* se·pi
quit *berhenti* ber·hen·ti
Qur'an *al Qur'an* al koo·ran

R

rabbit *kelinci* ke·lin·chi
race (sport) n *perlombaan* per·lom·ba·an
racetrack *trek balap* trek ba·lap
racing bike *balap sepeda* ba·lap se·pe·da
racism *rasisme* ra·sis·me

racquet *raket* ra·ket
radiator *radiator* ra·di·a·tor
radio n *radio* ra·di·o
railroad *jalan kereta api* ja·lan ke·re·ta a·pi
railway station *stasiun kereta api*
 sta·si·oon ke·re·ta a·pi
rain n *hujan* hoo·jan
raincoat *jas hujan* jas hoo·jan
rally (demonstration) *demo* de·mo
rape n *perkosaan* per·ko·sa·an
rare (steak) *setengah masak*
 se·teng·ah ma·sak
rare (uncommon) *jarang* ja·rang
rash *ruam* roo·am
rat *tikus* ti·koos
raw *mentah* men·tah
razor *alat cukur* a·lat choo·koor
razor blade *silet* si·let
read *membaca [baca]* mem·ba·cha [ba·cha]
reading *bacaan* ba·cha·an
ready *siap* si·ap
real estate agent *agen perumahan*
 a·gen pe·roo·ma·han
rear (location) a *belakang* be·la·kang
reason n *alasan* a·la·san
receipt *kuitansi* koo·i·tan·si
recently *baru-baru* ba·roo ba·roo
recognise *mengenal* meng·e·nal
recommend *rekomendasikan*
 re·ko·men·da·si·kan
record *mencatat [catat]*
 men·cha·tat [cha·tat]
recyclable *bisa daur ulang*
 bi·sa da·oor oo·lang
red *merah* me·rah
red wine *anggur merah* ang·goor me·rah
referee n *wasit* wa·sit
reflexology *refleksologi* re·flek·so·lo·gi
reforestation *reboisasi* re·bo·i·sa·si
refrigerator *kulkas* kool·kas
refugee *pengungsi* peng·oong·si
refund n *pembayaran kembali*
 pem·ba·ya·ran kem·ba·li
refuse *menolak [tolak]* me·no·lak [to·lak]
region *wilayah* wi·la·yah
regional *daerah* da·e·rah
registered mail *pos tercatat* pos ter·cha·tat
rehydration salts *garam anti dehidrasi*
 ga·ram an·ti de·hi·dra·si
relationship *hubungan* hoo·boong·an
relax *bersantai [santai]* ber·san·tai [san·tai]
relic *peninggalan* pe·ning·ga·lan
religion *agama* a·ga·ma

religious *beragama* be·ra·ga·ma
remember v *ingat* ing·at
remote *terpencil* ter·pen·chil
remote control *remote control*
 re·mot kon·trol
rent v *menyewa [sewa]* me·nye·wa [se·wa]
repair v *memperbaiki* mem·per·ba·i·ki
republic *republik* re·poob·lik
request v *minta* min·ta
reservation (booking) *pesanan* pe·sa·nan
reserve v *memesan [pesan]*
 me·me·san [pe·san]
rest n *istirahat* i·sti·ra·hat
rest v *beristirahat [istirahat]*
 be·ri·sti·ra·hat [i·sti·ra·hat]
restaurant *restoran* re·sto·ran
retired *pensiunan* pen·si·oo·nan
return (ticket) *pulang-pergi*
 poo·lang per·gi
return v *pulang* poo·lang
rhythm *irama* i·ra·ma
rib (body) *tulang rusuk* too·lang roo·sook
rice (cooked) *nasi* na·si
rice (uncooked) *beras* be·ras
rich (food) *gurih* goo·rih
rich (money) *kaya* ka·ya
rickshaw *becak* be·chak
ride (vehicle) *perjalanan* per·ja·la·nan
ride (bike/horse) v *naik* na·ik
ride (in vehicle) v *menumpang [numpang]*
 me·noom·pang [noom·pang]
right (correct) *benar* be·nar
right (direction) *kanan* ka·nan
right-wing *sayap kanan* sa·yap ka·nan
ring (jewellery) n *cincin* chin·chin
ring (phone) v *membunyikan [bunyi]*
 mem·boo·nyi·kan [boo·nyi]
ripe *matang* ma·tang
risk *risiko* ri·si·ko
river *sungai* soong·ai
road *jalan* ja·lan
road map *peta jalan* pe·ta ja·lan
roasted *panggang* pang·gang
rob *merampok [rampok]*
 me·ram·pok [ram·pok]
rock *batu* ba·too
rock climbing *panjat tebing* pan·jat te·bing
rock group *band rock* band rok
roll (bread) *roti kadet* ro·ti ka·det
romantic a *romantis* ro·man·tis
roof *atap* a·tap
room *kamar* ka·mar
room number *nomor kamar* no·mor ka·mar

rope *tali* ta·li
round (drinks) n *giliran* gi·li·ran
route n *rute* roo·te
row v *mendayung [dayung]*
men·da·yoong [da·yoong]
rubbish *sampah* sam·pah
rubella *rubela* roo·be·la
rug *permadani* per·ma·da·ni
rugby *rugby* rag·bi
ruins *runtuhan* roon·too·han
rule n *peraturan* pe·ra·too·ran
rum *rum* room
run v *lari* la·ri
running *lari* la·ri
runny nose *hidung berair* hi·doong be·ra·ir

S

sad *sedih* se·dih
saddle n *pelana* pe·la·na
safe (vault) n *kotak deposit* ko·tak de·po·sit
safe a *aman* a·man
safe sex *seks aman* seks a·man
sail n *layar* la·yar
sailing boat *perahu layar* pe·ra·hoo la·yar
sailor *pelaut* pe·la·oot
saint *orang suci* o·rang soo·chi
salad *selada* se·la·da
salary *gaji* ga·ji
(on) sale *obral* ob·ral
sales assistant *pelayan toko* pe·la·yan to·ko
sales tax *pajak penjualan*
pa·jak pen·joo·a·lan
salmon *ikan salem* i·kan sa·lem
salt *garam* ga·ram
same *sama* sa·ma
sand n *pasir* pa·sir
sandals *sandal* san·dal
sanitary napkins *pembalut wanita*
pem·ba·loot wa·ni·ta
sarong *sarung* sa·roong
Saturday *Sabtu* sab·too
sauce n *saus* sows
saucepan *panci bergangang*
pan·chi ber·gang·ang
sausage *sosis* so·sis
say v *bilang* bi·lang
scalp n *kulit kepala* koo·lit ke·pa·la
scarf *selendang* se·len·dang
school *sekolah* se·ko·lah
science *ilmu* il·moo
scientist *ilmuwan* il·moo·wan
scissors *gunting* goon·ting

score v *membuat angka*
mem·boo·at ang·ka
Scotland *Skotlandia* skot·lan·di·a
scrambled *aduk* a·dook
sculpture *patung* pa·toong
sea *laut* la·oot
search v *mencari [cari]* men·cha·ri [cha·ri]
seasick *mabuk laut* ma·book la·oot
seaside *pinggir laut* ping·gir la·oot
season *musim* moo·sim
seat *tempat duduk* tem·pat doo·dook
seat belt *sabuk pengaman*
sa·book peng·a·man
second (unit of time) n *detik* de·tik
second (in order) a *kedua* ke·doo·a
second class n *kelas dua* ke·las doo·a
second-hand *bekas* be·kas
secretary *sekretaris* sek·re·ta·ris
see *melihat [lihat]* me·li·hat [li·hat]
self-employed *swasta* swa·sta
selfish *egois* e·go·is
self-service *pelayanan sendiri*
pe·la·ya·nan sen·di·ri
sell *menjual [jual]* men·joo·al [joo·al]
send *mengirim [kirim]* meng·i·rim [ki·rim]
sensible *bijaksana* bi·jak·sa·na
sensual *berhawa-nafsu* ber·ha·wa naf·soo
separate a *terpisah* ter·pi·sah
September *September* sep·tem·ber
serious *serius* se·ri·oos
serve n *melayani* me·la·ya·ni
service (assistance) *jasa* ja·sa
service (religious) *misa* mi·sa
service station *pompa bensin*
pom·pa ben·sin
several *beberapa* be·be·ra·pa
sew *jahit* ja·hit
sex *seks* seks
sexism *seksisme* sek·sis·me
sexy *seksi* sek·si
shade *teduh* te·dooh
shadow n *bayangan* ba·yang·an
shadow puppets *wayang kulit*
wa·yang koo·lit
shampoo *shampoo* sham·poo
shape n *bentuk* ben·took
share v *bagi* ba·gi
shave *mencukur [cukur]*
men·choo·koor [choo·koor]
shaving cream *sabun cukur*
sa·boon choo·koor
she *dia* di·a
sheep *domba* dom·ba

sheet (bed) *sepre* se·pre
sheet (paper) *lembar* lem·bar
ship n *kapal* ka·pal
shirt *kemeja* ke·me·ja
shoe(s) *toko* to·ko
shoelaces *tali sepatu* ta·li se·pa·too
shop n *toko* to·ko
shop v *belanja* be·lan·ja
shopping *belanjaan* be·lan·ja·an
shopping centre *toko serbaada* to·ko ser·ba·a·da
short (height/length) *pendek* pen·dek
shortage *kekurangan* ke·koo·rang·an
shorts (clothes) *celana pendek* che·la·na pen·dek
shoulders *bahu* ba·hoo
shout *berteriak [teriak]* ber·te·ri·ak [te·ri·ak]
show n *pertunjukan* per·toon·joo·kan
show v *menunjukan [tunjuk]* me·noon·joo·kan [toon·jook]
shower n *dus* doos
shrimp *udang* oo·dang
shrine *keramat* ke·ra·mat
shut a *tutup* too·toop
shy *malu* ma·loo
sick *sakit* sa·kit
sickness *penyakit* pe·nya·kit
side (of street) n *pinggir* ping·gir
sign n *tanda* tan·da
sign v *menandatangani* me·nan·da·tang·a·ni
signature *tanda tangan* tan·da tang·an
silk n *sutra* soo·tra
silver n *perak* pe·rak
SIM card *SIM kard* sim kard
similar *mirip* mi·rip
simple *sederhana* se·der·ha·na
since (time) *sejak* se·jak
sinkers *penenggelam* pe·neng·ge·lam
sing *menyanyi [nyanyi]* me·nya·nyi [nya·nyi]
Singapore *Singapura* sin·ga·poo·ra
singer *penyanyi* pe·nya·nyi
single (person) *bujang* boo·jang
single room *kamar untuk satu orang* ka·mar oon·took sa·too o·rang
singlet *kaos dalam* ka·os da·lam
sister (older) *kakak perempuan* ka·kak pe·rem·poo·an
sister (younger) *adik perempuan* a·dik pe·rem·poo·an
sit *duduk* doo·dook
size *ukuran* oo·koo·ran
skin *kulit* koo·lit

skirt *rok* rok
skull *tengkorak* teng·ko·rak
sky *langit* lang·it
sleep n&v *tidur* ti·door
sleeping berth *tempat tidur* tem·pat ti·door
sleeping car *kereta tidur* ke·re·ta ti·door
sleeping pills *obat tidur* o·bat ti·door
sleepy *mengantuk* meng·an·took
slice n *iris* i·ris
slide (film) *slide* slaid
slow a *pelan* pe·lan
slowly *pelan-pelan* pe·lan pe·lan
small *kecil* ke·chil
smell n&v *bau* ba·oo
smile v *senyum* se·nyoom
smoke v *merokok* me·ro·kok
snack n *snack* snek
snail *keong* ke·ong
snake *ular* oo·lar
snorkelling *snorkeling* snor·ke·ling
snow n *salju* sal·joo
soap *sabun* sa·boon
soap opera *sinetron* si·ne·tron
soccer *sepakbola* se·pak·bo·la
socialist n *sosialis* so·si·a·lis
society *masyarakat* ma·sya·ra·kat
socks *kaos kaki* ka·os ka·ki
soft-boiled *direbus setengah matang* di·re·boos se·teng·ah ma·tang
soft drink *minuman ringan* mi·noo·man ring·an
soldier *prajurit* pra·joo·rit
some *beberapa* be·be·ra·pa
someone *seseorang* se·se·o·rang
something *sesuatu* se·soo·a·too
sometimes *kadang-kadang* ka·dang ka·dang
son *anak laki-laki* a·nak la·ki la·ki
song *lagu* la·goo
soon *segera* se·ge·ra
sore a *sakit* sa·kit
sour a *asam* a·sam
south *selatan* se·la·tan
souvenir *cenderamata* chen·de·ra·ma·ta
souvenir shop *toko cenderamata* to·ko chen·de·ra·ma·ta
soy milk *susu kacang* soo·soo ka·chang
soy sauce *kecap* ke·chap
space (room) n *tempat* tem·pat
Spain *Spanyol* spa·nyol
speak (language) *berbahasa* ber·ba·ha·sa
speak (talk) *berbicara [bicara]* ber·bi·cha·ra [bi·cha·ra]

special *istimewa* i·sti·me·wa
specialist *ahli* ah·li
speed (velocity) *kecepatan* ke·che·pa·tan
speedometer *pengukur kecepatan* peng·oo·koor ke·che·pa·tan
spicy *pedas* pe·das
spider *laba-laba* la·ba la·ba
spinach *bayam* ba·yam
spoiled (food) *busuk* boo·sook
spoon *sendok* sen·dok
sport *olahraga* o·lah·ra·ga
sportsperson *olahragawan* o·lah·ra·ga·wan
sports store *toko olahraga* to·ko o·lah·ra·ga
sprain v *keseleo* ke·se·le·o
spring (season) *musim semi* moo·sim se·mi
square (plaza) *lapangan* la·pang·an
stadium *stadion* sta·di·on
stairs *tangga* tang·ga
stale *busuk* boo·sook
stamp (postage) n *perangko* pe·rang·ko
stand-by ticket *tiket stand-by* ti·ket stend bai
star n *bintang* bin·tang
starfruit *belimbing* be·lim·bing
start v *awal* a·wal
station *stasiun* sta·si·oon
stationer *toko alat tulis* to·ko a·lat too·lis
statue *patung* pa·toong
stay (overnight) v *menginap* meng·i·nap
stay (remain) v *tinggal* ting·gal
steak *bistik* bi·stik
steal *mencuri [curi]* men·choo·ri [choo·ri]
steep (hill) *curam* choo·ram
step n *langkah* lang·kah
stereo n *stereo* ste·re·o
still (yet) *masih* ma·sih
stolen *dicuri* di·choo·ri
stomach *perut* pe·root
stomachache *sakit perut* sa·kit pe·root
stone *batu* ba·too
stoned (drugged) *mabuk* ma·book
stop (bus/tram) n *halte* hal·te
stop (cease) v *berhenti* ber·hen·ti
stop (prevent) v *menghentikan* meng·hen·ti·kan
storm n *badai* ba·dai
story *cerita* che·ri·ta
stove *kompor* kom·por
straight (line) *lurus* loo·roos
straight ahead *terus* te·roos
strange *aneh* a·neh
stranger *orang tidak dikenal* o·rang ti·dak di·ke·nal

stream (creek) *kali* ka·li
street *jalan* ja·lan
(on) strike *mogok* mo·gok
string *tali* ta·li
stroke (health) *serangan jantung* se·rang·an jan·toong
stroller *kereta bayi* ke·re·ta ba·yi
strong *kuat* koo·at
student (school) *pelajar* pe·la·jar
student (uni) *mahasiswa* ma·ha·sis·wa
studio *studio* stoo·di·o
stupid *bodoh* bo·doh
style *corak mode* cho·rak mo·de
subtitles *translasi* trans·la·si
suburb *pinggir kota* ping·gir ko·ta
sugar *gula* goo·la
suitcase *kopor* ko·por
summer *musim panas* moo·sim pa·nas
sun *matahari* ma·ta·ha·ri
sunblock *krim terbakar matahari* krim ter·ba·kar ma·ta·ha·ri
sunburn *terbakar sinar matahari* ter·ba·kar si·nar ma·ta·ha·ri
Sunday *(hari) Minggu* (ha·ri) ming·goo
sunglasses *kaca mata hitam* ka·cha ma·ta hi·tam
sunny *cerah* che·rah
sunrise *matahari terbit* ma·ta·ha·ri ter·bit
sunset *matahari terbenam* ma·ta·ha·ri ter·be·nam
sunstroke *kelangar matahari* ke·lang·ar ma·ta·ha·ri
supermarket *pasar swalayan* pa·sar swa·la·yan
superstition *takhyul* takh·yool
supporter (politics) *pendukung* pen·doo·koong
supporter (sport) *penggembira* peng·gem·bi·ra
surf n *ombak* om·bak
surf v *berselancar [selancar]* ber·se·lan·char [se·lan·char]
surface mail *pos biasa* pos bi·a·sa
surfboard *papan selancar* pa·pan se·lan·char
surfing *surfing* soor·fing
surname *nama keluarga* na·ma ke·loo·ar·ga
surprise n *keheranan* ke·he·ra·nan
sweater *sweater* swe·ter
Sweden *Swedia* swe·di·a
sweet a *manis* ma·nis
sweets *manisan* ma·ni·san

swim *berenang [renang]*
be·re·nang [re·nang]
swimming (sport) *renang* re·nang
swimming pool *kolam renang*
ko·lam re·nang
swimsuit *baju renang* ba·joo re·nang
Switzerland *Swis* swis
synagogue *gereja Yahudi* ge·re·ja ya·hoo·di
synthetic *buatan* boo·a·tan
syringe *jarum suntik* ja·room soon·tik

T

table *meja* me·ja
tablecloth *kain meja* ka·in me·ja
tablet *tablet* tab·let
table tennis *tenis meja* te·nis me·ja
tail (animal) *ekor* e·kor
tailor *penjahit* pen·ja·hit
take (away) *mengambil [ambil]*
meng·am·bil [am·bil]
take (the train) *naik* na·ik
take a photo *memotret [potret]*
me·mo·tret [po·tret]
talk *bercakap [cakap]* ber·cha·kap [cha·kap]
tall *tinggi* ting·gi
tampon *tampon* tam·pon
tap *keran* ke·ran
tap water *air leding* a·ir le·ding
tasty *enak* e·nak
tax n *pajak* pa·jak
taxi *taksi* tak·si
tea *teh* teh
teach *mengajar [ajar]* meng·a·jar [a·jar]
teacher *guru* goo·roo
team n *tim* tim
teaspoon *sendok teh* sen·dok teh
technique *teknik* tek·nik
teeth *gigi* gi·gi
telegram *telegram* te·le·gram
telephone n *telpon* tel·pon
telephone v *menelpon [telpon]*
me·nel·pon [tel·pon]
telephone office *wartel* war·tel
telescope *teleskop* te·le·skop
television *televisi* te·le·vi·si
tell *memberitahu* mem·be·ri·ta·hoo
teller *kasir* ka·sir
temperature (fever) *demam* de·mam
temperature (weather) *suhu udara*
soo·hoo oo·da·ra
temple (body) *pelipis* pe·li·pis
temple (Buddhist) *candi* chan·di

temple (Chinese) *kelenteng* ke·len·teng
temple (Hindu) *pura* poo·ra
tennis *tenis* te·nis
tent *tenda* ten·da
terrible *buruk sekali* boo·rook se·ka·li
terrorism *terrorisme* te·ro·ris·me
thank *berterima kasih* ber·te·ri·ma ka·sih
that (one) *itu* i·too
theatre *gedung sandiwara*
ge·doong san·di·wa·ra
their *mereka* me·re·ka
there (distant) *di sana* di sa·na
there (nearby) *di situ* di si·too
there is/are *ada* a·da
there isn't/aren't *tidak ada* ti·dak a·da
they *mereka* me·re·ka
thick *tebal* te·bal
thief *pencuri* pen·choo·ri
thin *tipis* ti·pis
think *berpikir [pikir]* ber·pi·kir [pi·kir]
third *ketiga* ke·ti·ga
thirsty *haus* ha·oos
this (one) *ini* i·ni
thread n *benang* be·nang
throat *tenggorokan* teng·go·ro·kan
thrush (health) *guam* goo·am
thunderstorm *hujan badai guntur*
hoo·jan ba·dai goon·toor
Thursday *Kamis* ka·mis
ticket *karcis* kar·chis
ticket collector *pemungut karcis*
pe·moong·oot kar·chis
ticket office *loket* lo·ket
tide n *pasang* pa·sang
tie v *ikat* i·kat
tie-dye n *ikat* i·kat
tiger *harimau* ha·ri·mow
tight *sempit* sem·pit
time *jam* jam
time difference *perbedaan waktu*
per·be·da·an wak·too
timetable *jadwal* jad·wal
tin (can) *kaleng* ka·leng
tin opener *pembuka kaleng*
pem·boo·ka ka·leng
tiny *kecil sekali* ke·chil se·ka·li
tip (gratuity) *uang rokok* oo·ang ro·kok
tire n *ban* ban
tired *capek* cha·pek
tissues *tisu* ti·soo
to *ke* ke
toad *kodok* ko·dok
toast (bread) *roti bakar* ro·ti ba·kar

toaster *pemanggang roti* pe·mang·gang ro·ti
tobacco *tembakau* tem·ba·kow
tobacconist *penjual tembakau* pen·joo·al tem·ba·kow
today *hari ini* ha·ri i·ni
toe *jari kaki* ja·ri ka·ki
tofu *tahu* ta·hoo
together *bersama* ber·sa·ma
toilet *kamar kecil* ka·mar ke·chil
toilet paper *tisu* ti·soo
tomato *tomat* to·mat
tomorrow *besok* be·sok
tongue *lidah* li·dah
tonight *malam ini* ma·lam i·ni
too (also) *juga* joo·ga
too (excessive) *terlalu* ter·la·loo
tool *alat* a·lat
tooth *gigi* gi·gi
toothache *sakit gigi* sa·kit gi·gi
toothbrush *sikat gigi* si·kat gi·gi
toothpaste *pasta gigi* pa·sta gi·gi
toothpick *tusuk gigi* too·sook gi·gi
torch (flashlight) *senter* sen·ter
touch v *menyentuh [sentuh]* me·nyen·tooh [sen·tooh]
tour n *tour* toor
tourist *turis* too·ris
tourist office *kantor pariwisata* kan·tor pa·ri·wi·sa·ta
toward *menuju* me·noo·joo
towel *handuk* han·dook
tower *menara* me·na·ra
track (path) *jalan kecil* ja·lan ke·chil
track (sport) *olahraga lari* o·lah·ra·ga la·ri
trade v *perdagangan* per·da·gang·an
tradesperson *pedagang* pe·da·gang
trade union *serikat buruh* se·ri·kat boo·rooh
traffic *kondisi lalu-lintas* kon·di·si la·loo lin·tas
traffic jam *macet* ma·chet
traffic lights *lampu lalu-lintas* lam·poo la·loo lin·tas
trail (route) *jalan* ja·lan
train n *kereta api* ke·re·ta a·pi
train station *stasiun kereta api* sta·si·oon ke·re·ta a·pi
transit lounge *ruang transit* roo·ang tran·sit
translate *menerjemahkan [terjemahkan]* me·ner·je·mah·kan [ter·je·mah·kan]
translator *penterjemah* pen·ter·je·mah
transport n *transportasi* trans·por·ta·si
travel v *jalan-jalan* ja·lan ja·lan

travel agency *agen perjalanan* a·gen per·ja·la·nan
travel sickness *mabuk jalan* ma·book ja·lan
travellers cheque *cek perjalanan* chek per·ja·la·nan
tree *pohon* po·hon
trek n *perjalanan* per·ja·la·nan
trip (journey) *perjalanan* per·ja·la·nan
trolley *kereta* ke·re·ta
trousers *celana panjang* che·la·na pan·jang
truck *truk* trook
true *benar* be·nar
trust v *percaya* per·cha·ya
truth *kebenaran* ke·be·na·ran
try (attempt) v *mencoba [coba]* men·cho·ba [cho·ba]
T-shirt *kaos oblong* ka·os ob·long
Tuesday *Selasa* se·la·sa
tumour *tumor* too·mor
tuna *ikan cakalang* i·kan cha·ka·lang
tune (song) *lagu* la·goo
turkey *kalkun* kal·koon
turn v *belok* be·lok
TV *televisi* te·le·vi·si
tweezers *penyepit* pe·nye·pit
twice *dua kali* doo·a ka·li
twin beds *tempat tidur untuk dua orang* tem·pat ti·door oon·took doo·a o·rang
twins *kembar* kem·bar
two *dua* doo·a
type n *macam* ma·cham
typhoid *penyakit tipus* pe·nya·kit ti·poos
typical *khas* khas
tyre *ban* ban

U

ugly *jelek* je·lek
ultrasound *ultrasound* ool·tra·sa·oond
umbrella *payung* pa·yoong
uncomfortable *tidak enak* ti·dak e·nak
understand *mengerti* meng·er·ti
underwear *celana dalam* che·la·na da·lam
unemployed *pengangguran* peng·ang·goor
unfair *tidak wajar* ti·dak wa·jar
uniform n *pakaian seragam* pa·kai·an se·ra·gam
universe *semesta alam* se·me·sta a·lam
university *universitas* oo·ni·ver·si·tas
unleaded *premium* pre·mi·oom
unsafe *tidak aman* ti·dak a·man
until *sampai* sam·pai
unusual *luar biasa* loo·ar bi·a·sa

up(hill) *naik* na·ik
urgent *segera* se·ge·ra
urinary infection *infeksi jalan perkencingan* in·fek·si ja·lan per·ken·ching·an
us excl *kami* ka·mi
us incl *kita* ki·ta
USA *Amerika Serikat* a·me·ri·ka se·ri·kat
useful *berguna* ber·goo·na

V

vacancy *kosongan* ko·song·an
vacant *kosong* ko·song
vacation *liburan* li·boo·ran
vaccination *pencacaran* pen·cha·cha·ran
vagina *liang peranakan* li·ang pe·ra·na·kan
valley *lembah* lem·bah
valuable *berharga* ber·har·ga
value n *nilai* ni·lai
veal *daging anak sapi* da·ging a·nak sa·pi
vegetable *sayur-mayur* sa·yoor ma·yoor
vegetarian (food) *makanan tanpa daging* ma·ka·nan tan·pa da·ging
vegetarian (person) *pengikut aliran vegetarian* peng·i·koot a·li·ran ve·je·ta·ri·an
vein *urat darah* oo·rat da·rah
venereal disease *penyakit kelamin* pe·nya·kit ke·la·min
venue *tempat* tem·pat
very *sangat* sang·at
video camera *kamera video* ka·me·ra vi·de·o
video recorder *video recorder* vi·de·o re·kor·der
video tape *kaset video* ka·set vi·de·o
view n *pemandangan* pe·man·dang·an
village (region) *kampung* kam·poong
village (town) *desa* de·sa
vinegar *cuka* choo·ka
virus *virus* vi·roos
visa *visa* vi·sa
visit v *mengunjungi [kunjung]* meng·oon·joong·i [koon·joong]
visually impaired *gangguan penglihatan permanen* gang·goo·an peng·li·ha·tan per·ma·nen
vitamin *vitamin* vi·ta·min
vodka *vodka* vod·ka
voice *suara* soo·a·ra
volcano *gunung api* goo·noong a·pi
volleyball (sport) *bola voli* bo·la vo·li
volume (sound) *volume* vo·loo·me

vomit n&v *muntah* moon·tah
vote v *memberikan suara* mem·be·ri·kan soo·a·ra

W

wage n *gaji* ga·ji
wait v *menunggu [tunggu]* me·noong·goo [toong·goo]
waiter *pelayan* pe·la·yan
waiting room *ruang tunggu* roo·ang toong·goo
wake up *bangun* bang·oon
walk v *jalan kaki* ja·lan ka·ki
wall (inside) *dinding* din·ding
wall (outside) *tembok* tem·bok
wallet *dompet* dom·pet
want *mau* mow
war *perang* pe·rang
wardrobe *lemari* le·ma·ri
warm *hangat* hang·at
warn *memperingatkan [ingatkan]* mem·pe·ring·at·kan [ing·at·kan]
wash (something) *mencuci [cuci]* men·choo·chi [choo·chi]
wash (oneself) *mandi* man·di
wash cloth (bath) *kain cuci* ka·in choo·chi
washing machine *mesin cuci* me·sin choo·chi
wasp *tabuhan* ta·boo·han
watch n *jam tangan* jam tang·an
watch v *menonton [nonton]* me·non·ton [non·ton]
water *air* a·ir
water bottle *botol air* bo·tol a·ir
waterfall *air terjun* a·ir ter·joon
watermelon *semangka* se·mang·ka
waterproof *tahan air* ta·han a·ir
waterskiing *waterskiing* wa·ter·ski·ing
wave (beach) n *ombak* om·bak
wax (surfing) *wax* waks
way *jalan* ja·lan
we excl *kami* ka·mi
we incl *kita* ki·ta
weak *lemah* le·mah
wealthy *kaya* ka·ya
wear *memakai [pakai]* me·ma·kai [pa·kai]
weather *cuaca* choo·a·cha
weaving *tenunan* te·noo·nan
wedding *perkawinan* per·ka·wi·nan
wedding cake *kue pengantin* koo·e peng·an·tin

wedding present *hadiah pernikahan* ha·di·ah per·ni·ka·han
Wednesday *Rabu* ra·boo
week *minggu* ming·goo
weekend *akhir minggu* a·khir ming·goo
weigh *menimbang [timbang]* me·nim·bang [tim·bang]
weight *berat* be·rat
welcome v *sambutan* sam·boo·tan
welfare *kesejahteraan* ke·se·jah·te·ra·an
well adv *sehat* se·hat
west *barat* ba·rat
Westerner (colloquial) *bule* boo·le
Westerner (standard) *orang barat* o·rang ba·rat
wet *basah* ba·sah
wetsuit (surfing) *pakaian surfing* pa·kai·an soor·fing
what *apa* a·pa
wheel *roda* ro·da
wheelchair *kursi roda* koor·si ro·da
when (in answer) *waktu* wak·too
when (in question) *kapan* ka·pan
where *di mana* di ma·na
which *yang mana* yang ma·na
while *saat* sa·at
whisky *whisky* wis·ki
white *putih* poo·tih
white wine *anggur putih* ang·goor poo·tih
who *siapa* si·a·pa
whole *seluruh* se·loo·rooh
why *kenapa* ke·na·pa
wide *lebar* le·bar
wife *istri* ist·ri
win v *menang* me·nang
wind n *angin* ang·in
window *jendela* jen·de·la
windscreen *kaca depan* ka·cha de·pan
windsurfing *selancar angin* se·lan·char ang·in
wine *anggur* ang·goor
wing *sayap* sa·yap
winner *pemenang* pe·me·nang
winter *musim dingin* moo·sim ding·in
wire n *kawat* ka·wat
wish v *ingin* ing·in
with *dengan* deng·an
within (an hour) *dalam (satu jam)* da·lam (sa·too jam)

without *tanpa* tan·pa
woman *wanita* wa·ni·ta
wonderful *bagus sekali* ba·goos se·ka·li
wood *kayu* ka·yoo
wool *wol* wol
word *kata* ka·ta
work n *kerja* ker·ja
work v *bekerja [kerja]* be·ker·ja [ker·ja]
work-out n *latihan* la·ti·han
workshop *lokakarya* lo·ka·kar·ya
world *dunia* doo·ni·a
World Cup *kejuaraan dunia* ke·joo·a·ra·an doo·ni·a
(intestinal) worms *cacing* cha·ching
worried *khawatir* kha·wa·tir
worship n *ibadat* i·ba·dat
worship v *sembahyang* sem·bah·yang
wound n *luka* loo·ka
wrist *pergelangan tangan* per·ge·lang·an tang·an
write *menulis [tulis]* me·noo·lis [too·lis]
writer *penulis* pe·noo·lis
wrong a *salah* sa·lah

Y

year *tahun* ta·hoon
yellow *kuning* koo·ning
yes *ya* ya
yesterday *kemarin* ke·ma·rin
yoga *yoga* yo·ga
yogurt *yogurt* yo·goort
you sg inf *kamu* ka·moo
you sg pol *Anda* an·da
you pl inf *kalian* ka·li·an
you pl pol *Anda sekalian* an·da se·ka·li·an
young *muda* moo·da
your sg inf *kamu* ka·moo
your sg pol *Anda* an·da
your pl inf *kalian* ka·li·an
your pl pol *Anda sekalian* an·da se·ka·li·an

Z

zip/zipper *rits* rits
zodiac *bintang kelahiran* bin·tang ke·la·hi·ran
zoo *kebun binatang* ke·boon bi·na·tang
zoom lens *lensa zoom* len·sa zoom

You'll find the English words marked as adjective a, noun n, verb v, singular sg, plural pl, informal inf, polite pol, adverb adv, exclusive excl and inclusive incl where necessary. All Indonesian verbs are provided as root words – for more information, see the **phrasebuilder**. For any food items, refer to the **culinary reader**.

A

abu-abu a·boo a·boo *gray • grey*
ada a·da *there is • there are*
adalah a·da·lah *be*
adat a·dat *custom • tradition*
adik laki-laki a·dik la·ki la·ki *little brother*
agama a·ga·ma *religion*
agen berita a·gen be·ri·ta *newsagency*
agen perjalanan a·gen per·ja·la·nan *travel agency*
ahli ah·li *specialist*
— **jamu** ja·moo *herbalist*
— **kacamata** ka·cha·ma·ta *optometrist*
— **kandungan** kan·doong·an *gynaecologist*
— **kimia** ki·mi·a *chemist*
— **nujum** noo·joom *fortune teller*
— **rias rambut** ri·as ram·boot *hairdresser*
air a·ir *water*
— **dingin** ding·in *cold water*
— **leding** le·ding *tap water*
— **matang** ma·tang *boiled water*
— **panas** pa·nas *hot water*
— **penyulingan** pe·nyoo·ling·an *purified water*
— **putih** poo·tih *boiled, drinkable water*
— **terjun** ter·joon *waterfall*
ajar a·jar *teach*
akhir a·khir *end* n • *finish* n
— **minggu** ming·goo *weekend*
aki a·ki *battery (car)*
alam a·lam *nature*
alamat a·la·mat *address* n
alasan a·la·san *excuse* n • *reason* n
alat a·lat *tool*
— **bantu dengar** ban·too deng·ar *hearing aid*
— **cukur** choo·koor *razor*

— **pacu jantung** pa·choo jan·toong *pacemaker*
— **pembuka botol** pem·boo·ka bo·tol *bottle opener*
— **pembuka kaleng** pem·boo·ka ka·leng *can opener*
— **selam** se·lam *diving equipment*
alat-alat makan a·lat a·lat ma·kan *cutlery*
alkitab al·ki·tab *Bible*
aman a·man *safe* a
ambil am·bil *take* v
anak a·nak *child*
— **laki-laki** la·ki la·ki *boy • son*
— **perempuan** pe·rem·poo·an *daughter • girl (preteen)*
anak-anak a·nak a·nak *children*
Anda an·da *you* sg pol • *your* sg pol
— **sekalian** se·ka·li·an *you* pl pol • *your* pl pol
aneh a·neh *strange*
anggaran ang·ga·ran *budget* n
anggota ang·go·ta *member*
anggur ang·goor *grape • wine*
angin ang·in *wind* n
angkot ang·kot *minibus*
anjing an·jing *dog*
— **penuntun** pe·noon·toon *guide dog*
antar an·tar *deliver*
antara an·ta·ra *between*
anting-anting an·ting an·ting *earrings*
antri an·tri *queue* n
apa a·pa *what*
— **saja** sa·ja *any • anything*
api a·pi *fire*
arus a·roos *current (electricity)*
asal a·sal *come from* v • *origin* n
asbak as·bak *ashtray*
asing a·sing *foreign*
asli as·li *indigenous • original*
atap a·tap *roof*
atasan a·ta·san *employer*

atau a·tow *or*
atur a·toor *arrange • organise*
awal a·wal *start* n
awan a·wan *cloud* n
ayah a·yah *father*

B

babi ba·bi *pig*
baca ba·cha *read* v
bacaan ba·cha·an *reading*
badai ba·dai *storm* n
badan ba·dan *body*
bagaimana ba·gai·ma·na *how*
bagasi yang diijinkan ba·ga·si yang
　di·i·jin·kan *baggage allowance*
bagi ba·gi *share* v • *deal (cards)* v
bagian ba·gi·an *part* n
bagus ba·goos *good*
　— sekali se·ka·li *great • wonderful*
bahan ba·han *ingredient • material*
　— kecantikan ke·chan·ti·kan *cosmetics*
bahasa ba·ha·sa *language*
Bahasa Indonesia ba·ha·sa in·do·ne·si·a
　Indonesian (language)
bahu ba·hoo *shoulders*
baik ba·ik *fine* a • *good • nice*
　— hati ha·ti *kind* a
baju pelampung ba·joo pe·lam·poong
　life jacket
baju renang ba·joo re·nang
　bathing suit • swimsuit
baju rok ba·joo rok *dress* n
bakar ba·kar *burn* n
balap sepeda ba·lap se·pe·da *racing bike*
balsem bibir bal·sem bi·bir *lip balm*
ban ban *tire* n • *tyre*
　— dalam da·lam *inner tube*
bandara ban·da·ra *airport*
bangun bang·oon *build* v • *wake up* v
banjir ban·jir *flood* n
bantah ban·tah *argue*
bantal ban·tal *pillow*
bantu ban·too *assist • help* v
bantuan ban·too·an *aid* n • *help* n
banyak ba·nyak *a lot • many • much*
Bapak ba·pak *Mr*
bapak ba·pak *dad • father*
　— mertua mer·too·a *father-in-law*
barang ba·rang *goods (possessions)*
　— simpanan sim·pa·nan *left luggage*
barang-barang kulit ba·rang ba·rang
　koo·lit *leathergoods*

barat ba·rat *west*
baring ba·ring *lie (not stand)* v
baru ba·roo *new • just (recently)*
baru-baru ba·roo ba·roo *recently*
basah ba·sah *wet* a
batal ba·tal *cancel*
batas kecepatan ba·tas ke·che·pa·tan
　speed limit
batu ba·too *rock* n • *stone* n
batuk ba·took *cough* n&v
bau ba·oo *smell* n&v
bawa ba·wa *bring*
bayangan ba·yang·an *shadow* n
bayar ba·yar *pay* v
bayaran ba·ya·ran *payment*
bayi ba·yi *baby*
bea dan cukai be·a dan choo·kai
　customs (immigration)
bebas be·bas *available • free*
bebek be·bek *duck*
beberapa be·be·ra·pa *several • some*
becak be·chak *rickshaw*
bedak bayi be·dak ba·yi *baby powder*
beguk be·gook *mumps*
beha be·ha *bra*
bekas be·kas *second-hand*
beku be·koo *freeze* v
belajar be·la·jar *learn* v
belakang be·la·kang *rear (location)* a
Belanda be·lan·da *Netherlands*
belanja be·lan·ja *go shopping*
belanjaan be·lan·ja·an *shopping*
beli be·li *buy* v
belok be·lok *turn* v
belum be·loom *not yet*
bemo be·mo *minibus*
benang be·nang *thread* n
benar be·nar *correct • right • true*
bendera ben·de·ra *flag*
bengkak beng·kak *swelling*
bengkel beng·kel *garage*
bensin ben·sin *gas • petrol*
benteng ben·teng *castle • fort*
bentuk ben·took *shape* n
beracun be·ra·choon *poisonous*
beragama be·ra·ga·ma *religious*
berangkat be·rang·kat *depart*
berani be·ra·ni *brave* a
berapa be·ra·pa *how much • how many*
berat be·rat *heavy • weight*
berawan be·ra·wan *cloudy*
berbahasa ber·ba·ha·sa *speak (language)*
berbahaya ber·ba·ha·ya *dangerous*

berbeda ber·be·da *different*
bercerai ber·che·rai *divorced*
berdekatan ber·de·ka·tan *close* a • *nearby*
berguna ber·goo·na *useful*
berharga ber·har·ga *valuable*
berhawa-nafsu ber·ha·wa naf·soo *sensual*
berhenti ber·hen·ti *quit • stop (cease)* v
berhutang ber·hoo·tang *owe* v
beri be·ri *give • pass (kick/throw)* v
berita be·ri·ta *news*
— **hangat** hang·at *current affairs*
berjemur ber·je·moor *dry (oneself)* v
berkabut ber·ka·boot *foggy*
berluka ber·loo·ka *injured*
bermalam ber·ma·lam *stay (overnight)* v
berpacaran ber·pa·cha·ran *date (person)* v
bersalah ber·sa·lah *guilty*
bersama ber·sa·ma *together*
bersejarah ber·se·ja·rah *historical*
bersenang-senang ber·se·nang se·nang *have fun*
bersepeda ber·se·pe·da *cycling*
bersih ber·sih *clean* a • *pure*
bertemu ber·te·moo *meet (first time)* v
berterima kasih ber·te·ri·ma ka·sih *be grateful • thank*
bertunangan ber·too·nang·an *engaged (to marry)*
beruntung be·roon·toong *lucky*
besar be·sar *big • large*
besok be·sok *tomorrow*
betina be·ti·na *female (animal)* n&a
biara bi·a·ra *convent • monastery*
biarawan bi·a·ra·wan *monk*
biarawati bi·a·ra·wa·ti *nun*
biasa bi·a·sa *ordinary*
biaya bi·a·ya *cost (service)* n
bibi bi·bi *aunt*
bibir bi·bir *lips*
bicara bi·cha·ra *speak*
bijaksana bi·jak·sa·na *sensible*
bilang bi·lang *say* v
binatang bi·na·tang *animal*
binatu bi·na·too *laundry (place)*
bintang bin·tang *star* n
— **kelahiran** ke·la·hi·ran *zodiac*
bioskop bi·os·kop *cinema*
bis bis *bus • coach*
— **antar kota** an·tar ko·ta *intercity bus*
bisa bi·sa *can (be able)*
— **daur ulang** da·oor oo·lang *recyclable*
bisu bi·soo *mute*
blitz blits *flash (camera)*

bodoh bo·doh *idiot • stupid*
bohong bo·hong *lie (not tell the truth)* v
bola lampu bo·la lam·poo *light bulb*
boleh bo·leh *can (have permission)*
boneka bo·ne·ka *doll*
bosan bo·san *bored*
buah boo·ah *fruit*
buat boo·at *for • make* v
buatan boo·a·tan *made • synthetic*
— **tangan** tang·an *handmade*
bujang boo·jang *single (person)*
buka boo·ka *open* a&v
bukan boo·kan *not (with nouns)*
bukit boo·kit *hill*
buku boo·koo *book* n
— **harian** ha·ri·an *diary*
— **panduan perjalanan** pan·doo·an per·ja·la·nan *guidebook*
bulan boo·lan *month • moon*
— **madu** ma·doo *honeymoon*
— **puasa Masehi** poo·a·sa ma·se·hi *Lent*
bule boo·le *Westerner (colloquial)*
bumi boo·mi *Earth*
bunga boong·a *flower*
bungkus boong·koos *packet (general)*
bunuh boo·nooh *kill* v • *murder* v
bunyi boo·nyi *ring (phone)* v
buruk boo·rook *bad (weather)*
burung boo·roong *bird • penis (colloquial)*
busuk boo·sook *off • spoiled • stale*
buta boo·ta *blind* a

C

cacad cha·chad *faulty*
cacat cha·chat *disabled*
— **kaki** ka·ki *paraplegic*
cacing cha·ching *worms*
cahaya cha·ha·ya *light (natural)* n
cairan cha·i·ran *lotion*
cakap cha·kap *talk* v
campak cham·pak *measles*
campur cham·poor *mix* v
canda chan·da *joke*
candi chan·di *temple (Buddhist)*
cangkir chang·kir *cup*
cantik chan·tik *beautiful • pretty*
capek cha·pek *tired*
cari cha·ri *look for • search* v
— **hiburan** hi·boo·ran *go out*
catat cha·tat *record* v
catur cha·toor *chess*

cek perjalanan chek per·ja·la·nan
  travellers cheque
celana che·la·na *pants (trousers)*
  — dalam da·lam *underwear*
  — panjang pan·jang *trousers*
  — pendek pen·dek *shorts*
cenderamata chen·de·ra·ma·ta *souvenir*
cepat che·pat *fast* adv • *quick* adv
cerah che·rah *sunny*
cerai che·rai *divorce* n
cerita che·ri·ta *story* • *talk* n&v
cermin cher·min *mirror*
cetakan che·ta·kan *print* n
cewek che·wek *girl (teenage & older)*
cincin chin·chin *ring (jewellery)*
cinta chin·ta *love* n&v
cium chi·oom *kiss* v
ciuman chi·oo·man *kiss* n
coba cho·ba *try (attempt)* v
coklat chok·lat *brown* • *chocolate* • *cocoa*
contoh chon·toh *example*
copet cho·pet *pickpocket*
cuaca choo·a·cha *weather*
cuci choo·chi *develop film* • *wash* v
cucian choo·chi·an *laundry (clothes)*
cucu choo·choo *grandchild*
cukup choo·koop *enough*
cukur choo·koor *shave* v
curam choo·ram *steep (hill)*
curi choo·ri *steal* v

D

dada da·da *breast* • *chest*
dadu da·doo *dice*
daerah da·e·rah *region* • *regional*
  — luar kota loo·ar ko·ta *countryside*
daftar makanan daf·tar ma·ka·nan *menu*
daging da·ging *meat*
dalam da·lam *deep* • *in* • *within*
damai da·mai *peace*
dan dan *and*
danau da·now *lake*
dandanan dan·da·nan *make-up* n
dapat da·pat *find* v • *get*
dapur da·poor *kitchen*
darah da·rah *blood*
dari da·ri *from*
darurat da·roo·rat *emergency*
datang da·tang *arrive* • *come*
datar da·tar *flat* a
dataran tinggi da·ta·ran ting·gi *plateau*
daun da·oon *leaf* n

dekat de·kat *near* adv
demam de·mam *fever* • *temperature*
  — kelenjar ke·len·jar *glandular fever*
denda den·da *fine* n
dengan deng·an *with*
dengar deng·ar *hear* • *listen to*
depan de·pan *front* • *next (time)*
derajat de·ra·jat *degrees (temperature)*
desa de·sa *village*
detik de·tik *second (unit of time)* n
dewa de·wa *god (general)*
dewasa de·wa·sa *adult* n&a
di di *at* • *on*
  — atas a·tas *aboard* • *above* • *on top of*
  — bawah ba·wah *at the bottom* • *below*
  — belakang be·la·kang
  at the back • *behind*
  — dalam da·lam *indoor* • *inside*
  — depan de·pan *ahead* • *in front of*
  — mana ma·na *where*
  — mana saja ma·na sa·ja *anywhere*
  — samping sam·ping *beside* • *next to*
  — sana sa·na *there (distant)*
  — sini si·ni *here*
  — situ si·too *there (nearby)*
dia di·a *he* • *him* • *his* • *she* • *her* • *hers*
dial langsung di·al lang·soong *direct-dial*
dibuat (dari) di·boo·at (da·ri) *made (of)*
dicuri di·choo·ri *stolen*
dijamin di·ja·min *guaranteed*
dikunci di·koon·chi *locked*
dilarang merokok di·la·rang me·ro·kok
  nonsmoking
dinding din·ding *wall (inside)*
dingin ding·in *cold* n&a
dipesan penuh di·pe·san pe·nooh
  booked out
doa do·a *prayer*
dokter gigi dok·ter gi·gi *dentist*
domba dom·ba *sheep*
dompet dom·pet *purse* • *wallet*
dorong do·rong *push* v
dosen do·sen *lecturer*
dot dot *dummy* • *pacifier*
drama dra·ma *play (theatre)* n
dua doo·a *two*
  — kali ka·li *twice*
  — minggu ming·goo *fortnight*
dua-duanya doo·a doo·a·nya *both*
duduk doo·dook *sit*
dunia doo·ni·a *world*
dus doos *shower* n
duta besar doo·ta be·sar *ambassador*

E

ekor e·kor *tail (animal)*
emas e·mas *gold* n
ember em·ber *bucket*
enak e·nak *delicious • nice • tasty*

F

fam fam *family name*

G

gading ga·ding *ivory* n
gaji ga·ji *salary • wage* n
gambar gam·bar *picture*
gampang gam·pang *easy*
— **pecah** pe·chah *fragile*
gang gang *aisle • alley*
gangguan gang·goo·an *harassment*
ganteng gan·teng *handsome*
garam ga·ram *salt*
garpu gar·poo *fork*
gatal ga·tal *itch* n
gedung ge·doong *building*
— **sandiwara** san·di·wa·ra *theatre*
gegar ge·gar *concussion*
gelap ge·lap *dark (night)* a
gembok gantung gem·bok gan·toong
padlock
gempa bumi gem·pa boo·mi *earthquake*
gemuk ge·mook *fat* a
gerbong ger·bong *van*
gereja ge·re·ja *church*
geretan ge·re·tan *cigarette lighter*
gigi gi·gi *tooth • teeth*
gigit gi·git *bite* v
gigitan gi·gi·tan *bite (dog/insect)* n
gila gi·la *crazy • delirious*
gincu gin·choo *lipstick*
ginjal gin·jal *kidney*
golongan darah go·long·an da·rah
blood group
gonceng gon·cheng *hitchhike* v
gua goo·a *cave* n
guam goo·am *thrush (health)*
guci goo·chi *pot (ceramics)*
gula goo·la *sugar*
gunting goon·ting *scissors*
gunung goo·noong *mountain*
— **api** a·pi *volcano*
gurih goo·rih *rich (food)*

H

hadiah ha·di·ah *gift • present*
hak asasi manusia hak a·sa·si ma·noo·si·a
human rights
hakim ha·kim *judge (court)* n
halaman ha·la·man *page (book)*
halte hal·te *stop (bus, tram)* n
HAM ham *human rights*
hama ha·ma *bug* n
hamil ha·mil *pregnant*
hampir ham·pir *almost*
handuk han·dook *towel*
hangat hang·at *warm*
hanya ha·nya *only*
harga har·ga *cost* n • *price* n
hari ha·ri *day*
— **ini** i·ni *today*
— **raya** ra·ya *holiday*
— **ulang tahun** oo·lang ta·hoon
birthday
harian ha·ri·an *daily*
harimau ha·ri·mow *tiger*
Hari Natal ha·ri na·tal *Christmas Day*
Hari Tahun Baru ha·ri ta·hoon ba·roo
New Year's Day
hati ha·ti *liver*
haus ha·oos *thirsty*
hidung hi·doong *nose*
hidup hi·doop *alive • life • live* v • *on (power)*
hijau hi·jow *green*
hitam hi·tam *black*
hitam-putih hi·tam poo·tih *B&W (film)*
hitung hi·toong *count* v
HP ha·pe *mobile phone*
hubungan hoo·boong·an
connection • relationship
hujan hoo·jan *rain* n
— **badai guntur** ba·dai goon·toor
thunderstorm
hukum hoo·koom *law (profession/rule)* n
hutan hoo·tan *forest*
— **lindung** lin·doong *protected forest*

I

ibadat i·ba·dat *worship* n
Ibu i·boo *Mrs • Ms*
ibu i·boo *mother • mum*
— **mertua** mer·too·a *mother-in-law*
— **rumah tangga** roo·mah tang·ga
homemaker

ijin i·jin *licence* n • *permission* • *permit* n
ikan i·kan *fish* n
ikat i·kat *tie* v • *tie-dye* n
iklan ik·lan *advertisement*
ikut i·koot *accompany* • *follow*
ilmu il·moo *science*
 — **sastera** sa·ste·ra *humanities*
ilmuwan il·moo·wan *scientist*
indah in·dah *beautiful*
induk telur in·dook te·loor *ovary*
infeksi jalan perkencingan
 in·fek·si ja·lan per·ken·ching·an
 urinary infection
ingat ing·at *remember*
ingatkan ing·at·kan *warn*
ingin ing·in *wish* v
ini i·ni *it* • *this (one)*
irama i·ra·ma *rhythm*
iri hati i·ri ha·ti *jealous*
iris i·ris *cut* v • *slice* n
isi i·si *fill* v
istana i·sta·na *palace*
istimewa i·sti·me·wa *special*
istirahat i·sti·ra·hat *intermission* • *rest* n&v
istri i·stri *wife*
itu i·too *it* • *that (one)*

J

jadwal jad·wal *timetable*
jago ja·go *great (fantastic)*
jagung ja·goong *corn*
jahit ja·hit *sew*
jala ja·la *net*
jalan ja·lan *go* v • *road* • *street* • *trail* n • *way*
 — **gunung** goo·noong *mountain path*
 — **kaki** ka·ki *walk* v
 — **kecil** ke·chil *path* • *track*
 — **kereta api** ke·re·ta a·pi *railroad*
 — **raya** ra·ya *highway* • *main road*
 — **setapak** se·ta·pak *footpath*
jalan-jalan ja·lan ja·lan *travel* v
jam jam *clock* • *hour* • *time* n
 — **buka** boo·ka *opening hours*
 — **tangan** tang·an *watch* n
jamu ja·moo *herbal medicine* • *herbs*
janji jan·ji *appointment* • *date* n • *promise* v
jantan jan·tan *male (animal)* n&a
jantung jan·toong *heart*
jarak ja·rak *distance* n
jarang ja·rang *rare (uncommon)*
jari ja·ri *finger*
 — **kaki** ka·ki *toe*

jaringan ja·ring·an *network*
jarum ja·room *needle (sewing/syringe)*
 — **suntik** soon·tik *injection* • *syringe*
jas jas *coat* n
 — **hujan** hoo·jan *raincoat*
jasa ja·sa *service (assistance)*
jatuh ja·tooh *fall (down)*
jauh ja·ooh *far*
jawab ja·wab *answer* v
jawaban ja·wa·ban *answer* n
jelek je·lek *bad* • *ugly*
jembatan jem·ba·tan *bridge (structure)* n
jemur je·moor *dry (clothes)* v
jendela jen·de·la *window*
jenewer je·ne·wer *gin*
jingga jing·ga *orange (colour)*
jual joo·al *sell* v
juga joo·ga *also* • *too*
jujur joo·joor *honest*
Jumat joo·mat *Friday*
jumpa joom·pa *meet (get together)* v
juru bahasa joo·roo ba·ha·sa *interpreter*
jururawat joo·roo·ra·wat *nurse* n
jurusan joo·roo·san *direction*
juta joo·ta *million*

K

kabut tipis ka·boot ti·pis *gauze*
kaca ka·cha *glass (material)*
 — **depan** de·pan *windscreen*
 — **mata** ma·ta *glasses* • *spectacles*
 — **mata hitam** ma·ta hi·tam *sunglasses*
 — **mata renang** ma·ta re·nang
 swimming goggles
kacoa ka·cho·a *cockroach*
kadang-kadang ka·dang ka·dang
 sometimes
kain ka·in *cloth* • *fabric*
 — **cuci** choo·chi *flannel* • *wash cloth*
 — **tempat tidur** tem·pat ti·door *bedding*
kakak laki-laki ka·kak la·ki la·ki
 big brother
kakak perempuan ka·kak pe·rem·poo·an
 big sister
kakek ka·kek *grandfather*
kaki ka·ki *foot* • *leg*
kalau ka·low *if*
kaleng ka·leng *can* • *tin*
kali ka·li *stream*
kalian ka·li·an *you* pl inf • *your* pl inf
kalkun kal·koon *turkey*
kalung ka·loong *necklace*

kamar ka·mar *room*
— **ganti pakaian** gan·ti pa·kai·an *changing rooms*
— **kecil** ke·chil *toilet*
— **mandi** man·di *bathroom*
— **tidur** ti·door *bedroom*
— **untuk dua orang** oon·took doo·a o·rang *double room*
— **untuk satu orang** oon·took sa·too o·rang *single room*
kambing kam·bing *goat*
kami ka·mi *we* excl • *our* excl • *us* excl
Kamis ka·mis *Thursday*
kampung kam·poong *village area*
kamu ka·moo *you* sg inf • *your* sg inf
kamus ka·moos *dictionary*
kanan ka·nan *right (direction)*
kancing kan·ching *buttons*
kandung kemih kan·doong ke·mih *bladder*
kantor kan·tor *office*
— **kehilangan barang** ke·hi·lang·an ba·rang *lost property office*
— **pariwisata** pa·ri·wi·sa·ta *tourist office*
— **penitipan barang** pe·ni·ti·pan ba·rang *left-luggage office*
kantung ka·toong *pocket*
kaos dalam ka·os da·lam *singlet*
kaos kaki ka·os ka·ki *socks*
kaos oblong ka·os ob·long *T-shirt*
kapal ka·pal *boat* • *ship*
— **feri** fe·ri *ferry* n
— **penyelam** pe·nye·lam *diving boat*
kapan ka·pan *when (question)*
— **saja** sa·ja *anytime*
kapas kesehatan ka·pas ke·se·ha·tan *cotton balls*
kapas pembersih telinga ka·pas pem·ber·sih te·ling·a *cotton buds*
karcis kar·chis *ticket*
karena ka·re·na *because*
Kartu Tanda Penduduk kar·too tan·da pen·doo·dook *identification card*
karya seni kar·ya se·ni *artwork*
karyawan kar·ya·wan *employee* • *labourer*
— **pabrik** pab·rik *factory worker*
kasih ka·sih *give* v
kasur ka·soor *mattress*
kata ka·ta *word*
kawat ka·wat *wire* n
kawin ka·win *married* • *marry*
kaya ka·ya *rich* • *wealthy*

kayu ka·yoo *wood*
— **bakar** ba·kar *firewood*
ke ke *to*
keadilan ke·a·di·lan *justice*
keahlian teknik ke·ah·li·an tek·nik *engineering*
kebangsaan ke·bang·sa·an *nationality*
kebenaran ke·be·na·ran *truth*
keberangkatan ke·be·rang·ka·tan *departure*
kebiasaan ke·bi·a·sa·an *habit*
kebun ke·boon *farm* n • *garden* n
— **binatang** bi·na·tang *zoo*
— **raya** ra·ya *botanic garden*
kecanduan ke·chan·doo·an *addiction*
kecelekaan ke·che·le·ka·an *accident*
kecepatan ke·che·pa·tan *speed (velocity)*
kecil ke·chil *little* • *small*
kedatangan ke·da·tang·an *arrival*
kedokteran ke·dok·te·ran *medicine (profession/study)*
kedua ke·doo·a *second (in order)* a
keduanya ke·doo·a·nya *both*
kedudukan perkawinan ke·doo·doo·kan per·ka·wi·nan *marital status*
kedutaan ke·doo·ta·an *embassy*
keguguran ke·goo·goo·ran *miscarriage*
keheranan ke·he·ra·nan *surprise* n
kehilangan ke·hi·lang·an *loss* • *lost (object)*
keju ke·joo *cheese*
kejuaraan ke·joo·a·ra·an *championships*
— **dunia** doo·ni·a *World Cup*
kekasih ke·ka·sih *lover*
kekurangan ke·koo·rang·an *shortage*
kelambu ke·lam·boo *mosquito net*
kelangar matahari ke·lang·ar ma·ta·ha·ri *sunstroke*
kelebihan ke·le·bi·han *excess (baggage)*
kelenteng ke·len·teng *temple (Chinese)*
kelompok ke·lom·pok *band* • *group* n
keluarga ke·loo·ar·ga *family*
keluh ke·looh *complain*
keluhan ke·loo·han *complaint*
kemah ke·mah *camp* v
kemarin ke·ma·rin *yesterday*
kematian ke·ma·ti·an *death*
kembali kem·ba·li *back (position)*
kembar kem·bar *twins*
kemeja ke·me·ja *shirt*
kemiskinan ke·mis·ki·nan *poverty*
kenal ke·nal *know (someone)*
kenapa ke·na·pa *why*

kencing manis ken·ching ma·nis *diabetes*
kendi ken·di *jar*
kenyang ke·nyang *full (of food)*
keong ke·ong *snail*
kepala ke·pa·la *head*
kepanasan ke·pa·na·san *heat* n
kepurbakalaan ke·poor·ba·ka·la·an *archaeological*
kerajinan ke·ra·ji·na·an *crafts*
— **tangan** tang·an *handicrafts*
keramahtamahan ke·ra·mah·ta·ma·han *hospitality*
keramat ke·ra·mat *shrine*
keran ke·ran *faucet • tap*
keranjang ke·ran·jang *basket*
keras ke·ras *hard • loud*
— **kepala** ke·pa·la *stubborn*
kereta ke·re·ta *trolley*
— **api** a·pi *train* n
— **tidur** ti·door *sleeping car*
kering ke·ring *dried • dry* a
kerja ker·ja *work* n&v
kertas ker·tas *paper*
kesehatan ke·se·ha·tan *health*
kesejahteraan ke·se·jah·te·ra·an *welfare*
keseleo ke·se·le·o *sprain* v
kesempatan ke·sem·pa·tan *chance* n
— **yang sama** yang sa·ma *equal opportunity*
ketentuan ke·ten·too·an *provisions*
keterangan ke·te·rang·an *information*
ketidaksamaan ke·ti·dak·sa·ma·an *inequality*
ketiga ke·ti·ga *third*
ketinggian ke·ting·gi·an *altitude*
keturunan ke·too·roo·nan *descendent*
keuntungan ke·oon·toong·an *profit* n
kewarganegaraan ke·war·ga·ne·ga·ra·an *citizenship*
khas khas *typical*
khawatir kha·wa·tir *worried*
khayalan kha·ya·lan *hallucination*
kios koran ki·os ko·ran *newsstand*
kipas angin ki·pas ang·in *fan (machine)*
kipas tangan ki·pas tang·an *fan (handheld)*
kiri ki·ri *left (direction)*
kirim ki·rim *mail* v • *post* v • *send*
kiriman ki·ri·man *mail* n
kista induk telur ki·sta in·dook te·loor *ovarian cyst*
kita ki·ta *our* incl • *we* incl • *us* incl
kodok ko·dok *frog • toad*
koki ko·ki *chef*

kolam renang ko·lam re·nang *pool*
kompor kom·por *oven • stove*
kondisi lalu-lintas kon·di·si la·loo lin·tas *traffic*
kontan kon·tan *cash* n
— **kecil** ke·chil *change (coins)* n
— **kertas** ker·tas *banknote • bill (note)*
— **logam** lo·gam *coins*
— **rokok** ro·kok *tip (gratuity)*
kopeling ko·pe·ling *clutch (car)*
kopor ko·por *suitcase*
koran ko·ran *newspaper*
korek api ko·rek a·pi *matches (lighting)*
kosong ko·song *empty* a • *vacant*
kosongan ko·song·an *vacancy*
kota ko·ta *city*
kotak ko·tak *box* n
— **pertolongan pertama** per·to·long·an per·ta·ma *first-aid kit*
kotor ko·tor *dirty* a
kotrek ko·trek *corkscrew*
kretek kre·tek *clove cigarettes*
krim terbakar matahari krim ter·ba·kar ma·ta·ha·ri *sunblock*
KTP ka·te·pe *identification card*
kuasa koo·a·sa *power*
kuat koo·at *strong*
kuburan koo·boo·ran *cemetery • grave*
kucing koo·ching *cat*
kuda koo·da *horse*
kuitansi koo·i·tan·si *bill • check* n • *receipt*
kuliah koo·li·ah *attend a lecture • lecture* v • *study* v
kulit koo·lit *leather* n • *skin* n
— **kepala** ke·pa·la *scalp* n
kulkas kool·kas *refrigerator*
kunci koon·chi *key • lock* n
kuning koo·ning *yellow*
kunjung koon·joong *visit* v
kuno koo·no *ancient*
kupu-kupu koo·poo koo·poo *butterfly*
kurang koo·rang *less*
kurs koors *exchange rate*
kursi koor·si *chair* n
— **roda** ro·da *wheelchair*
kutu koo·too *flea • lice*

laba-laba la·ba·la·ba *spider*
ladang la·dang *field*
lagi la·gi *again*
lagu la·goo *song • tune*

lain la·in *other*
laki-laki la·ki la·ki *male (person)* n&a
lakukan la·koo·kan *do* v
lalat la·lat *fly* n
lama la·ma *long (time)* • *old (thing)*
lampu lam·poo *light (electric)* n
— **besar** be·sar *headlights*
— **lalu-lintas** la·loo lin·tas *traffic lights*
lancar lan·char *fluent*
langganan lang·ga·nan *client*
langit lang·it *sky*
langkah lang·kah *step* n
langsung lang·soong *direct* a
lantai lan·tai *floor* n
lapangan la·pang·an *field* • *main square*
lapar la·par *hungry*
lari la·ri *run* v • *running*
larutan untuk lensa kontak
la·roo·tan oon·took len·sa kon·tak
contact lens solution
latihan la·ti·han *training* • *work-out* n
laut la·oot *sea*
lawan la·wan *oppose* • *opposite*
layar la·yar *sail* n
lebar le·bar *wide*
lebih le·bih *more*
— **suka** soo·ka *prefer*
leher le·her *neck* n
lekas le·kas *early* • *fast* adv
lelucon le·loo·chon *joke* n
lem lem *glue* n
lemah le·mah *weak*
lemari le·ma·ri *cupboard* • *wardrobe*
lembab lem·bab *humid*
lembah lem·bah *valley*
lembar lem·bar *sheet (paper)*
lengan leng·an *arm (body)*
lengkap leng·kap *complete* a • *finished*
lepuh le·pooh *blister*
lewat le·wat *pass (go by)* v • *through*
liang peranakan li·ang pe·ra·na·kan
vagina
liburan li·boo·ran *holidays* • *vacation*
lidah li·dah *tongue*
lihat li·hat *look* v • *see*
lilin li·lin *candle*
lindung lin·doong *protect*
lingkungan ling·koong·an *environment*
listrik li·strik *electricity*
logam lo·gam *metal* n
lokakarya lo·ka·kar·ya *workshop*
loket lo·ket *ticket office*
longgar long·gar *loose*

losmen los·men *guesthouse*
luar loo·ar *outside*
— **biasa** bi·a·sa *extremely* • *unusual*
— **negeri** ne·ge·ri *abroad* • *overseas*
lucu loo·choo *cute* • *funny*
luka loo·ka *cut* n • *injury* • *wound* n
— **memar** me·mar *bruise* n
lukisan loo·ki·san *painting (picture)*
lumpur loom·poor *mud*
lupa loo·pa *forget*
lurus loo·roos *straight (line)*
lusa loo·sa *day after tomorrow*
lusin loo·sin *dozen*
lutut loo·toot *knee*
luwes loo·wes *charming*

M

mabuk ma·book *drunk* • *nauseous* •
stoned (drugged)
— **jalan** ja·lan *travel sickness*
— **laut** la·oot *seasick*
macam ma·cham *type (sort)*
macet ma·chet *traffic jam*
mahal ma·hal *expensive*
mahasiswa ma·ha·sis·wa *student (uni)*
main ma·in *play* v • *have sex (colloquial)*
majalah ma·ja·lah *magazine*
makan ma·kan *eat* v
— **malam** ma·lam *dinner*
— **siang** si·ang *lunch*
makanan ma·ka·nan *food* • *meal*
— **tanpa daging** tan·pa da·ging
vegetarian food
malam ma·lam *evening* • *night*
— **ini** i·ni *tonight*
Malam Natal ma·lam na·tal *Christmas Eve*
Malam Tahun Baru ma·lam ta·hoon ba·roo
New Year's Eve
malas ma·las *lazy*
malu ma·loo *embarrassed* • *shy*
mandi man·di *bath* n • *wash oneself*
mangkuk mang·kook *bowl* n
manis ma·nis *sweet* a
marah ma·rah *angry*
masa depan ma·sa de·pan *future* n
masak ma·sak *cook* v
masakan ma·sa·kan *cooking* • *cuisine*
masalah ma·sa·lah *problem*
masa lalu ma·sa la·loo *past* n
masih ma·sih *still (yet)*
maskapai penerbangan ma·ska·pai
pe·ner·bang·an *airline*

masuk ma·sook *admission (price)* • *enter*
masyarakat ma·sa·ra·kat *society*
mata ma·ta *eye*
matahari ma·ta·ha·ri *sun*
— **terbenam** ter·be·nam *sunset*
— **terbit** ter·bit *sunrise*
matang ma·tang *ripe*
mati ma·ti *dead* • *off (power)*
mau mow *want*
mebel me·bel *furniture*
meja me·ja *table*
melayani me·la·ya·ni *serve* n
memaafkan me·ma·af·kan *forgive*
memberikan suara mem·be·ri·kan soo·a·ra *vote* v
memberi makanan mem·be·ri ma·ka·nan *feed* v
memberitahu mem·be·ri·ta·hoo *tell*
membersihkan mem·ber·sih·kan *clean* v
membosankan mem·bo·san·kan *boring*
membuat angka mem·boo·at ang·ka *score* v
memperbaiki mem·per·ba·i·ki *repair* v
memperkosa mem·per·ko·sa *rape* v
memutus me·moo·toos *decide*
menandatangani me·nan·da·tan·ga·ni *sign* v
menang me·nang *win* v
menara me·na·ra *tower*
menarik me·na·rik *interesting*
mencret mench·ret *diarrhoea*
mendaki men·da·ki *climb* v • *hike* v
— **gunung** goo·noong *mountaineering*
mendakian men·da·ki·an *climb* n • *hike* n • *hiking*
mendapat men·da·pat *earn*
mendaur ulang men·da·oor oo·lang *recycle*
menelpon dibayar oleh si penerima me·nel·pon di·ba·yar o·leh si pe·ne·ri·ma *collect call*
mengantuk meng·an·took *sleepy*
mengapa meng·a·pa *why*
mengenal meng·e·nal *recognise*
mengerikan meng·e·ri·kan *awful*
mengerti meng·er·ti *understand*
menghentikan meng·hen·ti·kan *stop (prevent)*
menghilangkan meng·hi·lang·kan *lose*
menginap meng·i·nap *stay (overnight)* v
mengunci meng·oon·chi *lock* v
menikah me·ni·kah *marry*
menikmati me·nik·ma·ti *enjoy (oneself)*
meninggal me·ning·gal *die* v

mentah men·tah *raw (food)*
menuju me·noo·joo *toward*
menyakitkan me·nya·kit·kan *hurt* a • *painful*
menyenangkan me·nye·nang·kan *comfortable* • *please* v
menyepak me·nye·pak *kick* v
menyopir me·nyo·pir *drive* v
merah me·rah *red*
— **muda** moo·da *pink*
merayakan me·ra·ya·kan *celebrate*
merayu me·ra·yoo *chat up* v
mereka me·re·ka *their* • *they*
merokok me·ro·kok *smoke* v
mesin me·sin *engine* • *machine*
— **cuci** choo·chi *washing machine*
— **hitung** hi·toong *calculator*
mesjid mes·jid *mosque*
mewah me·wah *luxury* a
mimpi mim·pi *dream* n&v
Minggu ming·goo *Sunday*
minggu ming·goo *week*
— **suci** soo·chi *Holy Week*
minta min·ta *ask (for)* • *request* v
minum mi·noom *drink* v
minuman mi·noo·man *drink* n
— **keras** ke·ras *alcoholic drink*
— **ringan** ring·an *soft drink*
minyak mi·nyak *oil*
— **harum** ha·room *perfume* n
— **tana** ta·na *kerosene*
mirip mi·rip *similar*
miskin mis·kin *poor (money)*
mobil mo·bil *car*
mogok mo·gok *break down (car)*
montir mon·tir *mechanic*
— **listrik** li·strik *electrician*
muak di waktu pagi moo·ak di wak·too pa·gi *morning sickness*
mual moo·al *nausea*
muda moo·da *young* a
mudah moo·dah *easy*
muka moo·ka *face*
mulai moo·lai *begin* • *start* v
mulut moo·loot *mouth*
mungil moong·il *cute*
mungkin moong·kin *maybe* • *possible*
muntah moon·tah *vomit* n&v
murah moo·rah *cheap*
musim moo·sim *season*
— **angin** ang·in *windy season*
— **angin barat** ang·in ba·rat *western wind season*

— **dingin** ding·in *winter*
— **gugur** goo·goor *autumn • fall*
— **hujan** hoo·jan *rainy season*
— **kemarau** ke·ma·row *dry season*
— **panas** pa·nas *hot season • summer*
— **panen** pa·nen *harvest season*
— **semi** se·mi *spring*

N

nabati na·ba·ti *vegetarian* a
nada pilih na·da pi·lih *dial tone*
naik na·ik *board (transport)* v • *climb* v •
ride v • *take (transport)* • *up* • *uphill*
nama na·ma *name* n
— **keluarga** ke·loo·ar·ga *surname*
— **panggilan** pang·gi·lan *nickname*
nanti nan·ti *later*
napas na·pas *breathe*
nasi na·si *rice (cooked)*
Natal na·tal *Christmas*
negara ne·ga·ra *country*
nenek ne·nek *grandmother*
nilai ni·lai *value* n
nomor no·mor *number* n
— **pelat** pe·lat *license plate number*
Nona no·na *Miss*
nonton non·ton *watch* v
numpang noom·pang *ride (vehicle)* v
nyamuk nya·mook *mosquito*
nyanyi nya·nyi *sing* v

O

obat o·bat *medication • medicine*
— **batuk** ba·took *cough medicine*
— **nyamuk** nya·mook
insect repellent • mosquito coil
— **pencahar** pen·cha·har *laxatives*
— **tidur** ti·door *sleeping pills*
obral ob·ral *(on) sale*
olahraga o·lah·ra·ga *sport*
— **lari** la·ri *track (sport)*
olahragawan o·lah·ra·ga·wan *sportsperson*
oli o·li *oil (crude)*
ombak om·bak *surf* n • *wave* n
ongkos ong·kos *cost* n • *fare* n
opelet o·pe·let *minibus*
orang o·rang *person*
— **asing** a·sing *foreigner*
— **barat** ba·rat *Westerner*
— **hukuman** hoo·koo·man *prisoner*
— **jalanan** ja·la·nan *homeless*
— **suci** soo·chi *saint*
— **tidak dikenal** ti·dak di·ke·nal *stranger*
— **tua** too·a *parent(s)*
otak o·tak *brain*
otot o·tot *muscle*

P

pabean pa·be·an *customs (immigration)*
pabrik pab·rik *factory*
pacar pa·char *partner (intimate)*
— **laki-laki** la·ki la·ki *boyfriend*
— **perempuan** pe·rem·poo·an *girlfriend*
pada pa·da *at (time)*
pagar pa·gar *fence* n
pagi pa·gi *morning*
pahit pa·hit *bitter*
— **seragam** se·ra·gam *uniform* n
— **upacara** oo·pa·cha·ra
ceremonial garment
pajak pa·jak *tax* n
— **bandara** ban·da·ra *airport tax*
— **penghasilan** peng·ha·si·lan
income tax
— **penjualan** pen·joo·a·lan *sales tax*
pakai pa·kai *wear* v • *use* v
pakaian pa·kai·an *clothing*
paling baik pa·ling ba·ik *best*
paling besar pa·ling be·sar *biggest*
pameran pa·me·ran *exhibition*
panas pa·nas *hot (temperature)*
panduan hiburan pan·doo·an
hi·boo·ran *entertainment guide*
panjang pan·jang *length • long (distance)*
panjat tebing pan·jat te·bing *rock climbing*
pantai pan·tai *beach • coast*
pantat pan·tat *bottom (body)*
papan angka pa·pan ang·ka *scoreboard*
papan catur pa·pan cha·toor *chessboard*
papan selancar pa·pan se·lan·char
surfboard
paru-paru pa·roo pa·roo *lung*
pasang pa·sang *place* v • *tide* n
pasar pa·sar *market*
— **gelap** ge·lap *black market*
— **loak** lo·ak *fleamarket*
— **swalayan** swa·la·yan *supermarket*
pasir pa·sir *sand* n
Paskah pas·kah *Easter*
pas naik pas na·ik *boarding pass*
pasta gigi pa·sta gi·gi *toothpaste*
patah pa·tah *break (bone)* n&v • *broken*

patung pa·toong *sculpture · statue*
payung pa·yoong *umbrella*
pedagang pe·da·gang
  businessperson · tradesperson
pedas pe·das *hot · spicy*
pegawai pe·ga·wai *office worker*
pegunungan pe·goo·noong·an
  mountain range
pekerjaan pe·ker·ja·an *job · profession*
  — kertas ker·tas *paperwork*
  — rumah tangga roo·mah tang·ga
  housework
pekerja kasar pe·ker·ja ka·sar
  manual worker
pelabuhan pe·la·boo·han *harbour · port*
pelacur pe·la·choor *prostitute* n
pelajar pe·la·jar *student (school)*
pelan pe·lan *slow* a
pelana pe·la·na *saddle* n
pelanggaran pe·lang·ga·ran *offense (legal)*
pelan-pelan pe·lan pe·lan *slowly*
pelatih pe·la·tih *coach* n *· instructor*
pelat nomor polisi pe·lat no·mor po·li·si
  numberplate
pelaut pe·la·oot *sailor*
pelayan pe·la·yan *waiter*
  — toko to·ko *sales assistant*
pelembab pe·lem·bab
  conditioner · moisturiser
pelicin pe·li·chin *lubricant*
pelihara pe·li·ha·ra
  care for someone · look after
pelipis pe·li·pis *temple (body)*
pelor gas pe·lor gas *gas cartridge*
peluk pe·look *hug* v
pelukis pe·loo·kis *painter (artist)*
  — potret po·tret *portrait sketcher*
pemain film pe·ma·in film *actor*
pemain musik pe·ma·in moo·sik *musician*
pemakaman pe·ma·ka·man *funeral*
pemancingan pe·man·ching·an *fishing*
pemandangan pe·man·dang·an *view* n
pemandu pe·man·doo
  guide (audio/person)
pembakaran mayat pem·ba·ka·ran
  ma·yat *cremation*
pembalut pem·ba·loot *bandage* n
  — tipis ti·pis *panty liners*
  — wanita wa·ni·ta *sanitary napkins*
pembangunan pem·bang·oo·nan
  construction
pembayaran kembali pem·ba·ya·ran
  kem·ba·li *refund* n

pembedahan pem·be·da·han
  operation (medical)
pembengkakan pem·beng·ka·kan *lump*
pembersihan pem·ber·si·han *cleaning*
pembohong pem·bo·hong *liar*
pembuka kaleng pem·boo·ka ka·leng
  tin opener
pembunuhan pem·boo·noo·han *murder* n
pemburuan pem·boo·roo·an *hunting*
pemenang pe·me·nang *winner*
pemeriksaan darah pe·me·rik·sa·an da·rah
  blood test
pemerintah pe·me·rin·tah *government*
pemilihan pe·mi·li·han *elections*
pemilik pe·mi·lik *owner*
pemilu pe·mi·loo *elections*
pemimpin pe·mim·pin
  leader · manager (business)
pemungut karcis pe·moong·oot kar·chis
  ticket collector
penanda bagasi pe·nan·da ba·ga·si
  luggage tag
penangkal infeksi pe·nang·kal in·fek·si
  antiseptic n
penawar sakit pe·na·war sa·kit *painkillers*
pencacaran pen·cha·cha·ran *vaccination*
pencuri pen·choo·ri *thief*
pendaftaran mobil pen·daf·ta·ran mo·bil
  car registration
pendapat pen·da·pat *opinion*
pendek pen·dek *short*
pendeta pen·de·ta *priest*
pendidikan pen·di·di·kan *education*
pendukung pen·doo·koong
  supporter (politics)
penebangan hutan pe·ne·bang·an
  hoo·tan *deforestation · logging*
penerbangan pe·ner·bang·an *flight* n
pengacara peng·a·cha·ra *lawyer*
pengadilan peng·a·di·lan *court (legal)*
pengakuan peng·a·koo·an
  confession (religious)
pengalaman peng·a·la·man *experience*
pengambilan barang peng·am·bi·lan
  ba·rang *baggage claim*
pengangguran peng·ang·goor *unemployed*
pengasuh anak peng·a·sooh a·nak
  babysitter
pengatur peng·a·toor *administrator*
pengemis peng·e·mis *beggar*
pengenalan peng·e·na·lan *identification*
penggemar peng·ge·mar
  supporter (politics)

penggembira peng·gem·bi·ra
supporter (sport)

penghubung peng·hoo·boong
operator (phone)

pengintai peng·in·tai _lookout_ n

pengukur kecepatan peng·oo·koor
ke·che·pa·tan _speedometer_

pengungsi peng·oong·si _refugee_

peninggalan pe·ning·ga·lan _relic_

penjagaan anak pen·ja·ga·an a·nak
childminding

penjahit pen·ja·hit _tailor_

penjara pen·ja·ra _jail_ n · _prison_

penjual pen·joo·al _vendor_
— **sayuran** sa·yoo·ran _greengrocer_
— **tembakau** tem·ba·kow _tobacconist_

penterjemah pen·ter·je·mah _translator_

penting pen·ting _important_ · _urgent_

penuh pe·nooh _full_

penukaran pe·noo·ka·ran _exchange_ n
— **uang** oo·ang _currency exchange_

penulis pe·noo·lis _writer_

penumpang pe·noom·pang _passenger_

penunjuk pe·noon·jook _indicator_

penutup bak mandi pe·noo·toop bak
man·di _plug (bath)_ n

penyakit pe·nya·kit _disease_ · _sickness_
— **jantung** jan·toong _heart condition_
— **kelamin** ke·la·min _venereal disease_

penyanyi pe·nya·nyi _singer_

penyepit pe·nye·pit _tweezers_

penyewaan mobil pe·nye·wa·an mo·bil
car hire

penyuka olahraga sepeda pe·nyoo·ka
o·lah·ra·ga se·pe·da _cyclist_

penyumbat telinga pe·nyoom·bat
te·ling·a _earplugs_

perahu pe·ra·hoo _boat_
— **layar** la·yar _sailing boat_

perak pe·rak _silver_ n

perang pe·rang _war_

perangko pe·rang·ko _postage_ · _stamp_

perasaan pe·ra·sa·an _emotions_ · _feeling_
— **sakit** sa·kit _pain_ n

peraturan pe·ra·too·ran _regulation_ · _rule_ n

perayaan pe·ra·ya·an _celebration_

perbatasan per·ba·ta·san _border_ n

perbedaan waktu per·be·da·an wak·too
time difference

percaya per·cha·ya _believe_ · _trust_ v

percobaan nuklir per·cho·ba·an nook·lir
nuclear testing

perdagangan per·da·gang·an _trade_ n

perdana menteri per·da·na men·te·ri
prime minister

perempat pe·rem·pat _quarter_ n

perempuan pe·rem·poo·an
female (human) n&a

pergelangan kaki per·ge·lang·an ka·ki
ankle

pergelangan tangan per·ge·lang·an
tang·an _wrist_

pergi per·gi _go_

perhentian jantung per·hen·ti·an
jan·toong _cardiac arrest_

perhiasan per·hi·a·san _jewellery_

periksa pe·rik·sa _check_ v

perincian pe·rin·chi·an _detail_

perjalanan per·ja·la·nan _journey_ · _ride (in
vehicle)_ n · _trek_ n · _trip_ n

perkawinan per·ka·wi·nan _marriage_

perkebunan per·ke·boo·nan _gardening_

perkosaan per·ko·sa·an _rape_ n

perlombaan per·lom·ba·an _race (sport)_ n

perlu per·loo _necessary_ · _need_ v

permadani per·ma·da·ni _rug_

pernikahan per·ni·ka·han _wedding_

peron pe·ron _platform_

perpanjangan per·pan·jang·an
extension (visa)

perpustakaan per·poo·sta·ka·an _library_

persamaan per·sa·ma·an _equality_

persediaan per·se·di·a·an _stock (food)_

persis per·sis _exactly_

pertama per·ta·ma _first_ a

pertandingan per·tan·ding·an _game_

Pertandingan Olympiade per·tan·ding·an
o·lim·pi·a·de _Olympic Games_

pertanian per·ta·ni·an _agriculture_

pertanyaan per·ta·nya·an _question_ n

pertengkaran per·teng·ka·ran _fight_ n

pertunangan per·too·nang·an
engagement (to marry)

pertunjukan per·toon·joo·kan
demonstration · _performance_ · _show_ n

perubahan pe·roo·ba·han _change_ n

perundang-undangan pe·roon·dang
oon·dang·an _legislation_

perusahaan pe·roo·sa·ha·an
company (firm)

perut pe·root _stomach_

pesan pe·san
book v · _message_ n · _order_ v · _reserve_ v

pesanan pe·sa·nan _order_ n · _reservation_

pesawat pe·sa·wat _airplane_

pesta pe·sta _festival_ · _party_

peta pe·ta *map*
petani pe·ta·ni *farmer*
pijat pi·jat *massage* n&v
pikir pi·kir *think* v
pikul pi·kool *carry*
pilek pi·lek *cold (flu)*
pilih pi·lih *choose*
pinggir ping·gir *edge • side (of street)*
— kota ko·ta *suburb*
pingsan ping·san *faint* v
pinjam pin·jam *borrow*
pintu pin·too *door • gate*
— keberangkatan ke·be·rang·ka·tan
departure gate
— keluar ke·loo·ar *exit* n
— masuk ma·sook *entrance*
piring pi·ring *dish* n • *plate*
pisau pi·sow *knife*
— lipat li·pat *penknife • pocket knife*
pohon po·hon *tree*
pola po·la *pattern*
pompa bensin pom·pa ben·sin
petrol station • service station
pondok pon·dok *hut*
popok po·pok *diaper • nappy*
pos pos *post (police, etc) • mail (system)* n
— biasa bi·a·sa *surface mail*
— kilat ki·lat *express mail*
— pemeriksaan pe·me·rik·sa·an
checkpoint
— tercatat ter·cha·tat *registered mail*
potong po·tong *cut* v
potongan po·tong·an *piece*
potret po·tret *take a photo*
prajurit pra·joo·rit *soldier*
pranama pra·na·ma *first name*
pria pri·a *man (male)* n
primbon prim·bon *horoscope*
pulang poo·lang *return* v
pulau poo·low *island*
puncak poon·chak *peak (mountain)*
punggung poong·goong *back (body)*
pungut poong·oot *collect • pick up* v
punya poo·nya *have*
— pilek pi·lek *have a cold*
pupur poo·poor *powder* n
pura poo·ra *temple (Hindu)*
pusat poo·sat *centre*
pusing poo·sing *dizzy*
putih poo·tih *white*
putus poo·toos *interrupted • cut off* v&a

Rabu ra·boo *Wednesday*
radang ra·dang *inflammation*
— hati ha·ti *hepatitis*
rahang ra·hang *jaw*
rakyat rak·yat *people*
ramai ra·mai *busy • crowded*
rambut ram·boot *hair*
rampok ram·pok *rob*
ransel ran·sel *backpack • knapsack*
rantai ran·tai *chain* n
rasa ra·sa *feel (touch)* v
ratu ra·too *queen*
ratus ra·toos *hundred*
reboisasi re·bo·i·sa·si *reforestation*
rebus re·boos *boil* v • *boiled*
recehan re·che·han *loose change*
rekan re·kan *companion*
rekening bank re·ke·ning bank
bank account
rem rem *brakes*
renang re·nang *swim* v • *swimming (sport)*
rencana perjalanan ren·cha·na
per·ja·la·nan *itinerary*
renda ren·da *lace (fabric)* n
rendah ren·dah *low*
resep re·sep *prescription*
retak re·tak *fracture (bone)* n
ribut ri·boot *noisy*
rindu rin·doo *miss (person)*
— kampung kam·poong *homesick*
ringan ring·an *light (weight)*
rits rits *zip • zipper*
roda ro·da *wheel*
rok rok *skirt*
rokok ro·kok *cigarette*
roti ro·ti *bread*
ruam roo·am *(nappy) rash*
ruang roo·ang *room*
— cuci choo·chi *laundry*
— tunggu toong·goo *waiting room*
rumah roo·mah *home • house*
— kos kos *boarding house*
— sakit sa·kit *hospital*
— sakit swasta sa·kit swa·sta
private hospital
runtuhan roon·too·han *ruins*
rusa roo·sa *deer*
rusak roo·sak *break down* v • *broken
down • damaged • out of order*
rute pendaki roo·te pen·da·ki *hiking route*

S

saat sa·at *moment • while*
Sabtu sab·too *Saturday*
sabuk pengaman sa·book peng·a·man
  seat belt
sabun sa·boon *soap*
  — **cukur** choo·koor *shaving cream*
sah sah *legal*
saja sa·ja *just (only)*
sakit sa·kit *ill • sick • sore • hurt* v
salah sa·lah
  fault (someone's) • mistake n • *wrong* a
  — **cerna** cher·na *indigestion*
saldo sal·do *balance (account)*
salib sa·lib *cross (religious)*
sama sa·ma *same*
sambungan (sam·boong·an
  connection (transport) n
sambutan sam·boo·tan *welcome* v
sampah sam·pah *garbage • rubbish*
sampai sam·pai *until*
samudera sa·moo·de·ra *ocean*
sandiwara san·di·wa·ra *theatre*
sangat sang·at *very*
santai san·tai *relax* v
sapi sa·pi *cow*
saran sa·ran *advice*
sarapan sa·ra·pan *breakfast*
sarung bantal sa·roong ban·tal *pillowcase*
satu sa·too *one*
satwa sat·wa *wild animal*
saya sa·ya *I • me • my*
sayap sa·yap *wing*
  — **kanan** ka·nan *right-wing* a
  — **kiri** ki·ri *left-wing* a
sayur-mayur sa·yoor ma·yoor *vegetables*
sebab se·bab *because*
sebelum se·be·loom *before*
sebelumnya se·be·loom·nya *last (previous)*
seberang se·be·rang *across*
sederhana se·der·ha·na *simple*
sedih se·dih *sad*
sedikit se·di·kit *few • little*
segala sesuatu se·ga·la se·soo·a·too
  everything
segar se·gar *fresh*
segera se·ge·ra *soon • urgent*
sehat se·hat *healthy • well*
sejak se·jak *since (time)*
sejarah se·ja·rah *history*
sejuk se·jook *cool (temperature)*
sekali se·ka·li *once • very*

sekarang se·ka·rang *now • present (time)*
sekolah menengah atas se·ko·lah
  me·nen·gah a·tas *high school*
sekolah tinggi se·ko·lah ting·gi *college*
seks aman seks a·man *safe sex*
selalu se·la·loo *always • forever*
selam se·lam *dive* v • *diving*
selama se·la·ma *for (length of time)*
selancar se·lan·char *surf* v
Selandia Baru se·lan·di·a ba·roo
  New Zealand
Selasa se·la·sa *Tuesday*
selatan se·la·tan *south*
selesai se·le·sai *finish* v
seluruh se·loo·rooh *whole*
sembahyang sem·bah·yang *worship* v
sembelit sem·be·lit *constipation*
semesta alam se·mes·ta a·lam *universe*
sempit sem·pit *narrow* a • *tight*
sempurna sem·poor·na *perfect*
semua se·moo·a *all*
  — **orang** o·rang *everybody*
semut se·moot *ant*
senang se·nang *glad • happy*
sendirian sen·di·ri·an *alone*
sendok sen·dok *spoon*
seni se·ni *art*
  — **bela diri rakyat** be·la di·ri rak·yat
    martial arts
  — **lukis** loo·kis *painting (the art)*
  — **pertunjukan** per·toon·joo·kan
    performance art
  — **prasejarah** pra·se·ja·rah *prehistoric art*
seniman se·ni·man *artist*
Senin se·nin *Monday*
senjata sen·ja·ta *gun*
senter sen·ter *flashlight • torch*
sentuh sen·tooh *touch* v
senyum se·nyoom *smile* v
sepakbola se·pak·bo·la *football • soccer*
sepanjang malam se·pan·jang ma·lam
  overnight n
sepasang se·pa·sang *pair* n
sepatu se·pa·too *shoe(s)*
  — **pendaki** pen·da·ki *hiking boot(s)*
  — **tinggi** ting·gi *boot(s)*
sepeda se·pe·da *bicycle*
sepi se·pi *quiet*
sepre se·pre *bed linen • sheet(s)*
serambi se·ram·bi *foyer*
serangan se·rang·an *assault* n
  — **jantung** jan·toong
    heart attack • stroke (health)

serangga se·rang·ga *insect*
serbuk sari ser·book sa·ri *pollen*
serikat buruh se·ri·kat boo·rooh *trade union*
sering se·ring *often*
serutu se·roo·too *cigar*
seseorang se·se·o·rang *someone*
sesuatu se·soo·a·too *something*
sesudah se·soo·dah *after*
setelah se·te·lah *after*
setengah se·teng·ah *half* n
setiap se·ti·ap *each • every*
setuju se·too·joo *agree*
sewa se·wa *hire* n&v • *rent* v
siang si·ang *midday • noon*
siap si·ap *ready*
siapa si·a·pa *who*
siapkan si·ap·kan *prepare*
sibuk si·book *busy (time/phone)*
SIM sim *drivers licence*
simpan sim·pan *put*
simpang sim·pang *intersection*
sinananga si·na·nang·a *shingles (illness)*
sinetron si·ne·tron *soap opera*
SMA *high school*
sogok so·gok *bribe* n&v
sore so·re *afternoon*
spiral spi·ral *IUD*
stasiun kereta api sta·si·oon ke·re·ta a·pi *railway station*
steker ste·ker *cigarette lighter • plug (electric)*
suami soo·a·mi *husband*
suara soo·a·ra *voice*
suasana soo·a·sa·na *atmosphere (of place)*
subuh soo·booh *dawn*
sudah soo·dah *already*
sudut soo·doot *corner*
suhu udara soo·hoo oo·da·ra *temperature (weather)*
suka soo·ka *like* v
suling soo·ling *flute*
sulit soo·lit *difficult*
sumberdaya manusia soom·ber·da·ya ma·noo·si·a *human resources*
sungai soong·ai *river*
suntik soon·tik *inject • injection*
surat soo·rat *letter (mail)*
— **keterangan** ke·te·rang·an *certificate*
— **lahir** la·hir *birth certificate*
Surat Ijin Mengemudi soo·rat i·jin meng·e·moo·di *drivers licence*
susah soo·sah *difficult*

sutra soo·tra *silk* n
swasta swa·sta *private* a • *self-employed*
syahwat shah·wat *orgasm*

T

tabrakan tab·ra·kan *crash* n
tabuhan ta·boo·han *wasp*
tahan air ta·han a·ir *waterproof*
tahu ta·hoo *know* v • *tofu*
tahun ta·hoon *year*
takhyul takh·yool *superstition*
takut ta·koot *afraid*
tali ta·li *rope • string*
— **jemuran** je·moo·ran *clothesline*
— **kipas** ki·pas *fanbelt*
— **sepatu** se·pa·too *shoelaces*
taman ta·man *park* n
— **kanak-kanak** ka·nak ka·nak *kindergarten*
— **nasional** na·si·o·nal *national park*
— **pra-sekolah** pra se·ko·lah *crèche*
— **umum** oo·moom *public gardens*
tamu ta·moo *guest*
tanah ta·nah *earth (soil) • land* n
tanda tan·da *sign* n
— **tangan** tang·an *signature*
tangan tang·an *hand*
tangga tang·ga *stairs*
tanggal tang·gal *date (day)*
— **kelahiran** ke·la·hi·ran *date of birth*
tangkap tang·kap *arrest* v • *catch* v
tanpa tan·pa *without*
tanya ta·nya *ask (question)* v
tari ta·ri *dance* v
tarian ta·ri·an *dance* n • *dancing*
tarik ta·rik *pull* v
taruh ta·rooh *bet* v
taruhan ta·roo·han *bet* n
tas tas *bag*
— **kantor** kan·tor *briefcase*
tatabahasa ta·ta·ba·ha·sa *grammar*
tawar ta·war *bargain* v
tawon ta·won *bee*
tebal te·bal *thick*
tebing te·bing *cliff*
teduh te·dooh *shade*
tekanan te·ka·nan *pressure (tyre)* n
telinga te·ling·a *ear*
telpon umum tel·pon oo·moom *public phone*
teman te·man *friend*
— **sekerja** se·ker·ja *colleague*

tembikar tem·bi·kar *porcelain • pottery*
tembok tem·bok *wall (outside)*
tempat tem·pat *place • space • venue*
— **cuci otomat** choo·chi o·to·mat *launderette*
— **duduk** doo·dook *seat*
— **kelahiran** ke·la·hi·ran *place of birth*
— **mendaftarkan diri** men·daf·tar·kan di·ri *check-in (desk)*
— **minum** mi·noom *pub*
— **penggantungan jas** peng·gan·toong·gan jas *cloakroom*
— **sampah** sam·pah *garbage can*
— **tidur** ti·door *bed • sleeping berth*
— **tidur gantong** ti·door gan·tong *hammock*
— **tidur untuk dua orang** ti·door oon·took doo·a o·rang *double bed • twin beds*
— **tinggal** ting·gal *quarter n*
tenaga nuklir te·na·ga nook·lir *nuclear energy*
tenang te·nang *calm*
tengah malam teng·ah ma·lam *midnight*
tenggorokan teng·go·ro·kan *throat*
tengkorak teng·ko·rak *skull*
tentang ten·tang *about*
tentara ten·ta·ra *military n*
tenun te·noon *weave v • woven*
tenunan te·noo·nan *weaving*
tepat waktu te·pat wak·too *on time*
terakhir te·ra·khir *last (final)*
terang te·rang *bright (colour)*
terbaik ter·ba·ik *best*
terbakar ter·ba·kar *burnt*
— **sinar matahari** si·nar ma·ta·ha·ri *sunburn*
terbang ter·bang *fly v*
terbesar ter·be·sar *biggest*
terdekat ter·de·kat *nearest*
tergesa-gesa ter·ge·sa ge·sa *in a hurry*
teriak te·ri·ak *shout v*
terima te·ri·ma *accept • admit (let in) v*
terjemahkan ter·je·mah·kan *translate*
terka ter·ka *guess v*
terkecil ter·ke·chil *smallest*
terkenal ter·ke·nal *famous*
terlalu ter·la·loo *too (excessive)*
terlambat ter·lam·bat *late (not on time) • miss (transport) v*
termasuk ter·ma·sook *included*
teropong te·ro·pong *binoculars*
terpencil ter·pen·chil *remote*

terperinci ter·pe·rin·chi *itemised*
terpisah ter·pi·sah *separate a*
tersesat ter·se·sat *lost (person)*
tertawa ter·ta·wa *laugh v*
tertunda ter·toon·da *delayed*
terus te·roos *straight ahead*
tes kehamilan tes ke·ha·mi·lan *pregnancy test kit*
tetapi te·ta·pi *but*
TI te·i *IT*
tidak ti·dak *no • not*
— **ada** a·da *nothing • there isn't/aren't*
— **aman** a·man *unsafe*
— **bersalah** ber·sa·lah *innocent a*
— **enak** e·nak *uncomfortable*
— **menerima tamu** me·ne·ri·ma ta·moo *no vacancy*
— **mungkin** moong·kin *impossible*
— **pernah** per·nah *never*
— **satu pun** sa·too poon *none*
— **wajar** wa·jar *unfair*
tidur ti·door *asleep • sleep n&v*
tikar ti·kar *mat n*
tiket ti·ket *ticket*
— **pulang-pergi** poo·lang per·gi *return ticket*
— **satu kali jalan** sa·too ka·li ja·lan *one-way ticket*
tikus ti·koos *mouse • rat*
tim tim *team (sport)*
timbang tim·bang *weigh*
timur ti·moor *east*
tinggal ting·gal *live (reside) • stay v*
tinggi ting·gi *high • tall*
tingkat ting·kat *floor (storey) • level n*
tinju tin·joo *boxing (sport)*
tipis ti·pis *thin*
tipu ti·poo *cheat n&v*
tipuan ti·poo·an *rip-off n*
titip ti·tip *deposit (luggage) v*
toko to·ko *shop n*
— **alat tulis** a·lat too·lis *stationer*
— **barang-barang elektronik** ba·rang ba·rang e·lek·tro·nik *electrical store*
— **mainan** ma·i·nan *toy shop*
— **pangan** pang·an *grocery*
— **perkakas** per·ka·kas *hardware store*
— **serbaada** ser·ba·a·da *department store • shopping centre*
olak to·lak *refuse v*
tolong to·long *help v • please (request)*
tombak ikan tom·bak i·kan *gig*
topeng to·peng *mask n*

topi to·pi *hat*
tua too·a *dark (colour)* a • *old (person)*
tuan rumah too·an roo·mah *landlord*
tugas tentara too·gas ten·ta·ra *military service*
Tuhan too·han *God*
tujuan too·joo·an *destination*
tukang bangunan too·kang bang·oo·nan *builder*
tukang cat too·kang chat *painter (trade)*
tukang cukur too·kang choo·koor *barber*
tukang daging too·kang da·ging *butcher*
tukang kayu too·kang ka·yoo *carpenter*
tukang kebun too·kang ke·boon *gardener*
tukang masak too·kang ma·sak *cook* n
tukang patri too·kang pa·tri *plumber*
tukang pijat too·kang pi·jat *masseur • masseuse*
tukang potret too·kang po·tret *photographer*
tukang sihir too·kang si·hir *magician*
tukar too·kar *change (money)* v • *exchange* v
tulang too·lang *bone*
  — **rusuk** roo·sook *rib (body)*
tuli too·li *deaf*
tulis too·lis *write*
tumbuh toom·booh *grow*
tumbuhan toom·boo·han *plant* n
tunangan too·nang·an *fiancé • fiancée*
tunggang kuda toong·gang koo·da *horse riding*
tunggu toong·goo *wait* v
tunjuk toon·jook *point* v • *show* v
turun too·roon *down* adv • *get off (bus, etc)*
  — **gunung** goo·noong *downhill*
tustel too·stel *camera*
tutup too·toop *close* v • *closed • shut* a

uang oo·ang *money*
  — **kecil** ke·chil *change (coins)* n
  — **kertas** ker·tas *banknote • bill (note)*
  — **logam** lo·gam *coins*
  — **rokok** ro·kok *tip* n
  — **sokongan** so·kong·an *dole*
udara oo·da·ra *air*

ujian oo·ji·an *test (exam)* n
ukuran oo·koo·ran *size*
ular oo·lar *snake*
ulung oo·loong *excellent*
umur oo·moor *age* n
undang oon·dang *invite*
ungu oong·oo *purple*
untuk oon·took *for (purpose)*
untung oon·toong *luck • lucky • profit* n&v
urat darah oo·rat da·rah *vein*
usus buntu oo·soos boon·too *appendix*
utama oo·ta·ma *main* a
utara oo·ta·ra *north*

wajan wa·jan *frying pan*
waktu wak·too *time* n • *when*
walikota wa·li·ko·ta *mayor*
wanita wa·ni·ta *woman*
warna war·na *colour*
warnet war·net *Internet café*
wartawan war·ta·wan *journalist*
wartel war·tel *telephone office*
warung wa·roong *food stall • store*
wawancara wa·wan·cha·ra *interview* n
wayang golek wa·yang go·lek *wooden puppet*
wayang kulit wa·yang koo·lit *leather puppet • shadow puppets*
weker we·ker *alarm clock*
wilayah wi·la·yah *region*

ya ya *yes*
yang berikutnya yang ber·i·koot·nya *next*
yang lain yang la·in *another*
yang lalu yang la·loo *ago • last (time)*
yang mana yang ma·na *which*
yang terpenting yang ter·pen·ting *essential*

zakar za·kar *penis*

INDEX

What kind of traveller are you?

A. You're eating chicken for dinner *again* because it's the only word you know.

B. When no one understands what you say, you step closer and shout louder.

C. When the barman doesn't understand your order, you point frantically at the beer.

D. You're surrounded by locals, swapping jokes, email addresses and experiences
– other travellers want to borrow your phrasebook or audio guide.

If you answered A, B, or C, you NEED Lonely Planet's language products ...

- **Lonely Planet Phrasebooks** – for every phrase you need in every language
  you want
- **Lonely Planet Language & Culture** – get behind the scenes of English as it's
  spoken around the world – learn and laugh
- **Lonely Planet Fast Talk & Fast Talk Audio** – essential phrases for short trips and
  weekends away – read, listen and talk like a local
- **Lonely Planet Small Talk** – 10 essential languages for city breaks
- **Lonely Planet Real Talk** – downloadable language audio guides from
  lonelyplanet.com to your MP3 player

... and this is why

- **Talk to everyone everywhere**
  Over 120 languages, more than any other publisher
- **The right words at the right time**
  Quick-reference colour sections, two-way dictionary, easy pronunciation,
  every possible subject – and audio to support it

Lonely Planet Offices

Australia
90 Maribyrnong St, Footscray,
Victoria 3011
☎ 03 8379 8000
fax 03 8379 8111
✉ talk2us@lonelyplanet.com.au

USA
150 Linden St, Oakland,
CA 94607
☎ 510 250 6400
fax 510 893 8572
✉ info@lonelyplanet.com

UK
2nd fl, 186 City Rd,
London EC1V 2NT
☎ 020 7106 2100
fax 020 7106 2101
✉ go@lonelyplanet.co.u

lonelyplanet.com